Happy Together

Daily Insight for Families from Scripture

to Carol + Vern
Stay happy together!
Ann + Bryan Norford

Ann and Bryan Norford

HAPPY TOGETHER
Daily Insight for Families from Scripture

Copyright © 2009 Ann and Bryan Norford

ISBN-10: 1-897373-81-3
ISBN-13: 978- 1-897373-81-1

Printed by Word Alive Press

WORD ALIVE PRESS
Just Write!

131 Cordite Road, Winnipeg, Manitoba, R3W 1S1
www.wordalivepress.ca

Printed in Canada

Table of Contents

WE DEDICATE THIS BOOK TO
OUR BELOVED DAUGHTERS
HEATHER, KAREN AND ALEXANDRA
AND THEIR FAMILIES

Acknowledgements:

To our dear friend Marilyn Gloer
for encouragement and critique of the original manuscripts

To the competent folk at Word Alive
for valuable advice and editing

To Dr. Jim Packer of Regent College, Vancouver,
for kindly contributing the foreword

Foreword

It has often, and truly, been said that what you get from the Bible, God's word of revelation, old yet ever new, depends on what you bring to it and what questions you ask it. This book, which the Norfords have laid out as a year's course of practical and devotional Bible readings, centres on the quest for wisdom about sex, marriage and the family, as one very important part of the life of faith and holiness. Their comments on the chosen passages yield a wealth of wisdom on these themes, far more, I guess, than most of us ever dreamed was there.

Christianity is truth and power: truth about our Creator God and his redeeming love for us, and power from Jesus Christ through the Holy Spirit for remaking our relationships— relationships with God, with our fellow humans (neighbours), and with ourselves. All life, looked at realistically, is relationships, and all our relationships are at first out of joint, due to sin in everyone's moral and spiritual system; thus they all need redirection and some measure of reconstruction. Until the self–centredness of grab–and-exploit is dethroned, and the other–centredness of love established in its place, relationships will be consistently distorted. This includes parent–child and child–parent relationships, just as it includes relationships between spouses. For though spouses pledge themselves to each other "till death do us part," as the Anglican Prayer Book put it, they are flawed human beings like the rest of us, and need the renewing grace of our Lord Jesus Christ as much as any.

The Bible's teaching about marriage and the family starts on its opening page and continues into the pastoral letters of the New Testament. The climax of it is the revelation that the husband–wife relationship is meant to reflect the mutual covenant love of Jesus Christ the Saviour and his church, while the parent–child relationship is meant to reflect the response of Christians to God the Father, whose adopted sons and heirs they are in the spiritual royal family. This book, used as prescribed, will impart a very rich understanding of these things.

Asked after the first fifty years to characterize their married relationship, Billy and Ruth Graham described themselves as "happily incompatible." I suspect that if the Norfords were asked the same question they would give substantially the same answer; I know that my wife and I would. The Grahams coined a telling phrase for something that is in fact quite typical. Opposites attract, and marital affection grows from the sense, not just of having a lot in common, but also of being significantly different from each other, in ways that both want to explore further. When agape–love—patient, kind, forbearing, forward–looking, habitually seeking the best for the loved one—rules the roost for them both, their marriage will yield mutual gifts of joy, peace, strength and contentment in abundance, even as they grow in awareness of how unlike each other they really are. Vive la difference, say the French (and the Norfords too), and they are right; for the sense that the loved one is still a bit of a mystery adds what you might call pepper, salt and sweet sauce (pardon my pun; it's intentional) to their relationship with each other. Any pair of incompatibles who want to go deeper into happy togetherness in their marriage will do well to take the Norfords' one-year course.

Marriage in the Western world is rocky today, as much from our personal immaturity and lack of common sense as from any other cause, and there could hardly be a more strategic time for this book, with all its down–to–earthness anchored deep in God, to come on the market. The good it could do is very great, and I heartily commend it. May it have the rich, wide ministry that it deserves.

J. I. Packer
Regent College, Vancouver, January 2009

About Our Book

You have doubtless noticed that family relationships—with partners, parents or children—can be the most rewarding and yet the most exasperating of life's experiences; the closer the relationship, the greater the challenge. While some couples and families appear to sail through life, other marriages seem to be a series of disasters. In answer to this there are hundreds of books, tapes, videos, TV shows and counsellors devoted to helping marriages succeed. Yet even the amount of help available often confuses rather than clarifies issues. Written as a daily devotional for a year, this book does not replace the many resources available to marriages, but daily considers a variety of family issues from Bible passages that may mend or improve relationships progressively.

Many Christian approaches to marriage simply use Scripture to provide a Christian veneer to sociological schemes. In doing so, the transcendent meaning of marriage is missed. All relationships, but supremely marriage, are meant to reflect God himself and the relationship that he has with his people. This basis for relationships provides the most effective approach for significant marriage—for both the partners' happiness and as a meaningful contribution to family, community and culture.

The original contents of this book were assembled for our golden wedding anniversary in 2005 and given to our children and grandchildren as a heritage from our life together. We gratefully recall our marriage with joy and our family with pleasure, recognizing that without our commitment to God, and more especially his faithfulness to us, the outcome would have been far less gratifying. Not that we have avoided mistakes or achieved a particular level of excellence, but we consider God's design for marriage both the basis and mainstay of our union.

The first week selects some passages from Proverbs and Romans to set a context for the meditations that follow. The remainder of the book works its way through the Bible, reviewing passages from Genesis to Revelation that have a bearing on marriage and family. It combines the benefits of a devotional format together with incremental teaching on the subject of marriage, exploring what the Bible says about marriage and family as well as ideas about God himself. The more we know about his attributes, attitudes and actions, the more we will understand ourselves, for we are made in his image, and the better we will grasp how our relationships are meant to work. We have chosen a readable daily format and simple observations about life or true personal stories to illustrate the principles being discovered. The material is primarily addressed to young adults—either married or considering marriage—and young families with limited time or theological background.

The format provides five scriptural meditations weekly for Monday to Friday. The weekend gives time to investigate other areas, change your routine or simply catch up. Alternatively, exploring footnotes supporting the week's meditations may extend your grasp of each day's reading. For the weekend, we have included some insights about marriage or anecdotes from life that may loosely relate to a meditation from the week. The stories you will encounter are all taken from life and, apart from those about us, the names of people involved have been changed. You can start reading the book any time of the year, as the weeks are undated.

Bryan roughed out the original manuscript and the singular pronoun "I" refers to him. Ann's review and critique provided constructive insights and the work is the thoughtful product of us both. Scripture portions are taken from the New International Version of the Bible. We trust that these thoughts from Scripture and over fifty years of life together will give you an appreciation of both the foundation and the ongoing safeguards for the relationships that are most meaningful to you—as partners or parents, single or married.

Ann and Bryan Norford,
Lethbridge, Alberta, Canada, March 2008

Opening Weekend

Beginning the Journey

You may have worked your way through the Bible before or used devotionals that have given general comfort or direction for your life. But you are now embarking on a journey that is unlike any other you have undertaken, for it is directed specifically to family life. If you are married, thinking about marriage or even living common law, this journey will identify from Scripture areas of success and failure that most of us encounter in life with our partners and children. While the Bible has some instructions about married life, from Old Testament legal requirements to New Testament guidance, it more often records stories of men and women who ran into the same joys and sorrows of life together common to us all.

While these people may have lived up to four thousand years ago, their problems and responses were as human and recognisable as ours—sometimes handled well, but often not. We will learn from Jacob, whose actions produced a dysfunctional family history of pain and misery, and from David, whose adultery created major problems for the rest of his life. Yet both these men were men of great faith who fell for the same temptations we all face. Love stories such as Ruth and Boaz and Solomon's love song to his bride will remind us of the depth and allure of faithful love for each other.

But these stories are not just about human relationships. As we will learn from the second week's meditations, family is part of the image of God created within us. God teaches us about families from who he is and his love and reactions to our faith and failures. So the more we learn of him, the better we will understand ourselves and be able to find our greatest joy in our closest relationships. Join us on this adventure through the Bible, discovering love, failure and recovery by lovers and families just like us.

Week One

Monday: Proverbs 1:1–7, 20–33

One of the major issues affecting each of our lives is relationship to others. Most of us have probably noticed that the closer the relationship, the greater the opportunity for tension and conflict, and the closest relationships are found in marriage and families, where most of us live.

Does it make a difference who we listen to? What are the wrong ideas that may undermine our relationships? What actions can we change to improve our enjoyment of one another? What are the lasting benefits of strong families, both for us as individuals and for our society?

Those of you that have had the opportunity to buy a new car doubtless spent some time poring over the instruction manual; the cost of the vehicle was probably enough to ensure you drove carefully and maintained the car diligently to provide long and trouble-free service. Similarly, to obtain the maximum benefit out of life for the time we have, we need to seek wisdom from the One who created us. As we start reading in Proverbs, we find wisdom in "the fear of the Lord" for it "is the beginning of knowledge." The fear of the Lord is also the beginning of wisdom and a "fountain [or source] of life"; it "leads to [fullness of] life" and even adds length to life.[1]

---

[1] Proverbs 9:10, Proverbs 14:27, Proverbs 19:23, Proverbs 10:27

The expression "fear of the Lord" in this context means a reverence for God's ultimate knowledge and wisdom. This attitude stands in contrast to those who would reject or scorn him as irrelevant to life. Today's reading carries a warning against rejecting his wisdom. Wisdom is personified as one who "would have poured out my heart to you and made my thoughts known to you" if we responded to her call. But if we reject her call, she will mock at our calamity when it overtakes us. The writer of Proverbs is simply telling us that if we do not absorb God's wisdom as a regular practice in life, we will be totally unprepared for the tough times. This wisdom can be found in his instruction manual to us, the Bible. Here is where we find God's plan for making those close relationships work.

Tuesday: Proverbs 3:1–10

Much of what we discussed yesterday is summarized in verses 5 and 6 of today's reading. These texts present two ways of ensuring a commitment to the Bible's wisdom in practical terms. Firstly, trusting the Lord prevents us from depending on our own wisdom. We probably pray earnestly about the tasks that we feel ill-equipped for, but we more often blithely sail through those that we are gifted for with little more than a perfunctory prayer. Yet we need God's guidance as much for the latter as for the former in order to avoid our tendency to misuse our stronger gifts or take credit for the outcome. Recognizing this will assist us to rely on him, not ourselves.

This leads to the second thought. When we have sought his guidance, it will be natural to acknowledge him as our guiding influence. But recognizing his overall control of our destiny must also lead to thankfulness to him in *all* things, for praise and gratitude to God are the primary means of maintaining allegiance to him; neglect of these disciplines is the beginning of folly.[1] This compels us to acknowledge God as the Creator of our family and

---

[1] Romans 1:18–21

express thankfulness to him for it—even though at times we may feel the opposite.

If ever there was an area where we needed to have our paths straightened, it is in the process of family relationships. We may lack parenting skills or fail to adequately live up to the standards God requires of us and so jeopardize a secure outcome for our family. But God is gracious to us, responding to our feeble and often failing attempts to trust him, and this gives us hope. It is when we come to realize that we have no alternative to trusting him more than ourselves that we receive the promise of God's guidance for the future of our partners and children.

Wednesday: Romans 3:21–28; Ephesians 2:1–9

It must be obvious to all but the most deluded that there is something terribly wrong with the human race, and this clearly affects how well humankind reflects the image of God. It doesn't take much introspection to realize that each of us is a flawed creation. Not that God's creation was originally flawed; he saw it to be very good—including his human creation.[1] If we are to affect our relationships for the better, we need to deal with our own failure to measure up first. It is as we recognize that we have fallen short of God's creation ideal that we realize that we need to be reconciled to God, and this is the first step to reconciling with others.

Scripture tells us that God not only created all things well, but when man sinned, God also saw the need to remedy human failure. Jesus Christ came and paid the penalty on the cross for our failure, paving the way for God to forgive and reconcile us to himself. Today's readings remind us that upon recognition and repentance of our sinfulness, and subsequent simple faith—belief and trust in Jesus Christ's sacrifice for us—we become a new

---

[1] Genesis 1:31

creation.[1] This is the first step in the process that allows God to restore his image in us.[2]

Coming to this point in life and committing ourselves to God's creation ideals marks the commencement of a new journey of hope. We discover how the wisdom of God is basic to our living as it begins to untangle the threads of life and provide joy in relationships, support through adversity and comfort in sorrow. Above all, our lives change as the image of God is restored in us, re-adjusting our attitudes and outlook to be more like Christ, the One who supremely displayed God's image.[3] This is the beginning of new understanding and renewal as we foster our relationships.

Thursday: Proverbs 4:1–9

You may recall that Solomon was commended by God for wanting wisdom rather than prestige as he gained the throne following the death of his father, David.[4] This passage reminds us that it was David who taught the young Solomon to seek after wisdom. As Solomon taught *his* son, he recalled that his father, David, had taught him while "still tender and cherished by [his] mother." So as Solomon ascended the throne and recognized his limited ability to fulfill the requirements of the monarchy, he knew where to turn for the wisdom he needed.

Wisdom is often associated with grey hair, probably because most of us learn over time by our mistakes instead of learning from others. But wisdom is not confined to the elderly; it is to be found in Scripture by those of any age who make the effort and take the time to grasp it. Although Solomon was later seduced from the faith, he began well, looking to his father's teaching for direction. It was David who discovered that wisdom is the basis

---

[1] 2 Corinthians 5:17–19
[2] Ephesians 4:22–24; Colossians 3:9–10
[3] John 14:6–9
[4] 1 Kings 3:10–12

for all that we desire from this life: protection, God's oversight of our lives, dignity, honour and a fitting end to a worthwhile existence.

What we convey to our children may extend through succeeding generations, as with David and Solomon, though our children may choose to either follow or ignore it. What sort of wisdom are we passing to them? Is it that which we have learned through the experience of God's Word? Or are we teaching them a convenient pragmatism or simply allowing them to absorb current cultural values without comment? If we love them, we will teach them values that will hold them in good stead and provide meaning throughout their lives—not only for themselves, but also for the families that *they* may have.

Friday: Proverbs: 7:1–27

In many proverbs Solomon addresses his son. He probably had daughters that he could have advised, but he reserved his comments for the son who would probably succeed him on the throne. It is a pity Solomon did not heed his own advice, for women were his downfall.[1] Even so, his advice was well placed— men tend to be the predators when it comes to sex. They are usually the rapists, stalkers and voyeurs. Yul Brunner, in the film musical *The King and I*, summed it up: "Women are like flowers, and men are like bees that go from flower to flower to flower . . ."[2]

The Bible confirms this general tendency by recording the adulteries of Reuben[3] and David,[4] the rape of David's daughter Tamar by her half-brother Amnon,[5] the rape of Jacob's daughter

---

[1] 1 Kings 11:1–3
[2] Quoted in the 1956 Rodgers and Hammerstein musical The King and I, based on Margaret Langdon's 1944 novel *Anna and the King of Siam* (Scarborough, ON: Harper Collins Canada, 1969).
[3] Genesis 35:22
[4] 2 Samuel 11:2–4
[5] 2 Samuel 13:1–19

Dinah by Shechem[1] and the abhorrent abduction of wives by the Benjamites during a period of Israel's anarchy.[2] Other examples could be given. Given the lessening of cultural restraints and personal discipline, men easily resort to animal behaviour, living by instinct rather than honour.

When a society reveres family and respects women, men are inspired to achieve their greatest nobility. A respectful society must depend on personal discipline infused by the culture; it cannot satisfactorily be imposed by law. Christianity based on a trust in the Bible develops a culture that respects all human life, especially the vulnerable: women, children and the unborn, sick and elderly. As these virtues are instilled within the culture, marriage and family become the norm and predatory behaviour is stigmatized and restrained. Marriage is known as the "tender trap." Every woman who draws her man into a faithful lifelong union and channels his energies into building a strong family pays us all a valuable service.

Weekend ~ Finding Wisdom

It is unnatural for me to be religious, as I am given more to reason than emotion or intuition. I can easily identify with the New Ager who sees Christianity as one religion among many and adapts or invents their own system according to personal logic. Or, like the secularist, it is just as easy to accept that some higher power brought the world into being but life generally belies the fact that God is still involved in our sorry state. This produces a practical atheism—believing in God but living as though he does not exist. To a thoughtful observer these seem like reasonable conclusions.

So why am I a Christian? Those who lack the experience of a Christian home may inherit a scepticism that inoculates them from considering Christ's claims. However, I was brought up in a

---

[1] Genesis 34:1–2
[2] Judges 21:15–25

Christian home that gave me a view of Christianity from the inside, so I did not have the disadvantage of a critical view from outside. I found that the Bible carried its own authority and gave the only meaningful explanation of life as we know it. All other philosophies that I have examined pale in comparison. Further, it is the only religion or philosophy I can find that deals effectively with the problem of evil—both its cause and its cure.

But I am not devoid of emotion. At ten years of age, the claims of Christ made sense to me, but in addition, his love demonstrated to me by the cross was emotionally compelling and I made a decision for him. Since that time the Bible's wisdom and authenticity has become clearer as the years have advanced. In fact, if I had not accepted Christ and the Bible's guide for life, I doubt if life would have provided the satisfaction and joy it does today; it would more likely be in the same disarray that too many exhibit.

Monday: Genesis 1:1–4; John 1:1–5

It's almost certain that you have puzzled over the concept of the Holy Trinity, the idea that God is one in essence but three persons: Father, Son and Holy Spirit. It is one of the mysteries of the Christian faith for most of us, yet today's readings show all three persons of the Trinity existed and were present at creation. If this is true, then it shouldn't be surprising to find evidence of the Trinity in the world we inhabit. For instance, all creation is comprised of space, matter and time. But space is also divided into three dimensions: length, width and height. Matter is composed of solid, liquid and gas, and some substances like water take on all three forms. Then, of course, time is also divided into three: past, present and future.

Of even greater significance, the Trinity can also be seen in us: our make-up is body, mind and spirit and we determine our actions by our intellect, emotions and will. But perhaps the most telling concept is the idea of male and female becoming one flesh and the children also being part of the same flesh. This mimics the Trinitarian God by the creation of father, mother and child (one or more). Obviously, the roles of human family members are quite different from the role of each person of the Trinity. This limited analogy also takes into account neither the state of singleness affirmed in Scripture nor human sin.

Nevertheless, the idea of God in relationship within the Trinity prefigures the dependence we have on others, particularly within family relationships. We need another person with whom to reproduce children and enjoy companionship and friendship. Family relationships find their meaning in the fundamental relationship of God himself—one of love and cooperation within the Trinity as well as expressed outside of himself by sacrifice for those he created. Without these qualities, relationship is no longer companionship but simply a convenience. One disgruntled wife expressed this recently by complaining: "Living with my husband is more like having a roommate!"

Tuesday: Genesis 1:24–27

If you are a man, you have probably growled the words "women drivers" in a derogatory manner during a traffic incident involving the opposite sex. If you are a woman, you are probably rolling your eyes at this brainless expression. That little phrase is only a symptom of the wider debate as to whether women are equal to men in their ability to handle life. There are some pretty entrenched views about the equality and role of the sexes on both sides of the argument—each often claiming support from Scripture. However, contrary to some views, this passage and some thoughts on passages to come show decided support for the equality of the sexes.

The word "man" in this passage is generic and includes male and female as indicated by verse 27, so both were created in God's own image. With no indication that women were in some way inferior to men, they were created equal. This is in contrast to the earlier creation of the animal world, which was not stamped with the image of God. In fact, the Scriptures clearly show that humankind was appointed to rule the animal world, suggesting a level of superiority for humans.

This command to rule the earth and its non-human inhabitants was given equally to both the male and female "man"—"let *them* rule"—they are equally co-responsible for nature. Unfortunately, the word "rule" is frequently associated with some form of dictatorship, but in Scripture it includes the need to care for the governed who depend on their ruler. When we apply this primary command to families, there is a clear necessity to provide protection and provision to the weaker and dependent ones, for they are also made in the image of God.

Wednesday: Genesis 1:28

This verse continues God's mandate to humankind, adding "subdue" to "rule." "Subdue" is often considered to mean "exploit," and it seems some men consider this their right within the family. Subdue clearly means to bring under control, but included in rulership, it still carries a responsibility for those dependent on that rule. Further, new instructions given to the man and woman confirmed that equality of the sexes included equal responsibility for governing. All the imperative verbs in this verse—be fruitful, increase, fill, subdue, rule—are plural in the original Hebrew, emphasizing marriage as an equal partnership. The need for co-operation in these commands is illustrated by the complementary need to multiply.

But this passage also has a bearing on family in the instruction to "be fruitful and increase in number." Children were not an afterthought to ensure the human race continued following the fall and impending death of Adam and Eve. Children were part of the original creation that God saw and considered "very good." This affirms what we previously noted, that families are also part of the image of the Triune God: father, mother and child (or children) forming a three-part analogy of the Trinity.

Thursday: Genesis 1:29–30

God is difficult for us to comprehend, so perhaps the reason for similarity between the Trinity and family is that we might come to some understanding of his relationship to us. For as the relationship within a family pictures for us the relationship within the Trinity, Scripture also tells us that the same love that exists between members of the Trinity is extended from God to us.

The Bible uses two helpful pictures to describe God's relationship to us: marriage and the child/parent relationship. God's people are frequently referred to as God's wife in the Old Testament[1] and as the Bride of Christ[2] in the New Testament. Similarly, they are seen as God's children in both the Old[3] and New Testaments.[4] In each of these cases, we can recognize the extent of God's love, care and guidance for his people by the human relationships that we experience.

But these verses also remind us that God's love is practical in that he not only gave instruction for rulership of the earth but also provided the resources needed for it. This promise of provision reminds us of Jesus' promise for provision for us and our families as we seek his desires.[5]

Friday: Genesis 2:4–22

We read previously that the equality of men and women is established within the opening chapters of the Bible. In particular, the image of God stamped on all men and women is the basis for treating all persons with reverence. It is notable that even secularists, who deny any meaningful reality beyond what is perceived by our five senses, see something transcendent in humanity. The Canadian Charter of Rights and Freedoms, similar to documents in other nations, points to an indefinable sacrosanct quality in humanity, both male and female.

But many cultures make women subservient, and even some Christians believe in the superior role of men and point to this passage to support their belief. For instance: Doesn't the fact that the female was taken from the body of the male make her derived

---

[1] Hosea 1:2–3; 3:1–3; Ezekiel 16:1–19
[2] 2 Corinthians 11:2–3; Revelation 19:7
[3] Isaiah 49:15; 66:13
[4] John 1:12; 1 John 3:1
[5] Matthew 6:31–33

and therefore inferior? But Paul reminds us that men and women are interdependent, for all men since Adam have come from the female.[1] Well then, doesn't the fact that she was created second give her secondary status? But the animals were created before Adam, and this didn't give them superior rank.

Ah, but the woman was created to be a helper. Doesn't this indicate a subservient *role* even if she was *created* equal? Sorry, it can't, for several psalms remind us that God is our helper[2] and he is not subservient to us. Likewise, the woman being designated as a helper is not a sign of subservience to the man. Each sex has qualities and resources that dovetail in completing the tasks of life and fulfilling God's commission to order and sustain the earth. "Helper" can mean both a supporter who is less skilled and one who has required superior skills, and in a good marriage this works both ways. Not only does procreation require both sexes, but the complementary skills and psychologies created in the male and female are ideally necessary for raising a family.

Weekend ~ Finding Equality

Ann and I were born, raised and married in England, in an entirely different culture to the current North American culture. It was a Christian culture—not one in which everyone was a Christian but where Christian values were universally accepted. However, the marriage partnership was definitely patriarchal; the wife was expected to support decisions made by the husband. For example, although we discussed it together, the decision to emigrate to Canada in the 60s was my decision. Ann dutifully went along, although she confided later that she thought I was crazy—I had just completed my architectural training and was ready to develop a career. At that point our union was clearly not illustrating the equal partnership of the Bible.

---

[1] 1 Corinthians 11:11–12
[2] Psalms 33:20; 46:1; 70:5; 118:7; 121:1–2

After we arrived in Canada, things changed. Ann noticed the independence of North American women and realized the lopsided arrangement of our marriage. With assertion on her part and bewilderment on mine, things began to change. If she was uncomfortable with a projected decision of mine, I heard about it, and so began an education on my part and a balancing of the marriage responsibilities. Despite my Christian background, I had not yet come to an understanding of the relationship between husband and wife that the Bible taught, rather accepting the patriarchal version of biblical interpretation that was current—and convenient—at the time.

I could have considered this change too belittling to my manhood, but I found that the injection of female ideas and intuition into our plans contributed to better decisions. Not only that, I became more and more appreciative of the abilities and plain commonsense of the lovely and talented wife God had given me. How could I have been so ignorant of the great resources Ann brought to our marriage and blind to the guidance Scripture gave me? The simple answer is arrogance; I used to believe that I always had the better and final answers to all of life's questions.

Monday: Genesis 2:23–24

For most of my life I puzzled over the meaning of "one flesh" referred to in the verses of today's reading. Eventually though, it became clear that the consummation of marriage by intercourse effectively instituted the "one flesh" idea. As Eve was taken from Adam's side, both she and Adam were literally one piece of flesh being made from the same lump of clay. In a similar way, the sexual union between a man and wife makes the two as though *they* were both made from the same piece of soil or the same flesh.

The Greek philosopher Aristophanes, in an amusing and delightful parody on the one flesh principle, suggested that human beings originally had four arms and legs, moving about in cartwheel fashion. Eventually, the gods split them in two, roughly into the form we know today, but leaving the halves forever seeking to be reunited with their other split half. This reunification then provided the intercourse that became marriage and enabled the furtherance of the human race.

What is clear from our reading is that the marriage relationship is so strong that it breaks the natural parent/child relationship, this despite the fact that the child is physically part of the flesh of the parents. This lends emphasis to the idea that the marriage relationship is not only stronger than the parent/child relationship, but marriage creates a greater "one flesh" relationship than that of parents and child. This is the one flesh status of marriage partners the Genesis writer understood and Jesus affirmed.[1]

Tuesday: Genesis 3:1–13

Why is there so much tension between the sexes? If they were meant to live in companionship together, why is there constant friction and break-up? As we shall see from today's reading, there are good reasons: Adam and Eve's fall into sin radically altered the bond between them as well as their relationship with God. What process brought this about?

First, there was the failure to make a joint decision whether to eat the forbidden fruit. Eve's choice was made without consulting Adam, in violation of the joint responsibility given to them. Equally, Adam abdicated his responsibility for Eve's welfare by participating after the fact instead of interceding for her. By blaming Eve rather than protecting her, Adam developed antagonism between them. Eve passed the blame down the line— "the devil made me do it." By playing the "blame game," both Adam and Eve tried to absolve their guilt while effectively admitting it.

Adam and Eve's sin not only drove a wedge between them but also interfered with their communion with God. At first that communion was close, desired by God and enjoyed by them as they walked together "in the cool of the day." But their sin turned joy to fear, innocence to shame and severed direct communion with God. He was the One who could steer them through the jungle of existence they had now penetrated. This was not a complete break with God, but it altered their relationships. Self-centredness interfered with the bond between the couple, and independence from God threatened to cut off contact with him. Recognizing similar attitudes that may exist within our marriage is the first step to increasing the joy of the relationship.

---

[1] Matthew 19:5

Wednesday: Genesis 3:14–16

There were consequences to Adam and Eve's disobedience. For Adam, it meant toil to provide for his family. For Eve, it meant pain in childbirth and a change in her relationship with her husband. It was not that God imposed the change, but rather, he forecast what the results of her sin would be. Specifically, he declared this enigmatic phrase, "Your desire will be for your husband, and he will rule over you."

Did this "desire" mean sexual attraction or the need for protection? Would it mean a need to emulate her husband? All these could be understood from the phrase, but there is probably a more sinister meaning. God's response to Cain before he killed Abel[1] is a pointed comparison. The phrase "it desires to have you, but you must master it" is the identical Hebrew grammatical construction to the phrase used in speaking to Eve, and domination is clearly in view. It seems obvious from today's Western culture that the battle of the sexes is one of domination, but in the natural order of things, because men are physically stronger, they will generally continue to dominate.

Also, in the words to Eve there was a promise that Satan would be destroyed by a Descendant of hers at some future time, predicted by God in his words to the serpent: "He will crush your head." This foreshadowed the death of Jesus that brought freedom for women and restored the equality that was lost at the fall. There is no longer any difference between the status of male and female as all human divisions were cancelled at the cross.[2] The recognition of equality in Christ is the cornerstone, not only of women's freedom from domination, but also of equitable treatment within the family—a restoration of creation as God intended it to be.

---

[1] Genesis 4:7
[2] Galatians 3:28

Thursday: Genesis 3:17–19

While much has been made of women's suffering as a result of the fall, men did not escape without penalty. Adam learned that sin pollutes the environment[1] and distresses the people involved. In Adam's case, the ground would be destabilised, not operating the way it was designed, creating undesirable products and necessitating toil to ensure growth. The unstable environment possibly accounts for the floods, drought, earthquakes and hurricanes that we still experience as nature operates contrary to its design, for "the whole creation has been groaning as in the pains of childbirth right up to the present time."[2]

It should be noted that the toil to produce provisions for life was designated to Adam. Eve would have her hands full in childbirth and child-rearing. This passage, together with yesterday's, indicates the distinctive roles that sin conferred on men and women, but I doubt that these passages are meant to deny women the possibility of pursuing fulfilling roles and service both inside and outside of the family.[3] Rather, male toil would be the primary source of food for the family, relieving women of heavy physical work. Too many women today are forced into menial tasks in order to put bread on the table, particularly those in poor families and single-mother households.

Feminism has also tended to denigrate the male role, resulting in many wives underestimating the load that working husbands carry. Men's work is often unfulfilling, stressful and sometimes humiliating. Hard physical labour or heavy mental effort drain a man of energy he would like to spend on his family. A husband's career is not always what it is cracked up to be, and he covets his home as a retreat from the rigours of business life.

---

[1] Cf. Leviticus 18:26–28; Numbers 35:33–34; Deuteronomy 21:22–23
[2] Romans 8:22
[3] Compare the varied roles of the virtuous woman, Proverbs 31:10–31

Friday: Genesis 3:20–4:2

The first verse of our reading today is probably best known in its King James Version (KJV) translation: "And Adam knew Eve his wife; and she conceived." Other translations use "had relations,"[1] "had sexual intercourse"[2] or "lay"[3] in place of the KJV's use of "knew." While the KJV is technically correct—translating the Hebrew word *yada* for "he knew"—*yada* here clearly means intercourse, and other translations seek to bring out this meaning.

The Hebrew word for "know" is also used for a variety of other related meanings. The Bible describes Adam as "knowing good and evil"[4] and uses the word "know" in the sense of simple acquaintance,[5] a close relationship like that between Moses and God,[6] and also God's total knowledge of humanity and human ways—even before birth.[7] This use of the same word for many aspects of life, including sex, raises the idea that the Hebrews recognised sexual intercourse as a part of the whole of life.

In contrast, our Western culture today exhibits sex as an isolated event, a social recreational device like bowling or a game of cards. But for women particularly, intimacy is companionship, caring and cosseting, a place of protection and support for their own yearnings. They do not easily divorce sex from the overall events of married life and there is little fulfilment for them in sexual activity without fulfilment in these other areas.

When a husband fails to appreciate this need in his partner, sex becomes simply a relief device for the him; his wife feels used and it is no longer a shared activity. It may also signify a breakdown in the shared closeness and companionship both men and women yearn for.

---

[1] New American Standard Bible
[2] The Living Bible
[3] New English Bible and New International Version
[4] Eve also; see Genesis 3:5
[5] Exodus 1:8
[6] Deuteronomy 34:10
[7] Psalm 139:1–4.

Weekend ~ Feminism

This week we have discussed the war between the sexes that the sin of Adam and Eve generated. The latest manifestation of this conflict is the rise of feminism during the latter part of the last century and continuing today. Plainly, men's domination of women in the world is a major cause for concern. The equality promoted at creation is far from complete, even in Western societies, and the effort for greater equality is a scriptural mandate. Not only is equality a part of the image of God lost at the fall, but it is also restored at the cross.[1]

However, extreme feminism concludes that, as men generally rule the world, they are the cause of the world's evil—men are a necessary evil to propagate the race and the world would be a safer and happier place if women replaced them. This clearly falls into the same error as male domination. Inequality in marriage cuts both ways, with stories of "henpecked husbands" and women "wearing the pants" now being commonly used as caricatures. Despite this, it is true that the major offenders in inequality are male, as predicted in Scripture.[2] Worse, some claim that it is the male role to fulfill this prophecy and they distort Scripture to support it.

Feminism only errs when it distorts the God-given roles of the sexes or elevates women above men. Its desire to seek equality of value and function for women in society is to be commended, but it is in the family relationships we can make the biggest difference. A discussion between you and your partner on what equality should look like in your marriage can only enhance the relationship. In the short run, it may be a source of friction as any underlying resentments are aired, but an agreement—even compromise—can only improve the companionship and enjoyment of working together.

---

[1] Galatians 3:28
[2] Genesis 3:16

Monday: Genesis 4:1–8

It is evident from this passage that, even though Cain and Abel's parents communicated God's requirements to them both, it was no guarantee that the boys would be godly children. Criticism is often levelled at God for his unwillingness to accept an offering from Cain's trade while accepting Abel's. It has been suggested that a sacrificial lamb was necessary from both of them to atone for their sin. This may have been true later in Israel's history, but there is nothing in our reading requiring it in this case. Rather, there is the assertion that Abel brought firstborns from his flock, while Cain brought his offering "in the course of time"—perhaps leftovers at the end of the season. It is most likely that the lack of a "firstfruit" offering of thanks for the harvest was Cain's downfall.

Our first parents experienced sibling rivalry in the same way many of us have. In this case, there was opportunity for Cain to be restored. He had the choice to "do what is right" or to give in to his anger and let sin shape his actions. Here again, God, the perfect parent, could only give wise alternatives; Cain retained freedom of choice as all children eventually do. In this case, Cain chose wrongly: Abel was murdered and his parents grieved.

When siblings are born close together, rivalry may start at an early age. As a general rule, the greater the age between siblings, the less severe rivalry becomes. Children can be taught at an early age to restore relationship with each other after disagreements, especially as part of their service to God. If this is instilled early in life, significant breaks in sibling relationships are unlikely. The problem in Adam's household may have been that knowledge of God and his ritual requirements was passed to the boys without the practical application of obedience to God in daily life.

Tuesday: Genesis 4:10–24

Cain was unrepentant. He was fearful of his punishment and God was gracious to ensure his life was spared. But there is no indication that his attitude toward God changed. What is worse, those who descended from him carried the same attitude towards God and life. This is particularly noticeable in Lamech, who justified his violent behaviour by referring back to God's sevenfold punishment of Cain's potential killers. But that assurance to Cain was specific to him and at God's prerogative. Not only was it out of context for Lamech to use, Lamech took the liberty of increasing its severity. Here we have a specific example of the sin of the father being repeated in succeeding generations.

The question arises as to why God allowed Cain to survive; after all, later punishment for murder was death. There is no easy answer to this—it is an early example of the pervasiveness of evil and the apparent ability of perpetrators to avoid its consequences. What is clear is that there existed for Cain, Lamech and other violent people the freedom of conscious choice that is available to every human; their choices simply summarized their attitude towards God and brought suffering to others. As humankind is made in the image of God, violence against a person is violence against God, and the person responsible will face the penalty for it—often at human hands,[1] and if not, eventually from God himself.[2]

The importance of godly parental examples cannot be emphasized enough; it comes through frequently in Scripture and will be often advocated in these pages. A godly life is not only

---

[1] Genesis 9:6
[2] Exodus 20:5

more likely to be a happy one, but of greater importance, it may provide for godly generations to come. Unfortunately, the opposite is also true. What legacy are we leaving to our children and grandchildren and those who follow them?

Wednesday: Genesis 4:25–26; 5:18–24

We are saddened by the exploits of Cain and Lamech, whose arrogance led to rejecting God's direction and increased violence and misery around them. But the birth of Adam's third son heralded a new beginning as "men began to call on (or proclaim) the name of the Lord." Eve's recognition that her children came from God[1] indicates that Adam and Eve retained some relationship with their Creator, which they endeavoured to pass on to their sons. While the image of God was stamped upon humankind, note the sobering addition that Seth was created in Adam's likeness. The lingering image of God was still evident, but marred by the sin that Adam and Eve had introduced into the human race.

The stage was set for the future as Seth, born with a sinful nature, sought to develop the relationship of humanity with God. Clearly, the faith was handed down through many generations (Enoch "walked with God"), but Seth's example was not copied by all of his descendents and many died in the flood. They included Methuselah, Enoch's son, who at the time of the flood was 969 years old. Had he followed in his father's faith, he might have reached 1000. Even Noah's father was more concerned with God's curses than his care.[2] Still, the faith was carried down the line to Noah, who walked with God[3] and was saved from the flood.

Thus, in these few verses we have sketched out the dilemma that we all face today: we desire to reflect God's likeness but are

---

[1] See also Genesis 4:1
[2] Genesis 5:28–29
[3] Genesis 6:9

continually distracted by our innate sinfulness, whether on a personal basis or on a community level. All this is a reminder that, like Seth, we need to maintain and demonstrate our faith to our children, even if it is not guaranteed that they will follow in our footsteps. Consider this: without our example, we can almost guarantee they won't.

Thursday: Genesis 5:1–4

F amily was God's idea. Even before the fall, Adam and Eve were instructed to be fruitful.[1] Although this reading reminds us that God created man in his own image, Adam eventually gave birth to children in *his* own likeness. What was the difference? Seth probably carried some physical similarity to Adam just as children today inherit similarities from their parents. But in the cryptic comparison between God's image and Adam's image there is more likely a contrast between the perfection that God created and the fallen race that now came into being as a result of Adam's sin. Later on, King David also recognised in himself this tendency to sin from birth.[2]

When I retired, I took a course in Philosophy at the local university. I joined a class of about a hundred or so, mostly late teenagers and young adults. The question arose as to whether children were born good or evil. Aware of the Bible's teaching on this subject, I volunteered that I had tried to raise three children and that my experience was that they were born evil. I expected a sharp rebuttal from some, but was greeted instead with a burst of laughter from the whole class. It seemed that they recognized some truth in my assertion from their own memories of childhood—even the instructor suggested that their parents might agree with me.

The idea that children are born with a clean slate—that they have no inherent knowledge of good and evil—is a totally secular

---

[1] Genesis 1:28
[2] Psalm 51:5

idea with little to commend it. My father always held that children were the proof of the doctrine of depravity: they need to be instructed on how to be good; bad behaviour seems to come naturally. Ann's grandmother suggested that letting a child grow up without discipline was like expecting a garden to grow beautiful without planting or tending it. Like us, our children are born with a sinful nature.

Friday: Genesis 6:13–21

Verse 18 in today's reading contains the first biblical use of the Hebrew word for covenant. The idea of covenant is central to the Old Testament's message of salvation, God's plan to secure humankind's future with him in response to the sentence of death imposed for their sin.[1] The plan unfolds its complexity slowly throughout the Old Testament but commences here with a simple story of the saving of one family and animal life at a time of judgment on the earth. The provision of the ark for Noah and his family is a symbol of the provision for our safety from God's judgment in the death of Jesus Christ for our sin.

A covenant is different from a contract, which sets obligations on both parties. The astonishing feature of a covenant is its totally unconditional nature. Noah was not required to perform any special deed in order to obtain the safety of the ark other than simply accepting the covenant signified by entering into the ark. Conversely, he could have ignored and rejected God's covenant in the face of the resulting danger. A fuller extent of the covenant would become clearer to Noah after the flood. It would be amplified throughout the Old Testament and gain its fullest expression in the New Testament's offer of salvation to all who would receive it. Later readings will elaborate on the concept that marriage is also a covenant, based on the pattern of God's covenant to us that is the focal point of the Bible's message.

---

[1] Genesis 2:17

The ark ensured the continuation of the human race and life on planet earth. Not only were there sufficient animals and birds—either seven or two of both sexes[1]—but a full family of humans was included: Noah and his wife, their three sons and their wives, eight in all. While we are not advised of the spiritual status of Noah's family members at the time, Noah's faithfulness provided a shield for the whole family at least for a time.[2] The benefits to the children of a couple that maintains their faithful allegiance to God and to each other cannot be underestimated.

Weekend ~ Great Expectations

I'm sure that you have sought expertise from many sources to assist in childrearing. Unfortunately, many parenting "helps" assume a perfect parent stereotype that none of us match up to. Few recognise parents' individual limitations or the gap between theory and practice. In addition, much Christian teaching implies that every obstacle and limitation will be defeated with God's help. All these approaches produce unrealistic expectations. We can only influence, not determine, our child's future. We can only determine to be a good parent, not necessarily to raise a good child.

The period of greatest influence is in the earliest years when the child is the most dependant, approximately from birth to six years of age. Our influence wanes as the child ages, reducing fastest in the middle years until about twelve. It is between the years of twelve to eighteen, when the child reaches adulthood, that the loss of influence is most acute and gives parents the most stress.

Parents have limitations, sometimes determined by genetics and/or their family and cultural environments. We are constrained by our heredity and temperament. Any sickness or handicap we

---

[1] Genesis 7:2–3
[2] See Genesis 19:12–16. God promised deliverance for Lot's whole family although his sons-in-law rejected it.

have or accidents that happen will affect our parenting. Culture, school and peer pressure, family relationships and how we react to situations will shape results. Living conditions and the number and sequence of children will also establish parental effectiveness with each child.

No wonder we need all the help we can get. It is good to take advantage of the helps that are available, but when we meet intractable situations, we will ultimately find that our final "help comes from the Lord, the Maker of heaven and earth."[1]

---

[1] Psalm 121:2

Monday: Genesis 7:1–10

God works in families. This is evident in today's reading, as God told Noah to bring his whole family into the ark. We have no way of knowing the spiritual status of his family except for what we can surmise from Ham's later behaviour.[1] Other examples of God's interest in families abound. For instance, Lot's sons-in-law—and any others of Lot's family—were included in the escape from Sodom, although they refused to go.[2] Rahab's family was included in her escape from Jericho.[3] The Philippian jailer's whole family was included at his conversion.[4] Paul indicated that there is sanctification for an unbelieving partner for the sake of the children of the union; presumably that sanctification is for the period of childhood.[5]

Of course, it could be argued that God had to save Noah's family to ensure the continuation of the human race, but the same could hardly be said of Lot or Rahab. You may recall that we have already established that the stamp of God's Trinity is on the family and that the family is part of the image of God on humankind. This would certainly confirm the importance of the family to God. But Jesus also showed compassion for the close

---

[1] Genesis 9:20–23

[2] Genesis 19:12–14

[3] Joshua 6:22–23

[4] Acts 16:29–34

[5] 1 Corinthians 7:14

bond between parent and child. He raised two children back to life out of sympathy for their parents.[1]

This all illustrates that God is vitally interested in your family and looks upon them with compassion. This applies not just to parents and children, but as Lot and Rahab show, often to the extended family as well. As prayers for our families are always a priority, so also is God's interest in answering those prayers. We know parents who prayed for twenty years for the return of a child to the Lord. It seemed for so much of that time that the prayers were never going to be answered, but they learned that God answers in his own time, in his own way and for his own reasons.

Tuesday: Genesis 9:1–17

We are all familiar with the rainbow that often occurs when it rains. Many of us are also aware of the Bible story in today's reading, which identifies the rainbow with God's promise not to flood the earth again. Of continuing interest in this covenant is that, like the covenant with Noah, it is totally unconditional.

Myths about the rainbow have grown up since then, particularly about the pot of gold supposedly at its end. But that gold is as ephemeral as the rainbow itself, which is simply an image refracted through a million raindrops. It is not the rainbow that assures us that the flood will not recur, but God, who keeps his promise. Under certain atmospheric conditions the rainbow displays a full circle. It is a reminder of the ring of gold that promises a secure marriage. But the ring, like the rainbow, is not the basis of the promise; it is only a symbol. The promise is only as good as each partner's faithfulness to the other.

The basic intention of marriage is a promise of faithfulness — that pledges made to each other will be kept, particularly to retain sex within the bounds of the marriage. As God promised no more

---

[1] Mark 5:35–43; Luke 7:11–15

flood, so the man promises no more women—and vice versa. The promise made in the traditional marriage covenant is unconditional, even as God's rainbow covenant made no demands of Noah and his family. We all recognize that, in practice, marriage becomes a scene of give and take, and there are practical limits to human endurance. Nonetheless, it is sobering to recall that when we married we made a covenant to remain faithful irrespective of our partner's actions—for better or for worse.

Wednesday: Genesis 9:18–29

Nakedness has always engendered a sense of shame ever since Adam and Eve's sin in the Garden of Eden.[1] Today's reading gives an account of Noah's moment of weakness and Ham's apparent misuse of it. Was Ham's report to his brothers one of mirthful amusement, ridiculing his father's state? We don't know, but his brothers certainly took exception to it. They treated their father with honour rather than with Ham's indifference. Upon waking, Noah showed even greater concern about Ham's dishonour than his brothers did. This is the only story that we have of Noah's sons, and it is presumably added to show their ongoing attitude and relationship with their father and his faith.

Did Noah's blessings and curses on his sons fix their futures, or were Noah's remarks simply a prediction of the future for each of them if they continued the same course? As we have seen with Adam and Eve, God's curses on them were outcomes, not necessarily judgments, of their sinful act and its consequences. Perhaps we should think of outcomes and judgments as one and the same—there are natural outcomes for good or bad behaviour, although not always consistent in this unstable world. To put it another way, our lives generally go well or badly depending on whether or not we follow our Creator's instructions.

---

[1] Genesis 2:25; 3:7, 10

At the very least, Noah was giving his sons good advice, which is required of all fathers. When the joy of fatherhood is tempered with sadness and fear at a child's waywardness, we have to ask ourselves if we have been negligent in this area—we can always find some omission to raise our guilt. But the fact that children eventually make their own decisions does not release us from our responsibilities to point out the hazards of ignoring our Creator's requirements.

Thursday: Genesis 10:6–20

This passage must seem totally boring, consisting mainly of lists of unpronounceable names with little relevance to family life. What interest could we possibly have in exploring Noah's descendents? Yet genealogy is of interest to many who pore over ancestry lists to seek a background for themselves. Our sense of identity is often wrapped up in those who have gone before us, particularly our parents. This morning's list notes the influence of Ham upon his descendents.

Shem was the father of the Semitic races, which included the Jews and eventually gave birth to Jesus. From the little we know of Ham, he appears to be the black sheep of the family, and the enmity between Ham and Shem forecast by Noah follows them down to the descendents of today. The list of Ham's descendents is instructive. Two of his sons we are familiar with: Mizraim (Egypt) and Canaan, Israel's idolatrous tempters in Joshua's time and for the next 900 years. Nimrod, in verse 8, created the historic cities of Nineveh, capital of Assyria, and Babylon, both of which were responsible for the deportation and enslavement of Israel in the sixth century BC.

Egypt's descendents, the Casluhites, gave birth to the Philistines, who oppressed the Israelites during the time of the Judges and David's reign and gave name to present day Palestine. Canaan's descendents, verses 15–19, were an assortment of nations that also opposed Israel. Sidon provided Jezebel for Israel's queen. Several of the other nations eventually came under

God's judgment for their sin.[1] Eventually, the Canaanites peopled the cities of the plain that God destroyed by fire,[2] while others moved into present day Gaza.

It is unlikely that we will have the same influence in history. However, the list of fractious nations that descended from Ham repeats the warning to us that our attitudes can significantly influence our children and the generations that succeed them.

Friday: Genesis 11:27–32; 12:4–5

Ten years into our marriage and with two young children, Ann and I emigrated from England to Canada. My parents, together with brothers and sisters and Ann's grandmother and aunt who had raised her during her teenage years, were at the docks as we boarded the ship that would carry us to our new country. The excitement of the trip made me unmindful of the pain of parting that it brought to our families. It wasn't until several years later that my father told me of the lump in his throat that lasted for several days after we left with our children. Fortunately, the increasing ease of air travel made for frequent transatlantic flights to visit and enjoy some spectacular holidays together.

But the pain of separation is real. Reading between the lines, Terah mourned the loss of his first son by naming his final settlement, Haran, after him. So it would have been a second blow to him to lose his son Abram, his daughter Sarai[3] and his grandchildren as they completed the journey to Canaan that Terah had initiated. But unlike our journey to Canada, Abram's journey was less of a choice and more of a response to the call of God. Abram believed God's promise that the land would be given to

---

[1] Note the repetition of several nations in Genesis 15:12–21.

[2] Sodom, Gomorrah, Admah and Zeboiim, Deuteronomy 29:23.

[3] Sarai (later Sarah) was Abram's (later Abraham) stepsister as well as his wife, see Genesis 20:11–13.

his descendents, even when he discovered its fulfilment was centuries away.[1]

You may be feeling the pain of separation because your son or daughter has received a call from God for service abroad. Frequently that call is to hazardous lands—the world is an increasingly dangerous place. Today's electronic communications and ease of travel may soften the blow, but you are joining— perhaps less willingly—in the sacrifice that marks the Christian call. Our children will make their own decisions regarding life; we must prepare ourselves for the possibility of a call of God on their lives and support their sacrifice with our own.

Weekend ~ The Covenant Relationship

As you may have gathered, one of the aims of these devotionals is to review much of the Bible's guidance that relates to interpersonal relationships at large and then apply it to our relationships as husbands, wives and children. Most of us are aware that we frequently treat our family members with less respect than we treat others, even despite the fact that we have a covenantal arrangement with our marriage partners that we do not have with the population in general. This may not be true of common-law marriages or casual relationships, as there is no formal commitment and therefore no pledge to be upheld.

Like the promises to Noah, marriage is a covenant, not a contract. A contract is void if either party should fail to fulfill the contract requirements. Traditional wedding vows do not have conditions dependent upon which each partner remains faithful to the other. Rather, each makes a vow to the other without conditions and "for better or for worse." The greatest example is the covenants made by God to his people—the old covenant to Israel and the new covenant to Christians—called the Old and New Testaments. The source of the assurance of faith is built on

---

[1] Genesis 15:13–14

the knowledge that God will keep his promises despite our lapses in maintaining our side of the covenant.

Unlike a contract, the marriage covenant remains in force even if our partner breaks his or her vows. While there are times when a total breakdown is unavoidable, we are not obliged to break our vows in retaliation for promises broken by our partner. The strength of a marriage is in the ability to maintain covenant vows through difficult times, always assuming the possibility of reconciliation. Using God's secure covenant promises as our guide and his forgiveness as our pattern, we can not only make our marriages more secure but also witness to the faithfulness of God in the process.

Monday: Genesis 12:1–7

The covenant God made with Noah[1] may be viewed as an interim measure by God, pending a specific covenant with humankind. The promise contained in the rainbow simply forestalled judgment on earth similar to the deluge; it did not preclude a further judgment on a sinful earthly population, and the later destruction of Sodom[2] may be an indication of things to come.[3] What we needed was a way out of our sinfulness, not judgment for it, and today's reading begins that salvation history that many of us have come to claim for ourselves.

These seven verses begin the covenant that God made for humankind's deliverance as God called Abram to a new land and a new life. The promise to Abram, given again with variations in the years and centuries following, was that a nation would descend from him and be given a land to call their own, one of international scope that promised to bless all peoples through him. There was no further warning of judgment to come but a promise of deliverance without conditions, except for one. This condition was not so much one of action but one of faith confirmed by Abram's move to a new land. Provision by God's grace and acceptance by faith, clearly enunciated in the New

---

[1] Genesis 9:9–17
[2] Genesis 19:23–25
[3] 2 Peter 3:10

Testament,[1] started here, since Abram's belief was accepted as righteousness.[2]

The bride-to-be's "yes" is a confirmation of faith placed in her future husband that he will fulfil his promises to her. Her further preparations for the wedding and their future together are not done to earn her husband's promise. His promise is a gift of his love for her, and her actions are simply a response of faith. In this way, the marriage covenant that we enter into reflects the relationship that Abram enjoyed with God, which we enjoy now as Abram's spiritual descendants. Or put another way, our marriages are a witness to the relationship of love that God has with us.

Tuesday: Genesis 15:1–7

When Ann and I came to Canada, there were four of us including our two young girls. At our present stage of life, with most of our grandchildren grown and beginning to marry and have their own children, we now have a family of eighteen and expect more to come. We covet all of them for the faith, which drives our desire to pray for all of them regularly. For those of you starting out in marriage, it may be difficult to visualize that you will probably generate a large family of children, grandchildren and great-grandchildren. But that is the legacy most of us will leave. And there is a vaster legacy for which we may be responsible. In our reading today, Abram is reminded of the vast family that will descend from him—as countless as the stars in the sky—and for us as for him, it requires many generations to accomplish.

However, the message to Abram in today's reading is that his descendents are from God, according to God's promise. It is a reminder that all children are a gift from God,[3] even those born

---

[1] Ephesians 2:8
[2] Genesis 15:6
[3] Psalm 127:3

under adverse circumstances. The destruction of foetuses in the womb is a rejection of this gift and consequently a rebuff to God, which is part of the reason Christians condemn abortion. For Abram, the fact that he believed that God would provide an heir was accepted by God as righteousness—an early example of salvation by faith—especially as Sarai, his wife, was past her childbearing years.

We believe that all our children, however pleasing or disappointing, are also gifts from God. Perhaps even Abram, watching his children and grandchildren, had doubts about their being God's gift to him. But all three of today's monotheistic religions—Judaism, Christianity and Islam—revere Abram as a man of great faith and humble obedience to God. He has influenced countless generations since, and millions of the world's people have retained that same faith in God. Will our descendents want to follow in our faith?

Wednesday: Genesis 16:1–16

This passage raises awkward questions. Was Abram's intercourse with Hagar a lapse of faith in God's promise for a son? In giving Sarai permission to "Do with her whatever you think best," did Abram tacitly condone Sarai's treatment of Hagar? Why would God promise descendants to Ishmael to match that of Israel if he knew the friction it would cause? In these questions we get a picture of real life, which itself raises unanswered questions. However, we can at least find clues that will help us avoid similar situations in our own lives.

Abram may have thought that the liaison with Hagar—culturally acceptable in his day—would fulfil God's promise of a son. He was understandably incredulous of the later promise that Sarai would bear the promised child, so he sought God's blessing on Ishmael.[1] Whatever Abram's reason for intercourse with Hagar, Ishmael's example reminds us that children from today's

---

[1] Genesis 17:17–18

illicit relationships and broken marriages may carry scars and resentment for a lifetime unless God intervenes. Today, blended families face additional challenges raising their children, as Sarai, Hagar and Ishmael later exhibited.[1]

Why God allowed Ishmael to become a nation can only be partially answered by the fact that we all bear the consequences of our actions. To take action to restrict the outcomes of our behaviour is to undermine our gift of free will; for if actions have no consequences then they have no significance. Later, God told Abram that he would keep his promise to Ishmael because he was Abram's son, equal to Isaac,[2] although the covenant that brought us salvation would be through Isaac. Despite the difference in birth between the two, God would treat them with equal dignity. All children, irrespective of the conditions of their birth, are equal before God.

Thursday: Genesis 17:1–14

As God changed Abram's name to Abraham, God repeated his promise that all the earth would be blessed though a Descendant of his.[3] In our reading today, God restated his promise to Abraham that he would become a great nation and the land would be his. What is introduced at this point is a reciprocal agreement, opened by the phrases "As for me" (verse 4) and "As for you" (verse 9).

Until now, Abraham has been participating in the covenant by faith with little outward sign of that participation. It is important to note that God's promise remained the same—a gift of grace to Abraham, making no requirement of Abraham to act in a way that earned his place in God's covenant. Rather, a sign was required to indicate that Abraham accepted the promises of God and was willing to participate in his covenant. This sign was shown by

---

[1] Genesis 21:8–10
[2] Genesis 21:13
[3] Genesis 18:18; 22:18

circumcision, and Abraham's descendants still show this commitment in their flesh. Not to have this mark was a rejection of that partnership and rightly denied that person membership in God's community.

Marriage is signified by the exchange of rings. Just saying "yes" is insufficient. By accepting her groom's ring, the bride outwardly expresses her faith and participation in her new husband's promises to her. The same is true of his acceptance of her ring. From that time on they both wear on their flesh the sign of the covenant they both willingly entered.

Friday: Genesis 19:1–11

To any parent, I'm sure, the actions of Lot in offering his daughters to a mob of licentious men must appear outrageous. It can only be a parody of Middle Eastern hospitality that he would protect strangers before his family. From our standpoint, there can be nothing to excuse Lot's behaviour toward his girls, but even so, there may have been reasons. Lot's thinking may have been paralysed by fear, as verse 9 suggests the whole family could have been raped. Lot's actions could also have been pure cowardice; he could have offered himself in place of his visitors and his daughters. While the offer of his daughters is repulsive and intolerable, he may have gambled that it would not be accepted because the intruders were homosexual.

This gamble might not be as farfetched as we imagine and, in fact, the offer of his daughters was not accepted. It is clear that the city of Sodom—from which the word sodomy comes—was completely homosexual: "*all* the men from *every part* of the city of Sodom—both *young* and *old*—surrounded the house" (my emphasis). The writer is at pains to note that all the men practised both homosexuality and violence. Here was the reason for Sodom's destruction: sin had "reached its full measure."[1]

---

[1] Note the use of this clause in Genesis 15:16

In contrast, there are countless stories of parents who willingly gave their lives for their children. Both the maternal and paternal instinct to protect the young is necessary and God-given to preserve the species that he created, whether animal or human. But in addition to instinct, humans have been given the ability to reason, which may be used to rationalize bad behaviour. We may not be called upon to sacrifice our lives for our children, but are we prepared to make other sacrifices to ensure their wellbeing?

Weekend ~ Facing Reality

The wife of a pastor visiting us once clearly enunciated that she could never see herself involved in adultery—smaller sins, yes, but that, no. It reminded me of the Bible verse that tells us it is surprisingly easy to fall in areas where we think we are standing firm.[1] It seems so obvious to shield our weak positions that we may leave our strong zones unguarded. Bearing in mind our fallen nature and tendency to deceive ourselves, I suggest adding warnings to the marriage vows. As an exercise, I have included some warnings in the following "Revised Version" of these vows. This is done partly tongue-in-cheek, but I believe it helps to place our capricious nature into the picture.

> "I now take you to be my wife (husband) according to God's holy Word, to have and to keep from this time forward. I will love, esteem and respect you, I will be faithful to you; I will encourage you to become all that God intends, for as long as we both shall live.
>
> "Should I fail to love you, I can expect a deteriorating closeness of companionship; should I fail to esteem and respect you, you will exhibit a deteriorating personhood and dignity; should I fail to be faithful to you, our marriage and our children's future will be in jeopardy. Should I fail to encourage you to become all that God intends, you will lose your individual

---

[1] 1 Corinthians 10:12

*distinctness and our combined potential for him will be lost.
Should my actions or attitudes bring our marriage to an end
before death parts us, we will both experience misery, displaced
children and an enduring sense of loss.*

"I make this solemn vow and covenant to you and to God."

I'm sure you can refine this with your own words and vows,
but you should be able to pick up the general idea. Perhaps you
might like to recite these vows to your partner and sense the
response in your own heart.

Week Seven

Monday: Genesis 19:12–16

We noted earlier with Noah that God is interested in families. With that story and the one we read today, God shows a particular interest in the families of godly men and women, even though some family members were not so inclined. As the impending judgment of Sodom drew near, the angels sent to rescue Lot asked him about his family: "Do you have anyone else here—sons-in-law,[1] sons or daughters, or *anyone else* in the city who belongs to you?" (my emphasis). The promise of safety for Lot covered not only himself but his extended family also.

It is clear that most of his family had little interest in God's warning. Lot's sons-in-law laughed at his entreaty and he received no response from anyone else. In fact, after a night of attempted persuasion, only his wife and two daughters took the warning seriously enough to leave, and even then they had to be dragged from the city by the angels. Despite God's mercy extended to the remainder of Lot's family, they had the freedom of choice whether to leave or go—and to their loss, they decided to stay.

This story also opposes the frequent belief that God's judgment is not real. Even predictable calamities can be ignored by the most obstinate. We can recall old Harry Truman, who refused to leave his home in the path of the Mount St. Helens

---

[1] Lot must have had other daughters than the two in yesterday's reading, as they were both virgins.

eruption in Washington State, and others who have remained in the paths of hurricanes despite warnings and perished as a result. We have frequently heard the response of those hit by catastrophes: "I never thought it would happen to me!" This sense of invincibility follows us all to some degree, but particularly the young. To train children in godly living from an early age will help preserve them from drunkenness, reckless driving, sexual disease, drug addiction and other hazardous pursuits that they may believe will not harm them.

Tuesday: Genesis 19:26–38

The urgency of Lot and his family's flight from Sodom was so great that they were told not to look back.[1] There wasn't even time to view the spectacular fireworks that erupted over the cities of the plain. We're not sure how Lot's wife died. It was probably not just a glance to the rear but perhaps grief at the life left behind or fear at the alarming sight that transfixed her to the spot until the fallout from the destruction overtook her. We do know that her disobedience, resulting in her death, had other tragic consequences in the future that might have been avoided had she lived.

Today there is a growing recognition of the value of women and their contribution to life, and most of us realize that families are far more practical with a woman's input. It is doubtful that Lot's wife would have defended Lot's decision to live in a cave with two adult virgin daughters. In addition, it was Lot's lack of faith in the angels' promise not to overthrow his small city of refuge[2] that led him to flee to the mountains in fear that it, too, would be destroyed. These two events—the death of Lot's wife's due to disobedience and Lot's flight to the mountains due to lack of faith—precipitated a further event to plague Israel's history.

---

[1] Genesis 19:17
[2] Genesis 19:19–22

The girls were faced with the cultural pressure of the time to have children. The actions of Lot's wife left them in a dilemma, to which they responded improperly by incest with their father. The resulting children generated the nations of Moab and Ammon, nations that frequently oppressed the Israelites. Lot's wife's actions affected both her generation and the long term. We cannot know where our actions may lead; we can only act according to the guidelines laid down for us by our Creator. But whatever our choice, the results of our choosing will surely follow.

Wednesday: Genesis 22:1–19

Previous readings have provided a dismal litany of parental errors and their consequences. So it is with some relief that we come to a parental story of tragic potential but a bright outcome. Whatever lapses of faith we can ascribe to Abraham, this one illustrates for us the dogged determination Abraham had to establish his faith in God's promises. His challenge was this: God was asking him to slay his childless son, through whom God had promised nations and—for our benefit—the One who would bless the world.[1] The words of faith uttered by Abraham in verse 8 on his way up to this crucial sacrifice are legendary. He knew by faith that God would somehow provide for a resolution without which all God's promises to him and to the world would be terminated.

But in addition, his words were prophetic concerning the One who would be the ultimate sacrificial Lamb. The story of Christ's crucifixion and resurrection is woven all throughout this event. Isaac appears to be the willing sacrifice; as an only son he was not withheld from sacrifice and was symbolically received back from the dead.[2] The event was so significant that the covenant God had made with Abraham was again confirmed: a nation, land (inferred by conquest) and a blessing to all nations through his offspring— "because you have obeyed me." The irony is that Abraham's

---

[1] Genesis 12:2–3, 17:21, 18:18
[2] Hebrews 11:19

obedience to a command that would negate all God's promises became the basis of their certainty.

We can sense the darkness in Abraham's soul as he trudged up Mount Moriah, but it cannot be compared with the joy he had at the reclamation of his son and revitalized fellowship with God. The intensity of the struggle that family life may bring cannot be compared with the joy of fulfilling our responsibility to God and knowing the benefits that will eventually accrue for our loved ones.[1]

Thursday: Genesis 24:1–9

What father wouldn't like to find a wife of his own choosing for his son? Someone has said that youth is wasted on the young, and certainly youth does not seem to be the ideal time to make the most important choices of life. This suggests there is some merit in arranged marriages, although the practice is unlikely for Western culture in the foreseeable future. But Abraham had that freedom to choose for his son Isaac, and he took advantage of it. In reality, he did not make the final choice, but he made two stipulations regarding the marriage that were consistent with the covenant that he had entered into with God in order to promote Isaac's commitment to it.

He did not want Isaac to settle back in Haran, the place Abraham left to follow God's call. The country God had promised Abraham was the best environment to keep Isaac faithful to the covenant. This is in pointed contrast to the neglect that Isaac gave to the selection of wives for *his* sons. Esau selected wives for himself from other clans[2] and Jacob—later setting out for Haran—only came back to Canaan because of God's intervention.[3]

Particularly, Abraham wanted a wife for Isaac from his own clan. It could be considered racial discrimination that he didn't

---

[1] Romans 8:18
[2] Genesis 26:34
[3] Genesis 28:15, 20–21

want Isaac to marry a Canaanite. But his objection was not their race, but rather their religion, for it was highly idolatrous. He wanted a wife for Isaac who would continue living within the covenant to which God had called the family.

We may not be able to choose those whom our children will marry, but we can pray for our children and grandchildren. We need to pray that they would come to faith in Christ and also pray for the partners they will marry—that those partners will keep them faithful to God and to each other.

Friday: Genesis 24:32–66

Abraham sent his servant to his brother's household to find a wife for his son Isaac. In our reading the servant is recounting his story to Laban (who later deceived Jacob), hoping Rebekah would be allowed to return with him to become Isaac's bride. It is the story of an arranged marriage, Abraham's servant seeking God's guidance as he searched carefully for a wife for Isaac. As the end of today's story shows, the marriage had a "once upon a time" start: "so she became his wife and he loved her."

Isaac's love for Rebekah was confirmed by two incidents. When Isaac saw his wife was barren, he prayed for her and she became pregnant.[1] Later, while in a neighbouring country ruled by Abimelech, Isaac referred to Rebekah as his sister. As her husband, he thought he might be killed on account of her great beauty. Abimelech was alerted to their married status when he "saw Isaac caressing his wife Rebekah."[2] The caress was obviously more than a brotherly embrace.

Here is the beginning of an "ever after" relationship. Most couples who marry expect that their marriages will last, each expressing by marriage that they want to be with the other for life. Experience shows that this is not always the outcome, as many marriages end in separation, divorce or even a continuing

---

[1] Genesis 25:21
[2] Genesis 26:7–8

dysfunctional relationship. Initial attraction and sacrificial care for each other can be too easily lost, illustrated in the later story of Isaac and Rebekah.

Weekend ~ I Believe; Therefore I Understand

One of the paradoxes of the Christian faith is the necessity to believe in order to understand. This goes against our natural thought process; it is easier to believe what we understand. Certainly, it is in conflict with the basis of our scientific age, where belief depends on verification of the facts. Unfortunately, when it comes to spiritual things, we can provide circumstantial evidence but final proof is not available to us. The agnostic bases his scepticism about the existence or character of God on this issue— he cannot know for certain and has no proof of either God's existence or non-existence. At least in this he is being more honest than the atheist, for the absence of proof of God does not prove he does not exist.

To the non-Christian, faith doesn't make sense, and this has been true since Paul's day, when preaching the Gospel appeared foolish to the Greek intellectuals.[1] Abraham's trek up Mount Moriah went against all logical thinking and Paul's preaching on Mar's Hill in Athens was greeted with ridicule by many who heard it.[2] Jesus was clear about the need for faith to provide understanding by claiming that it is the Spirit of God that provides conviction of the need of a Saviour,[3] with which Paul also concurred.[4] Accepting the message of Christ's sacrifice on the cross for us opens the door to a new world of understanding about God, ourselves, others and the world around us.

For many people (and perhaps yourself) the Bible was a dry book that made little sense until they became Christian. But

[1] 1 Corinthians 1:23
[2] Acts 17:18, 32
[3] John 16:8
[4] 1 Corinthians 2:11–12

almost overnight, the Bible suddenly made sense, providing insights about ourselves and all aspects of life, which in turn nurtured a greater interest in spiritual things. This is simply a reflection of the need to believe in order to understand spiritual things and the fact that greater understanding leads us to deeper truths of our faith. Belief and understanding create an upward spiral of learning and change that develops the true reflection of the image of God in us.

Week Eight

Monday: Genesis 25:19–28

The blissful relationship of Isaac and Rebekah did not last. Today's story is a classic that exposes the dangers of favouritism. Isaac favoured Esau while Rebekah favoured Jacob, each making their choice based on the individual temperaments that neither son could change. Certainly, both sons could have tried to please both parents by responding to both parents' desires for them, but it would have been counterproductive for each son to unnaturally change his temperament. Of greater significance, it would have been wrong to expect the children to compensate for the parents' preferences. It is the responsibility of parents to love and provide opportunity equally, irrespective of personal inclination.

That is not to ignore the fact that we may have favourite children. A child that thinks and acts as we do is more likely to attract us than one whose direction in life is opposite to our preference. It is easy to draw a parallel with a family where a sports-oriented dad may have more difficulty relating to a studious bookworm son than a son whose love of outdoors and involvement in sport matches his own. Conversely, a mother may worry and fret more over a gregarious high energy risk-taker than a stay-at-home child that her motherly eye can protect.

It is not the natural affinity that we may have with one of our children that is wrong; it is the blatant exposure of that favouritism at the expense of another child. Worse still, with Isaac and Rebekah it was probably not just favouritism that influenced their actions towards their sons, but just as likely, they were using their sons as pawns in an established conflict with each other, as later events suggest. Parents who use their children against each other set both their children and themselves up for misery as the further accounts of Isaac and Rebekah illustrate.

Tuesday: Genesis 26:1–6

We have seen that God made a covenant with Abraham, repeating it twice more[1] to confirm it. Clearly, God wanted Abraham to be under no misapprehension regarding his promise. However, we might wonder if the promise died with Abraham if it was never mentioned again. But our reading today records the promise being repeated again to Abraham's son Isaac, particularly the promise: "All peoples on earth will be blessed through you and your offspring." Not only did this confirm the covenant to Isaac, it was also an affirmation that succeeding generations would continue to carry the promise. Not only would that promise be carried in their memory, but also in their flesh, for as long as the lineage was kept alive. The promise of an Offspring to bless the world remained alive for future generations.

From then on, God continually reminded Israel of the promise made with Abraham, Isaac and later to Jacob, by referring to himself as the God of Abraham, Isaac and Jacob.[2] It was this God who appeared to Moses and led Israel out of Egyptian slavery. In this way, the covenant was affirmed to succeeding generations as an enduring promise, a mainstay in times of trial and affliction.

It is this God—whose promise is permanent—who calls us to make a covenant with our partners that can be relied on for a lifetime, especially through the difficult times. Those difficulties become moments of choice: either we can opt out of the marriage to avoid coping with the trouble (usually *not* the easiest way out)

---

[1] Genesis 18:18; 22:18
[2] Typically Exodus 3:6, 15 and many references in the OT

or we can determine to keep our covenant and resolve the problem for the strengthening of the marriage. Just as a ship captain's skill is learned on rough—not calm—seas, strong marriages are built by working through the difficult times.

Wednesday: Genesis 27:1–17

Was the friction between Isaac and Rebekah a result of their differing favouritism for their two sons, or was there some pre-existing hostility that the boys exploited? We cannot know for sure. Whatever the cause, by the time of today's reading the gap between Isaac and Rebekah was well established to a point of competition, evidenced as she eavesdropped on Isaac to gain the advantage. Rebekah was well aware of the prophecy that Jacob would lead Esau,[1] so she probably rationalized that she was in some way fulfilling God's will. She reminds me of the rebellious teenager that justified her behaviour by claiming she was fulfilling the prophecy that children would turn against their parents.[2]

But the boys were not innocent in this farce. Jacob had already obtained the birthright by sharp dealing, which Esau considered of little worth at the time,[3] although he regretted it later.[4] Despite his transfer of the birthright to Jacob, Esau was quite willing to receive it from his father. Jacob also acquiesced in Rebekah's elaborate subterfuge, only questioning whether it would work.

Most children will try to come between their parents at some point in order to achieve their ends. Not that small children are that scheming; they seem to act instinctively. The initial scenario looks quite harmless: the parents disagree on some course of action for a child and one parent feels compelled to defend the child and does so openly. The stage is set for the child to despise the other parent, who is then humiliated. If this practice continues,

---

[1] Genesis 25:22–23
[2] Matthew 10:21
[3] Genesis 25:29–34
[4] Hebrews 12:16–17

resentment builds in the victimised parent and self-righteousness in the other. The child develops the skill, which eventually becomes a means of manipulating parents and others in later life. The answer? Always discuss affairs affecting the child privately and face the child with a united front—even if one parent does not entirely agree with the decision.

Thursday: Genesis 27:18–40

The full story of Jacob is of a "street-wise" individual who knew instinctively how to take advantage of situations. Whatever misgivings he had as to whether his mother's deception would work, he performed his act flawlessly, finally persuading his father even though he could not camouflage his voice. He lied consistently and convincingly, even bringing God into his deception. In response, he received Isaac's blessing, which was normally reserved for the firstborn, fulfilling God's prophecy. Here is a perfect example of pragmatism at work—the end justifies the means. It assumes that God does not have the resources to bring about his own desires.

Esau showed genuine grief at his loss. He would have been about 80 years of age at this point and, like many of us, regretted the rashness of his youth. Unfortunately, many of the decisions we make in our earlier years have consequences in later life, and it requires the grace of God to deal with them. Although time ameliorated Esau's anger, both his and Isaac's angry responses were the direct result of Rebekah and Jacob's connivance. Rebekah is no longer heard from, her actions no longer had any significant influence and Jacob later lived a life of much grief as a result of *his* sons' actions.

This incident, of course, raises the question of what would have happened if Rebekah and Jacob had not intervened. Would the prophecy of Jacob's pre-eminence have been denied? How would God have accomplished his purposes if Esau had received the blessing given to Jacob? The answers are all in the realm of fantasy—we cannot know. The story does point out that God can use our foolhardiness as well as our faithfulness to accomplish his purposes. Without either, he will still complete his mission, but our faithfulness is more likely to bring harmony in the long run as we work *with* him for the sake of our children.

Friday: Genesis 27:41–28:9

Despite being well on in years, it appears that Jacob had not yet married. However, Esau had, not waiting for his parent's selection but making his own. He married Hittite women who were not of his parent's faith and "were a source of grief to Isaac and Rebekah."[1] Esau now sought to kill Jacob in revenge for losing his father's blessing, and again Rebekah used deception to convince Isaac to send Jacob away. She could probably have simply stated the truth—she was afraid for Jacob's life—but she preferred to discredit Esau by using his choice of women as an excuse to send Jacob away for a wife in their own clan.

At this point it appears that Isaac's anger at Jacob had dissipated. Perhaps he had come to terms with God's desire to pass his blessing through Jacob rather than Esau. (God's covenant given to Abraham had been passed to Isaac[2] and was now about to be repeated to Jacob.[3]) In addition, Esau was having second thoughts about his earlier marriages to his Hittite wives and tried to improve his relationship with his parents by marrying a daughter of Ishmael. In fact, his relationship with Jacob eventually improved, as he was welcomed him back to Canaan some twenty years later[4] and the two buried their father together.[5]

As rebellious children age—especially when they have children of their own—it is not uncommon for friction with parents to soften. Hostile relations with a child can cause as much grief as losing a child; it is ongoing and has the added burden of

---

[1] Genesis 26:34
[2] Genesis 26:2–5
[3] Genesis 28:13–15
[4] Genesis 33:4
[5] Genesis 35:27–29

antagonism. As we trust that time will soften our children towards us, prayer for them will help us maintain a tender attitude towards them.

Weekend ~ Favouritism

We have dwelt at length on the subject of favouritism. The outcomes we have seen would appear to make favouritism a sin. Yet many of us will have favourite children, especially in large families. It is not the favouritism itself that is harmful but the blatant showing of it. A family we knew had two children, a boy and a girl, of which the girl was the more highly treasured. She was attractive and the parents dressed her up and made a fuss over her to the exclusion of attention to the boy. He resented his sex, becoming uncertain of his identity and developing a latent homosexuality. Eventually, his confusion and humiliation drove him to suicide. We don't know if the parents ever realized their part in his death.

What is important is to be aware that all children are different. We cannot always treat every child the same; effective encouragement and punishment varies from child to child. What one child may take as a warning, another may accept as a challenge. Birth order also has an effect on the attention that children get. First children tend to be "control freaks" and are often lumbered with more duties than younger siblings. Middle children in families of three often receive less attention than the older and younger ones. Siblings of a handicapped child may often receive insufficient notice. It is these children that may become the victims of inadvertent favouritism and place themselves at risk by seeking the attention they need elsewhere.

Attention paid individually on a regular basis to each child, especially in the earlier years, can pay dividends later on. A child that feels special to his or her parents will develop a sense of acceptance and identity that will help to shield them from the dangers outside the home.

Monday: Genesis 28:10–22

Most of you will recall this story of Jacob's ladder, but much as we eat the flesh of a plum and throw the pit away, few will recall the message God gave to Jacob. The pit is the life within the plum to ensure future growth, and similarly, the message that Jacob received from God at the top of the ladder contains the promise of life from God to the world. The ladder and angels were only trappings to draw attention to the message. The prophecy to Jacob's mother, Rebekah,[1] is fulfilled in this passage.[2]

Jacob was later named Israel, and his twelve sons became the progenitors of the nation of Israel. But considering the conniving nature of Jacob, he seemed an unlikely candidate. He had little knowledge or regard for God up to the time of his deception of Isaac, talking to Isaac of "your God."[3] Yet it appears that God chooses people on the basis of their future faithfulness rather than their past record; it was especially true of Paul, the fiercest persecutor of the early church as recorded in the New Testament.

God called Jacob's attention to his grandfather, who was chosen by God on the knowledge that Abraham would "direct his children and his household after him to keep the way of the Lord

---

[1] Genesis 25:21–23

[2] Jacob receives the same covenant promise repeated to Abraham three times (Genesis 12:1–3; 18:18; 22:15–18) and again to his father Isaac (Genesis 26:2–5).

[3] Genesis 27:20

by doing what is right and just."[1] Abraham's selection was not just because of his personal faithfulness but on the basis of his future allegiance—particularly passing the faith to his household and his children. The greatest thing we can do for our children is to maintain our faithfulness to God. But it is also necessary that we ensure our children understand the importance of their own commitment to God.

Tuesday: Genesis 29:16–20

The saying goes that absence makes the heart grow fonder. Absence is also a drag; each day of separation seems like a year, which is fuelled by an intense longing to be together. So at first glance, it is difficult to understand Jacob's love for Rachel making years appear like days. But it seems that Jacob was not counting the waiting time but placing a value on the price to pay for such a bride; in his mind seven years seemed like a trifle to pay for her. In contrast, Jacob may have considered seven *days* too high a price for Leah. As it happened, he was deceived into paying seven years for Leah and then placed in hock for another seven years for Rachel.

It becomes clear that Jacob was not measuring the worth of the girls so much as his love for them. All this raises the issue of the value we place on our partners and how that value is measured. During courtship most lovers wax eloquent on the lengths to which they will go to win their beloved. But ask that question again after a few years of marriage. As the Christian view of love is one of service, measuring love then becomes a matter of measuring the level of service we give to our partner. Conversely, the level of selfishness that we expend on ourselves measures the amount of love lost.

In those heady days of first love, many a lover will claim he is prepared to die for his beloved, placing the ultimate value on her. This experience gives us some sense of the love of God that

---

[1] Genesis 18:19

resulted in the giving of his life for those he loved.[1] But Jesus not only gave his life for us, he rose again so that he could live for us. Few of us are required to fulfill that lofty pledge to die for our beloved, but that ideal can be fulfilled by living for her—and that may be more drastic in its implications than dying for her.

Wednesday: Genesis 29:21–35

Jacob was the arch deceiver, outwitting both his brother[2] and father.[3] In this passage, he met his match in Laban, who used him to marry off his two daughters and simultaneously ensure that Jacob would work for him for fourteen years without pay. As a result of Laban's deception, Jacob was left with two wives—not the recipe for a happy family. Both wives were unhappy: Rachel because she was barren, Leah because she was unloved.

Leah's story is heart-wrenching, for she was the innocent victim of Laban's trickery. Hers is a journey from hope to despair, but she finally finds her peace in God. The births of her four sons tell the story of her desire and effort to earn Jacob's love. Surely the birth of her first son, Reuben, would win Jacob's love, but it did not. She took comfort in the birth of her second, Simeon, but when Levi was born she hoped that three sons would bond Jacob to her. When none of this worked, the birth of her fourth son, Judah—meaning praise to God—brought her to the point of simply leaving her case with God, recognizing that Jacob would obviously always prefer Rachel.

Physical attraction is not sufficient on its own to sustain a marriage, but it is nonetheless a necessary element, and the difference between Jacob's relationship with Leah and Rachel illustrates this. The relationship between love and allure will always be a mystery, some mistakenly assuming one or the other to be the "real thing." In our story, Jacob's behaviour is not

---

[1] Matthew 20:28; Romans 5:6–8
[2] Genesis 25:27–34
[3] Genesis 27:18–24

blameless. Jacob could have eased Leah's misery, providing some healing of the wrong done to them both. When we have been deceived by a third party, it is too easy to transfer our resentment and anger to our partner—the closest target. But our partner is also our closest ally. To bring him or her on side to face the incident together not only strengthens us, but also strengthens the marriage.

Thursday: Genesis 29:31–35

We read these verses yesterday, but we also need to note— like Esau and Jacob—that the birthright depended not only on birth order but also on behaviour. Recall the fraud played on Jacob by his uncle Laban. After working for Laban for seven years to marry Rachel, Laban substituted Leah (presumably veiled and in the dark) to ensure she was married off before Rachel. Jacob did marry Rachel within a week, but he had to work another seven years in order to pay his debt for Rachel. The unfortunate result of this deception was that "Leah was not loved." But God had pity on Leah, who bore Jacob his first four children—Reuben, Simeon, Levi and Judah—while Rachel remained barren.

It was these four children of Leah's that were the most significant in the later life of the nation of Israel—and for us. In particular, Judah's clan eventually became the kingly line, giving birth to the "Lion of Judah," Jesus, the Messiah and our Saviour. But Judah was fourth in line; the elder sons were denied this special birthright as a result of their behaviour and lack of repentance. Their future, as well as Judah's, was foretold by their father, Jacob, before his death[1] and is recorded in more detail later.

There is no account of Leah's death, so we do not know if she was alive for the actions of her sons, but Jacob certainly was. Jacob was dismayed by the behaviour of his sons, as many parents are, but what is important to note is that all Jacob's children— including Reuben, Simeon and Levi—remained within the

---

[1] Genesis 49:3–12

covenant that God made with their forefathers. Our children are distinct individuals who will make their own decisions in life and may well pay the price of their foolish ones, but God is merciful and is open to repentance. he ever desires to renew fellowship with himself.

Friday: Genesis 30:1–2

The Canadian Parliament's legislation to legalize gay marriage opened the door to other alternate marriage relationships; in particular, it raised the question of polygamy. The idea that legalizing gay marriage could also promote serious discussion about polygamy was considered "ridiculous" by one Canadian prime minister. However, at the time of writing, polygamy exists in the province of British Columbia, and although it is against the law, it is not pursued by the police. This is partly because to do so would provoke a challenge under the Canadian Charter of Rights and Freedoms. If one alternate form of marriage is approved, there is far less defence against others.

It is clear from our readings that polygamy was practised in Old Testament times, but this reading and others indicate that it was not very satisfactory.[1] Both of Jacob's wives were unhappy— Leah because she was not loved and Rachel because she was barren and jealous of Leah. While this arrangement appeared to be tolerated in the Old Testament, it was clearly illicit by New Testament times, when Jesus repeated the creation ideal of one man being married to one woman.[2] While polygamy may not yet be a serious issue, adultery is rampant and it repeats all the problems of polygamy: humiliation, jealousy and possible abandonment.

However, the problem is not restricted to the married partners; it has its effects on children of the marriage. Hagar's

---

[1] See also Hannah and Peninah, 1 Samuel 1:1–7.
[2] Matthew 19:4–6

child, Ishmael, copied the scorn of his mother,[1] and rival children from David's wives turned to violence and murder. Similarly, children in adulterous homes frequently suffer lifelong trauma and may develop the habits of the adulterous partner in adult life. The greatest security we can give children is a home that is established by steadfast parental relationships, one where both parents love and respect each other.

Weekend ~ Jacob and Charles

The story of Jacob and his wives has a remarkable counterpart in recent history. Prince Charles, the youthful heir to the British throne, fell in love with a young attractive Camilla Shand but failed to propose to her as she was not considered royal material. When he left for a year in the navy, Camilla married another friend, Andrew Parker-Bowles. Then, at 28 years of age, Charles met Diana Spencer, 16, of suitable royal heritage, and he later married her. The relationship between Charles and Diana, despite the much vaunted fairytale romance, was akin to Jacob and Leah: Camilla remained Charles' first and real love as Rachel did to Jacob.

Camilla divorced her husband in 1995, but she had already resumed her relationship with Charles. Diana, sick with bulimia and consumed by jealousy, attempted suicide several times and tried to find comfort in affairs of her own. This came to an end with Diana's death in a subway accident in Paris. Charles now faced a dilemma. As future head of the Church of England, he could not marry a divorced woman, so the relationship continued in stagnant fashion. Eventually, a compromise was arranged, which allowed Charles and Camilla to wed after 34 years of courtship.

It is easy to look upon these relationships as typical unfaithful behaviour, with blame to be scattered liberally over all the participants. But we have to ask: What different outcome might

---

[1] Genesis. 16:3–4; 21:8–10

there have been for both Jacob and Charles had there been no outside interference? The pressures of friends and family, however well meaning, can be disastrous for a marriage. While we may seek advice and counsel from those we trust, we should resist unsolicited "advice" from outsiders regarding our relationships. Only then can we be sure that our commitments are our own, since we must take responsibility for the outcomes.

Monday: Genesis 30:3–13

There is ample record in Scripture to illustrate that people often believe that God needs help to accomplish his purposes. We saw it with Abraham and Sarah and with Rebekah and Isaac, and we see it here again with Jacob and Rachel. These were not occasions where a faithful believer was simply fulfilling God's direction, but rather, instances of faithless subterfuge or manipulation to bring about what they considered a godly result. This frequently led to undesirable consequences—our world still labours under some of these outcomes 4000 years later. Probably, in Jacob's view, Rachel, as the chosen wife, was presumed the primary wife for the continuation of the covenant. If God wasn't providing a child to Rachel, then Jacob would provide his own option.

Unfortunately, the same attitude still prevails today; the cutting of ethical corners is acceptable if it yields good results. This may be as simple as tax evasion in order to financially support a Christian organisation. Joseph Fletcher, one of the early proponents of situational ethics, coined the phrase "therapeutic adultery," where adultery might offer solace or support to a needy woman. For the "Christian" manipulator, the end justifies questionable means if it results in some form of spiritual progress. As we have seen, this usually has undesirable results, equivalent to cutting off the tree branch on which one sits.

The children born to Rachel through her maid Bilhah made up the number of sons that formed the nation of Israel, but they had unremarkable lives and descendants. The children born later to Rachel herself, however, did have specific roles to play. Joseph saved the family from extinction when he became ruler of Egypt. Benjamin's descendants were the only full tribe to remain loyal to the kingly line of Judah when Israel split some 1,000 years later. All this underlines the necessity of living godly ethical lives if we are to make a mark for God's glory—even if it appears to be a losing proposition in the short term.

Tuesday: Genesis 30:14–16

You may have heard frequent accusations that the patriarchal system of the Old Testament exploited women as chattels. There is no doubt the system had its failings as much as any society—both they and we are fallen people—and women suffered from the effects of the fall. But the recorded experiences of the wives tell a different story to that of broad abuse. The wives of the patriarchs had their own households of servants and lived with freedom of action. Abraham conceded to Sarah's wishes regarding a son and Sarah had freedom to deal summarily with a scornful Hagar as she chose.[1] Rebekah had sufficient freedom to deceive Isaac.[2]

But our reading today is most illuminating and even a little humorous. Mandrakes were believed to have properties that increased fertility. Thus, Rachel wanted them for a future occasion of intimacy with Jacob in the hope of breaking her personal barrenness. She proposed Leah sleep with Jacob that night in exchange for the mandrakes. Both women clearly assumed Jacob would simply acquiesce in their scheme; clearly, the wives had control over who slept with Jacob and when.

---

[1] Genesis 16:1–6
[2] Genesis 27:5–10

As a wider reading of the story of Jacob and his wives shows, their home was not a happy one. Despite some freedom, the wives were fierce rivals for offspring and resorted to manipulation to achieve their ends. This is no surprise, noting Jacob's previous history of deceit. But we don't have to be in a patriarchal culture to find manipulation and game-playing as a formula for co-existence by some marriage partners. These methods of competition are more likely found and used in the marketplace. We have probably resorted to them ourselves at times, but is this form of co-existence really what we desire in our marriages?

Wednesday: Genesis 31:22–42

After twenty years of working for Laban, Jacob decided it was time to leave. This was not easy; Laban had manipulated him to stay several times and had manpower enough to force his tenure. Jacob, himself the master manipulator, had met his match.

This story really emphasises the way in which the habits of the parents rub off on their children. Jacob's deception of Isaac only perpetuated the deceptions of both Abraham[1] and Isaac[2] before him and provided an environment for Rachel to deceive her father about his household gods.

If Jacob ever had a desire to be "just like my dad," he certainly accomplished it! Not only did Jacob fall for his father's and grandfather's mistakes, his wives followed both his example and that of their father, Laban. Rachel—with Leah's agreement—justified her behaviour on the basis of her father's deceit.[3] Our children assume that the life they have and the way their parents act is normal. They may revise their ideas of what is normal as they reach puberty, but old habits die hard and justifying deceit as a reaction to another person's behaviour is compelling.

---

[1] Genesis 12:10–13; 20:1–2
[2] Genesis 26:7
[3] Genesis 31:14–16

Justifying all sorts of behaviour on the basis of other people's actions is universal. Our culture encourages taking the posture that we are victims when accused, thus placing blame for our behaviour on others and helping us avoid responsibility for our actions. If our children are to be responsible members of society, they must see that *we* are willing to own *our* actions. It is true that we are often provoked into undesirable actions by the behaviour of those around us. The response of the mature Christian is to recognise and accept anger, frustration or vindictive emotions and then channel them into positive responses that address injustice in a way that is ethically valid and spiritually acceptable. We want our children to live lives that they control, not to be victim to the whims of others.

Thursday: Genesis 32:1–31

The rivalry between Isaac and Rebekah over their favourite sons is an example of the effect of parents on their children's lives. Jacob and Esau were consequently separated for twenty years. While the sons were responsible for their behaviour as adults, Jacob clearly assimilated the example of Rebekah's conniving and Esau easily accepted the offer of Isaac's blessing, to which he was no longer entitled. Now, twenty years later, Jacob is about to return home, still facing Esau's threat of death. As parents, it is sobering for us to think that this twenty-year separation and the possibility of violence could have been avoided if Isaac and Rebekah had been united in their care of both sons.

However, no parents are perfect, and God's intervention in our children's affairs gives us hope. Even before he had news of Esau, Jacob met the angels of God, which gave him hope. Perhaps this was the trigger for his prayer and persistence with God in preparing to meet Esau. While his elaborate preparations to meet a hostile Esau reflect Jacob's old ways, his meetings with God had tempered his approach to his problems. While he made what preparations he could to ease what he feared would be a hostile meeting, eventually his faith was in God and he went forward to meet Esau. Esau also had a change of heart. The years—and perhaps a growing faith—had softened his attitude, and he was overwhelmed to meet Jacob.

But the brothers remained estranged, Jacob refusing Esau's offer of company and help. The only other recorded meeting of the two was at the funeral of their father, Isaac. Much later, the nations of Israel and Edom—the descendants of Jacob and Esau— became enemies, Obadiah[1] warning Edom of judgement for their cruel treatment of Israel. It should be a timely reminder to us again that our treatment of our children can have repercussions well beyond our generation.

Friday: Genesis 35:1–15

You have probably heard the suggestion that the patriarchs were so named because in their culture the husband was the boss. Unfortunately, this has been accepted by many Christians in the past to justify father-dominated households. The patriarchs are so named because they were the fathers of the covenant people—for Israel and for Christians. It should also be remembered that they were not just fathers of a simple family such as we are used to, but leaders of a great clan, and as such had leadership responsibilities for their descendants and employees. Even so, many of the Genesis stories show that the wives were not simply "yes–women"; they engaged in serious dialogue regarding their own and their children's futures.

The greater the following, the greater the responsibility to lead by example and even by direction if necessary. In this chapter, Jacob, as head of the family clan, decided it was time to make a fresh commitment of allegiance to God. It seems he made this decision unilaterally, but it must be noted that his entire household appeared to have agreed with his decision. Some members of the household would probably have been from other nations that served other gods—perhaps having even persuaded

---

[1] Obadiah 8–14

some of Jacob's own family to do so—and it was time to clean house. Presumably the earrings had some idolatrous significance, unlike the simple adornments of today.

Jacob returned to Bethel, where God had met him as he fled from Esau. It became a place, not only where he originally met God, but where he found communion with God for the rest of his life.

With the best of intentions, decisions and safeguards, we will frequently make the wrong decisions or fail to uphold our own standards. A return to the place of communion with God on a regular basis is the only way to maintain a sense of stability and steadiness in our family life, particularly during difficult and fractious times.

Weekend ~ A Story of Restoration

Angie and Gary were not Christians when they married. Angie was a gentle and kindly girl but she hankered after the freedom she had before marriage and subscribed to a current feminist view that self-fulfilment was a priority for her. If this was not attainable in marriage, the union should be dispensed with. She and her gregarious, adventurous single friend Barb took to a life together seeking the fulfilment that feminist ideology promised. Gary was left with two daughters to raise alone.

After a year or two of this life, both Angie and Barb came face to face with the claims of Christ, became Christians and joined a local church. As she grew in her understanding of Christian life, Angie realized she needed to restore her relationship with her husband. She wasn't sure by this time whether she still loved her husband, but she sought his agreement to return to the marriage. He had never wanted the separation to begin with and the two were reunited. Angie continued her church attendance and involvement, but Gary took an intellectual view against the claims of Christianity. However, Gary saw a change in his wife and over a period of time became sympathetic, if not in agreement, with the faith.

Eventually they had another child together and Angie was hospitalized for a while during the birth. By this time, Gary was concerned that his two daughters continue attending church, and in Angie's absence, he took them to church himself. The ultimate wisdom of the Christian faith suddenly made sense to him, and on Angie's return, she was reunited with a Christian husband. Despite her misgivings, Angie had come to a practical understanding of what submission to a husband meant for her: remaining with him to raise their family together and reflecting her relationship to Christ by her example of faithfulness to Gary.

Monday: Genesis 37:2–11

As we have discussed earlier, children tend to assimilate their parents' habits. Jacob is a prime example, repeating the favouritism of his parents. Even before the events of today's reading, there was estrangement between Leah's sons and Jacob. After the massacre of the men of Shechem, both Simeon and Levi showed no remorse and rejected their father's rebuke.[1] Joseph was still a child, but Jacob's favouritism of Joseph was probably already evident. Clearly, old habits die hard, and Jacob had not learned from the pain of his own parents' favouritism.

It seems from this passage that Jacob not only resented the fact that Leah had children while Rachel could not but suggested to his sons that they were second class by his special treatment of Joseph. At seventeen years of age, Joseph had picked up on his special status and as a teenager was not above exploiting it. Although the dreams were not of his making, his talking about them seems short-sighted. His brothers were enraged at his assertion of future power over them and even his father rebuked him. Just because the dreams were true did not justify Joseph humiliating his family. Consider the response had Mary freely rumoured her promise of the birth of Jesus.

However, Jacob's rebuke was out of place. He had already fostered the favouritism that Joseph used against his brothers but

---

[1] Genesis 34:30–31

was unaware of the impending tragedy he had unleashed. Showing favouritism among children has serious consequences. It will give a favoured child a false sense of importance while impeding a disfavoured child's development. As we will see, given the right circumstances, it can even be dangerous.

Tuesday: Genesis 37:12–30

The potential danger of Jacob's favouritism becomes real in today's reading. Only Reuben and Judah of the four eldest boys held any sense of responsibility for Joseph, the remainder apparently being quite happy to dispose of him. Particularly, Simeon and Levi, the second and third sons, maintained the violent streak they exhibited at Shechem. Neither the slaying of their own brother nor the imminent grief of their father eclipsed their anger, which was followed by the six younger sons. Eventually Joseph was sold as a slave as a compromise between the brothers.

Perhaps you are thinking that these actions were necessary to ensure Joseph was in a position to assist the family later during a time of famine. Certainly, God used these circumstances to bring about that outcome, an idea to which Joseph himself eventually agreed.[1] But to justify the brothers' actions on the basis of the outcome is also to justify Rebekah's deception to ensure Jacob received the blessing. It assumes that God has no other way to ensure the right outcome, and on this basis, even God would have to justify their actions. The end rarely justifies the means, and in this and similar cases, the participants are accountable for their actions. Jesus said that even Judas was accountable for his actions: "the Son of Man will go as it has been decreed. But woe to that man who betrays him."[2]

It is too easy for us to parrot the "it can't happen to me" syndrome, yet newscasts routinely report violence and death as

---

[1] Genesis 45:5–8
[2] Luke 22:22

results of anger or jealousy in family relationships. We can never know the adversity and dangers we pose to our children—and even beyond them—by playing favourites.

Wednesday: Genesis 37:31–35

The effect the loss of Joseph had on Jacob can be imagined without today's reading to inform us. But it must be remembered that Jacob's misery was partly of his own making. While we have dwelt on the effects of favouritism on children, it can also come back to haunt the parents. Obviously, we can assert that Jacob's favouritism was partly the cause of his loss, but there are other pointers in the text to show how other actions came home to roost.

Jacob knew the brothers were minding their sheep near Shechem.[1] This, of course, was the place they had to leave in fear following Simeon's and Levi's massacre in Shechem.[2] Recalling the Shechem incident made Jacob fearful for his sons and prompted him to send Joseph to ensure their safety. As it happened, Joseph was in far greater danger from his brothers than they were from the Shechemites. The final irony in this story is that Jacob was deceived by a goat, as he himself deceived *his* father Isaac with a goat.

It seems Jacob was still unaware of how his actions had precipitated events. He refused to be comforted and held the brothers' guilt over them for another twenty years.[3] If ever there was a dysfunctional family, this was it. When Jacob claimed that his years had "been few and difficult,"[4] it is clear that he realized that much was of his own making. Favouritism not only hurts children, it can return pain to the parents also.

---

[1] Genesis 37:12–14
[2] See Genesis 34 for the full story
[3] Genesis 42:36
[4] Genesis 47:9

Thursday: Genesis 39:6–23

Potiphar's wife was sufficiently affluent to have time on her hands but insufficiently fulfilled to seek entertainment outside of her marriage. In her case, advantage in life did not create integrity. On the other hand, Joseph, who had mostly disadvantages in life, showed remarkable reliability in his response to his master's wife. Given complete freedom to run Potiphar's household, he would not exploit it and refused the woman's advances. Perhaps William Congreave was thinking of Potiphar's wife and her subsequent treatment of Joseph when he penned the words: "Hell hath no fury like a woman scorned."[1]

Two things come to mind in relation to this incident. Firstly, Potiphar's wife's actions were a power play. This parallels the many cases of employees being sexually harassed by employers of either sex, not to mention the seduction of an employer by an employee for personal gain. But as in this case, because of authority or influence, an employer—by extension, Potiphar's wife was Joseph's employer—can easily take advantage of a susceptible employee who may fear losing his or her job. This was clearly her ploy with Joseph.

This leads us to the second thought. Joseph did, in fact, lose his job and his reputation. As expected, Potiphar believed his wife over Joseph, his slave. In addition, Joseph was thrown in jail for his alleged offence. Clearly, he could have taken advantage of the woman's advances, as the outcome was the same as his refusal to do so. The fact that he did not points to the internal integrity that motivated Joseph to the moral course. He was not motivated to this course by fear of retribution or the possible reward of praise for honourable action. Rather, Joseph's anguish at the thought of causing offence to God was greater than the allure of the woman's repeated attempts at seduction. As I once heard a preacher say:

---

[1] William Congreve, *The Mourning Bride* (1697) Act 3, Scene 2. Original reads: "Heaven has no rage like love to hatred turned, Nor hell a fury like a woman scorned."

"For the Christian to sin against God is not just regrettable; it is an agony."

Friday: Genesis 42:1–5

Today's reading centres on the continuing dynamics of Jacob's family. Jacob is still very much in control, and Benjamin has now replaced Joseph as Jacob's favourite. But the anger that the sons had over the first favourite, Joseph, has been replaced by guilt that their father's grief fosters. Jacob now uses his ongoing grief, in conjunction with their guilt, to manipulate and dominate his sons. He is not about to let them get away with their displeasure at his favouritism, and he drives the message home with his favour to Benjamin. The result is a family of disoriented adult children who "looked at each other," unsure of how to act without their father's direction.

Jacob, as self-centred as ever, refuses to let Benjamin out of his sight, and certainly will not trust him to the brothers for a lengthy journey to Egypt. He is partly justified; if he blames the brothers for Joseph's disappearance, how can he know whether he can trust them a second time? Despite the fact Jacob has still not accepted that his favouritism provoked their anger in the first place, the brothers are still responsible for their treatment of Joseph and must face up to it at some point. Although they don't know it, the journey to Egypt is going to be the test.

This family's dilemma is a classic example of how both sides of a dispute generally carry some blame. If the boys would come clean with their bitter secret and Jacob would admit the menace of his favouritism, the rift could be healed. But as long as one member of a family refuses to admit his or her own responsibility, the estrangement will remain. Life is too short to let barriers between ourselves and those we love to remain for long. For Jacob and his sons it lasted over twenty years. We all face that possibility as long as we harbour unresolved issues.

Weekend ~ Real People

You may have seen the television advertisement that has two angels discussing a third angel's wings. The comment is made that "they look so perky they can't be real!" The same accusation could be levelled at stories of people that "are so perfect they can't be real!" This is not the case for the characters we have been reading about in recent days. One of the factors supporting the reality of the stories we have been reading is their natural human conduct.

Abraham, the hero of faith in God, twice resorts to deception concerning Sarah to ensure his own safety. Isaac also follows his father's example. Isaac and Rebekah, in love in their early marriage, descend into partisan favouritism over their sons. Jacob shows flashes of extraordinary faith, yet retreats into stubborn permanent self-pitying grief to punish his sons at the loss of Joseph. Jacob's sons, reflecting the radical nature of youth, dispense with Joseph with callous disregard for the consequences. Yet with advancing years, their attitude is softened to both Joseph and Benjamin. Even so, their earlier fears appear to dog them to the end of the story.

It is often the erratic behaviour of these characters that betrays their reality. With some honest thought, we can see ourselves in them. And if we recognize the authenticity of the writings in the reality of these men and women, then we must accept the basic premise of the narrative: God has control over the events of these lives and uses them for his purposes. And his purposes were— and still are—specifically to fulfill his desire for reconciliation with us, those who have descended from Adam's all too human family, through the coming of Jesus Christ to earth.

Week Twelve

Monday: Genesis 42:6–17

At first reading, Joseph appears very harsh with his brothers. And reasonably so—anyone who had been treated as Joseph had been could be reckoned to deserve some revenge. What had happened to these men during the intervening years? Did they carry the same anger and violent behaviour of his last encounter with them? In a complete reversal of that event, he now had control of the situation. How was he going to use it? Would he turn them into slaves as they had once made him? Perhaps to give himself time to consider his options, he incarcerated them for three days.

Yet when he first saw his brothers, his memory was not of their treatment of him but his dream about them when he was seventeen. The prophecy of that dream was coming true as they bowed to the ground before him. As we shall see in later readings, his true feelings for them were not in his words to them but in his actions for them behind the scenes. He wept as they confessed their sin against him;[1] he returned their money, not willing to take it from his own family, paying for the grain himself[2] and then providing for their return journey.[3]

---

[1] Genesis 42:24
[2] See Genesis 43:23
[3] Genesis 42:25

It's unlikely that we will ever have the same control over our difficult family situations. However, we do have control over our own actions towards our loved ones. Some family feuds date back to childhood, because each party continually responds in kind, justifying their actions by the ongoing provocation received. While some of Joseph's actions remain to be explained later, it is clear that his actions were out of concern for his family—particularly those still in Canaan. To take some time to pray and think about our responses as Joseph did can provide us with options that ensure we act in the interests of our family relationships—even if they are not reciprocated.

Tuesday: Genesis 42:18–28

There is nothing like guilt to foster a sense of being punished. Clearly, their treatment of Joseph in his teen years continued to weigh on the brothers' consciences. One may wonder if they interpreted other calamities during that time as God's judgement on them. Certainly, the idea that Benjamin was to be a pawn in their dealings with this Egyptian would trigger thoughts of the previous episode with Joseph and further inflame their father's simmering resentment against them. Their dilemma seemed intractable as they became the pawns themselves in a long distance dialog between Joseph and Jacob.

Joseph was playing the part expected of him. As the premier official of the country, he was responsible for its security and his treatment of aliens such as his brothers was reasonable. He skilfully used their admission of a younger brother as an opportunity for proof of their claim to be "honest men, not spies."[1] But unknown to his brothers, he had a personal motive: he wanted to be sure that this youngest brother would not suffer the same fate he had. As long as the family needed food, Benjamin's life would be safe as a guarantee of further provisions.

---

[1] Genesis 42:10–11

Youth is a great time for sinning and old age a great time for regretting. The sins of the past come to haunt us as we grow older, and like Joseph's brothers, calamity is often seen as punishment for earlier failures. It seems, again like the brothers, that it takes adversity to bring us to a point of confession. In this sense, misfortune can be a blessing, bringing us face to face with the truth about ourselves. And there is nothing like family friction to give us the pain we need.

Wednesday: Genesis 42:29–43:14

Even the kindness of Joseph in returning the brothers' money became a threat for them. This, added to Jacob's refusal to let Benjamin go, made it doubly difficult to return to Egypt any time soon. But eventually the time would come when the need for food would drive their agenda. Somehow, it was necessary to persuade Jacob to release Benjamin to travel with them.

What follows is a dialog that shows why Reuben, the oldest, lost the leadership of the clan. He made an irresponsible and ineffective plea for the release of Benjamin. His timing was poor. There was no pressure to return as long as there was food for them and a final decision could be postponed. But specifically, to offer the life of his own sons for Benjamin's may sound high-minded at first hearing, but it was hardly likely to reassure Jacob; someone who would sacrifice his own sons' lives could hardly be trusted with someone else's son.

Judah, on the other hand, let the matter slide until no food was left. His assertion that "we could have gone and returned twice" indicates how much time had elapsed. But of greater importance, Judah was willing to take complete responsibility for Benjamin himself, placing his own life on the line. The pattern of Jesus' own sacrifice for us sets the pattern: we must be prepared to provide a sacrifice ourselves if we are to be effective in repairing broken relationships.

This marked the beginning of Judah wresting the leadership of the clan from Jacob's self-obsessive grasp. Jacob was less concerned with the family—note his easy acceptance of the loss of Simeon—than his own comfort. Judah's leadership did not simply capitulate to Jacob but used timing and circumstances to show up Jacob's selfishness. Judah's concern was sacrificial; he was willing to sacrifice himself if necessary to serve Jacob's ends as well as to ensure the continued well-being of the whole family.

Thursday: Genesis 44:1–17

This chapter is perhaps the hardest to read from the brothers' point of view. Joseph's treatment of the brothers seems unnecessarily harsh—was he taking some personal revengeful pleasure at their distress? It seems unlikely. His obvious delight at seeing Benjamin, the favourable treatment of the other brothers, his concern for their (his) father, the return of Simeon to them and his private weeping all suggest a deep love and care for the whole family.[1] So why did he use trickery, placing Benjamin—as it seemed to the brothers—in jeopardy?

Here was the final test. Benjamin had replaced Joseph as the favourite son, therefore the brothers' treatment of him when in peril would clearly indicate their state of heart towards the favourite son. Would it be different from their treatment of Joseph? The placing of Joseph's cup in Benjamin's' sack would ensure a decisive choice for the sons to make—themselves or Benjamin. Joseph further clarified the choice by offering to allow the brothers to return without Benjamin.

We are constantly tested regarding our relationships, mostly in small things but occasionally in major confrontations. And these tests come more often in family relationships; we generally see our families the most and they are usually the closest to us. Are we willing to make the occasional sacrifice to maintain relationship with them? Have we improved our attitudes over time? Remember Joseph's care for his family: he cared deeply for them but did not allow sentimental attachment to draw him into

---

[1] Genesis. 43:26–30

their dysfunctional relationship. Had he done so, his ability to care for them would have been compromised.

Friday: Genesis 44:18–45:2

We have previously noted that Judah was beginning to take control in Jacob's clan, and today's reading clinches his position as leader among the brothers. It is impossible not to be moved by Judah's eloquent intervention on behalf of Benjamin. It is both courageous and sacrificial. Not knowing that this ruler is actually his brother, in verse 18 he assumes that he faces possible death just for speaking out. Joseph held the power of life and death over the whole kingdom. But unknown to Judah, using his father as defence of his position was the most telling argument, and his obvious concern for the well-being of their father was God's way of reaching Joseph's heart.

The distraught pleading of Judah accomplished three things. It clearly established his leadership based on sacrificial concern for his charge and his father. It satisfied Joseph that the brothers had changed hearts towards their father and his favourites, completely undermining Joseph's subterfuge, which then provoked his emotional outburst. Finally, it satisfied Joseph's desire for true repentance, providing an admission of wrongdoing and a change in behaviour evidenced by their concern for Benjamin and their father.

The basis for reconciliation was set. Judah's honesty and Joseph's concern for the family provided the environment in which they could reunite. If these two prerequisites are present, there is no reason why any family split cannot be healed. But as we have witnessed, it requires all parties to come to that agreement. In the meantime, it is incumbent upon us to maintain our integrity until others come to that point. Remember, Joseph waited many years to meet his family, and even then it was more than a year before the final reconciliation took place.

Weekend ~ Forgiveness

If there is one human characteristic that causes us to stumble more than any other, it is the necessity for forgiveness. And yet, forgiveness is the foremost quality of grace, particularly the grace extended to us by God through the sacrifice of his Son, Jesus Christ. The grace of God to us *is* forgiveness. All other aspects of his goodness to us depend on this one attribute; he continues to give rain and sun to all, good and evil,[1] because his forgiveness is longsuffering.[2] Most of you have heard sermons on this subject urging forgiveness to those who have wronged you, for God's grace shown to us requires us to extend the same to others.[3]

What is also likely is that most sermons you have heard have failed to indicate that there is a condition for forgiveness: repentance. Whereas God's forgiveness is available and extended to all, it has to be accepted. When we became Christians, we recognized our sinfulness before God, repented of it and sought his forgiveness. In Jesus' parable of the servants, they both acknowledged their debt to their debtors.[4] It is not possible to receive forgiveness where there is no acknowledgement of real guilt.

But does this allow us to deny forgiveness and maintain bitterness and anger toward those who refuse to listen to our complaint? Hardly, for God has offered forgiveness to us whether we accept or reject it. It is necessary for us to reflect his image in this if we are to preserve our fellowship with God.[5] It is also necessary for us to forgive in our hearts because retained bitterness skews our thinking and damages our health. Thus, we need to deal with the conflict within ourselves, irrespective of outside acceptance.

---

[1] Matthew 5:45
[2] 2 Peter 3:9
[3] Matthew 6:12
[4] Matthew 18:21–35
[5] Matthew 6:12–15

The question for us is whether we can live in forgiveness with our partners. Most of the time we are really sorry if we have hurt our partners, recognizing that grievous wounds may take time to heal. However, if my partner is unwilling to acknowledge sin against me, he or she will bear the consequences of that denial. But ultimately, I am still responsible for the state of my own heart.[1]

---

[1] James 2:13

Week Thirteen

Monday: Genesis 45:3–15

My wife and I have been most privileged to have had several reunions with our family of children and grandchildren. It has become more difficult as both children and grandchildren marry and have lives of their own, although we take every opportunity to visit them individually. But the emotional reunion of Joseph and his brothers exceeds all others in its intensity and shock. The narrative at this point reveals its authenticity as it gives great detail of a real dialog between Joseph and his brothers.

Joseph's command for all his attendants to leave him must have raised the level of the brother's terror in the presence of this man. What was he planning to do? Quite understandably, their first response to his revelation of his identity was bewilderment and disbelief. For Joseph's part, his first concern was for his father; the question regarding Jacob was thrown in with obvious ignorance of the effect his revelation would have on his brothers. Knowing Joseph's real identity did not allay their fears. Now they feared not just a foreign tyrant but an abused brother. Then Joseph explained himself again, this time dismissing their fear of revenge by stating his recognition that "it was not you that sent me here but God." Once the shock had subsided, "his brothers talked with him."

Adversity that God allows in our lives is not meaningless. We know why God allowed it in Joseph's life, but reasons for our own conflicts are not always obvious to us; probably much of it will not be known this side of eternity. Family splits seem particularly meaningless, which only adds to their pain. Are you able to trust God with it and wait for the explanation? Joseph waited over twenty years.

Tuesday: Genesis 45:16–28

Joseph's integrity had impressed Pharaoh and his court so much that they were pleased at Joseph's reunion with his brothers. It was Pharaoh's insistence that sent the brothers back with the good news: the whole family was to move to Egypt to live on the best of the land, where they would have food throughout the remaining five years of famine. Pharaoh also provided carts for transporting the family back to Egypt and provisions for the journey. Even their needs for personal belongings would be supplied.

Upon their return from Egypt, the brothers' disclosure of Joseph's position was too much for Jacob. Jacob is the Old Testament's "Doubting Thomas." His years of sullen and obstinate refusal to be comforted had blunted his faith. Why should he believe his sons now? But there was one fact of evidence that eventually convinced him. As Thomas was able to see Christ's scars from the crucifixion and believe, so Jacob's spirit revived upon seeing the carts from Egypt.

It is all too easy to lose confidence that change will happen as the years go by. Our tendency to have disdain for Jacob belies our own reduction of faith over time. Jacob had over twenty years to lose heart that he would never see Joseph again. Can we sustain faith for that length of time? Prayer for a loved one will never go answered. George Müller, the great English philanthropist who provided for the orphans of Britain, firmly believed in answers to prayer and often prayed food into his orphanages for mealtimes. He believed God would answer his prayers for a close friend that he would become a Christian. And these prayers were answered—but not until after Müller's death.

Wednesday: Genesis 46:1–7

It is all too easy to follow the story of Jacob and dwell on the foolish mistakes he made and his obstinacy in refusing to be comforted over the loss of Joseph for so many years. If we are not careful, we can allow these apparent vices to overshadow both the overarching faithfulness of Jacob to God and the grace of God towards Jacob. I sometimes wonder if Jacob's continuous mourning over Joseph was a subconscious belief that he was not dead and that he would see him again.

However that may be, after his reunion with Joseph, the end of Jacob's life returned to the fellowship with God he had experienced earlier in life. Perhaps we should see those intervening years as a long test of faith, where Jacob responded badly at times, yet never renounced his faith. In this light it is easier to see ourselves, failing as we often do under pressure, yet always retaining that basic awareness that ultimately our lives are under God's control.

The mystics speak of the "long night of the soul," those periods when all we have believed and trusted in seems lost. We all experience this to some degree, but some of us feel tested to the limits of our endurance, the experience sometimes lasting for years. The times of estrangement from or conflict with our close family can be the greatest trials, occasionally provoking inappropriate responses from us. But we can be encouraged by God's words to Jacob, a reminder that God had not forgotten or left him. The day may not be far away when God will speak to your heart again as he spoke to Jacob.

Thursday: Genesis 49:1–12

As was customary towards the end of the patriarchs' lives, Jacob called his sons to him and gave them his blessing. He couched it in terms of "what will happen to you in days to come." In Jacob's pronouncements, the history of his four eldest sons caught up with them. Reuben lost his place as firstborn because of his adultery with Bilhah, Rachel's maidservant and Reuben's stepmother.[1] There is no record of his repentance for this act. Simeon and Levi lost their inheritance because of their slaughter of the Shechemites and display of arrogance rather than regret at this episode.[2] Simeon did not have his own land apportioned to him but rented space from Judah.[3] Levi's descendants also had no inheritance in the land, for they became priests for the emerging nation.

It is also true that Judah himself committed adultery with his daughter-in-law, an incestuous relationship. But the full story is given, particularly his recognition and repentance of the wrong he had done to her, provoking her subterfuge.[4] The possibility of forgiveness as a response to repentance is a common theme through Scripture. In addition, as we have seen already, Judah's growing leadership of the clan throughout his years was based on wisdom and concern for the family. Thus, Jacob set him apart as the leader of his brothers and as the progenitor of the kingship to come—clearly referring to David and eventually to Jesus.

Integrity is important, not only for our personal growth and position, but also to provide us with influence within our families. Our children have often indicated—and probably overrated—our stable example of faith as an influence in their adherence to their faith. Dedication to faith needs to be caught as well as taught.

Friday: Genesis 50:15–21

Old habits die hard, and old fears do too. Even after all they had experienced of Joseph's generosity of spirit, his brothers still feared possible reprisal from him. Their actions tell us more about them than about Joseph. Did Joseph really harbour a secret desire for revenge? Unlikely. What is more probable is that they

---

[1] Genesis 35:22
[2] Genesis 34:30–31
[3] Joshua 19:9
[4] Genesis 38:24–26

could not conceive of themselves acting in such a magnanimous way and so denied the possibility to Joseph. Their actions in approaching Joseph also betrayed their character, again resorting to subterfuge to try to block Joseph's possible future retaliation. They were not even able to speak to his face, sending a messenger with their story instead.

Joseph, true to his nature, wept when he received their message. His response was also consistent with his understanding of God's providence. He repeated his earlier assertion that God allowed his adversity in order to save the family. He was not "in the place of God" and so was not in a position to bring judgement on his brothers for their actions. Nonetheless, he clearly laid the responsibility on the brothers: "You intended it for harm."

We are always responsible for our actions, good or bad, even if God uses them for his purposes. He will use our faith-based actions, but it is comforting to know that he can also overrule actions that are less than faithful. Because family relationships are usually close, they are more likely to give rise to friction. When they do, we can fall into the trap of responding badly. But don't fall into the trap of thinking that others cannot respond better than us; accept genuine offers of reconciliation gladly.

Weekend ~ Children: Part of Spiritual Warfare

Whenever we give ourselves over to the sinful side of our nature, we give Satan opportunity to use us for his ends. In areas of the world where there is little or no government, gangs kill, rape and pillage. There is a litany of despotic rulers such a Hitler, Stalin, Mussolini, Idi Amin, Milosovich and the like whose dark side Satan exploited. We may also include the parasites on legitimate society who make their living and fortunes by defrauding and devastating the innocent.

It may be less obvious, but there are times when we all allow our dark passions to overwhelm our better judgement and give

Satan a foothold.[1] Acting out of uncontrolled anger, resentment, bitterness or rivalry when the well-being of others is in jeopardy because of our actions, we aid Satan in his plans. When we visualize the rage, slander and malice that is practiced worldwide by normally "decent" people, we begin to realize the extent of Satan's resources and the enormous damage done by loose talk.

I'm sure we all want our children to be beacons of light in so much darkness. They will not achieve this naturally. As the Bible recognizes the natural bent of human beings toward sin, so it admonishes the need for discipline. Discipline is not just staying away from the "bad guys" but a personal inner discipline of thoughts, words and actions in all situations. This is tough enough for ourselves, but it will be even more difficult for our children without their commitment to Christ and clear direction on acceptable motives and actions.

---

[1] Ephesians 4:25–32

Week Fourteen

Monday: Exodus 1:8–21

The Egyptians sought to limit the growth of the Hebrew nation by killing their male children. Although it seems the Egyptians initially did not desire to practice infanticide themselves, neither could they abort without knowing the child's sex. They put the task on the Hebrew midwives, who were told to kill all male Hebrew children "on the delivery stool," the closest thing to abortion. It appears that the midwives' excuse for not killing the male children—that Hebrew women were more vigorous than their Egyptian counterparts, giving birth before the midwives arrived—maintained male births and the Hebrew nation continued to flourish. Could the Egyptians have known the sex before birth, male foetuses would probably have been aborted, more successfully reducing the Hebrew birthrate.

Population control by abortion is commonly practised today in developing nations where the birthrate is high, often pressured by wealthier nations. But abortion produces population decline in developed countries also. Canada's births are well below the replacement rate of 2.4 live births per couple, Quebec leading the way with a birthrate of only 1.4. China and India are approaching a crisis because women frequently abort female fetuses since male children are preferred. This is leading to a shortage of marriageable women, with bartering and kidnapping girls growing in practice as a result.

Birth is simply a growing event in life, like puberty, the first sexual experience and sickness. Thus, there is only a fine line between abortion and infanticide, and abortion has opened the door to infanticide in Western nations, perhaps not on a widespread scale but sufficient to be of significant concern. Killing children is recognized as the most heinous of crimes—even in warfare—and those who prey on children are seen as the worst pariahs of society. Generally, the more defenceless the victim, the greater the sin. Yet despite the fact that the unborn are the most defenceless of all, they are often disposed of with the least regret, easing the way to infanticide. In the "Christian" West, we cannot point too many fingers at the king of Egypt.

Tuesday: Exodus 1:22–2:10

Once Pharaoh realized that the male Hebrew children were not being killed at birth by the Hebrew midwives, he went the next step, ordering his people to take the initiative and kill all newborn Hebrew males. We do not know at what age male children were allowed to live, but it is unlikely that this edict was fully complied with anyway. The country was widespread and observance would be erratic depending on local governors. Communications were not good, and bonds between local Egyptians and Hebrews would save many of the boys.

The story of Moses and Pharaoh's daughter is a prime example. Destroying a foetus can be a relatively objective procedure for the surgeon, but once the baby is born, seen and held, killing is far more difficult for the average person. Sending hardened soldiers to do the job, as Herod did in attempting to kill the infant Jesus, is far more effective than expecting caring adults to do the same.

Abortion is like divorce: the "one flesh" basis of marriage makes ending it seem like tearing flesh from flesh. So the physical procedure of abortion can be seen as symbolic of divorce, and much the same turmoil and pain involves a decision to abort. While some use abortion as a method of contraception, for most it is a very difficult decision, and compassion and help should be the Christian response to that dilemma.

Wednesday: Exodus 5:19–23; 6:9–12

Discouragement is most debilitating, for it undermines resolve, action and even faith. This passage is one in which even the great Moses is found questioning God. His previous approach to Pharaoh to release the Israelites from bondage had backfired, creating even more onerous conditions for them. Thus, the Israelites became cynical of Moses' promises. In turn, Moses became sceptical himself, complaining to God that he had not rescued Israel as promised and repeating to God the logical conclusion that if his own countrymen wouldn't listen to him, then why should he expect Pharaoh to?

We easily fall prey to the same discouragement, either seeing no results from our prayers or failing to come to grips with rational arguments that seem to preclude any meaningful answer. It is particularly true of those intractable problems that revolve around conflict with family members. Moses made two errors that we also easily fall into. Firstly, Moses assumed that freeing Israel was God's only purpose. Moses was later given another reason for the delayed promise: God would demonstrate to Pharaoh a power greater than his own.[1]

Secondly, we easily forget that God has ways of fulfilling his promises outside of our limited understanding. To the women who approached the tomb on the first Easter morning, the stone in front of the tomb was an insurmountable problem—they couldn't move it themselves. But with God's intervention, the stone was not a problem. God is still in the business of removing stones— obstructions that seem immoveable to us—perhaps even the rebellion within our own families.

---

[1] Exodus 7:3–5

Thursday: Exodus 6:6–8

There's an old song that goes: "You're nobody 'til somebody loves you!" Certainly our sense of self-worth is often reflected in what others think of us. This is particularly true of the opinions of those we respect the most, and it explains the disillusionment and despair we feel upon rejection and humiliation. So what creates a marriage that has meaning for both partners and becomes their source of joy? Our passage today describes the way God planned to demonstrate his love for Israel and illustrates some principles we can use to establish affirming relationships.

The passage describes three things that God promised to the Israelites: freedom from the Egyptians, a land of their own and the distinction of becoming his people. Freedom from oppression in Egypt meant that God would give protection from their enemies, not only from Egypt, but any group they encountered throughout their existence. A land of their own meant there would be provision for the necessities of life. These were both contingent on Israel's faithfulness to God, and their frequent loss of that protection and provision is a sad commentary on that relationship. Finally, he gave them purpose for their existence—as his people they would represent him to the world.[1]

Our primary mandate for our family is to protect them and provide for them. These are both legal and natural requirements, and many consider this the end of their responsibilities. But the greater requirement is to give purpose to our children. This can be imparted by both husband and wife, and meaning is given to life as we give and receive acceptance and approval. Our primary service to Christ is to our family, providing them with a sense of purpose that is only found in pursuing the will of God for their lives.

[1] Deuteronomy 4:5–8

Friday: Exodus 12:1–13

In an ironic reversal of Pharaoh's earlier edict to destroy the male Hebrew children, Moses predicted the death of the firstborn throughout Egypt while at the same time leaving the Hebrew families intact. In addition, Pharaoh showed a reversal of his earlier fear of the Hebrews by refusing to let them go, even despite a series of major calamities brought upon Egypt by God. Now the Egyptians were going to feel the same agony of loss that they had brought upon the Hebrews. This was going to be the final episode that would persuade Pharaoh to let the Hebrews leave Egypt. Moses had given Pharaoh plenty of warning.[1]

The episode of plagues that preceded this latest warning was a sign of God's supremacy over Egypt and Pharaoh. The failure of the previous plagues to gain the Hebrews' release was not a sign of God's weakness but of his power and patience.[2] Pharaoh, for that period, was living by the grace of God. It may be easy for us to be openly critical of the Egyptians, yet as we previously noted, the Western world has little to boast about when it comes to the treatment of children.

What is true on a national basis is also true personally. We can be thankful that we do not have the influence over a nation that Pharaoh did, but we do have influence over those closest to us. When we fail them, we may not cause the havoc that Pharaoh did, but our sin is the same; it differs only in degree. This is true of both parents and children, for children also have responsibility. We all live by the grace and patience of God and can avoid much of the trauma associated with life by conforming to God's requirements of us.

---

[1] Exodus 11:4–8
[2] Exodus 7:3–5

Weekend ~ Bondage

You may have identified with the Israelites during this week's readings. They lived in their state of bondage for an extended time before their release under Moses. Too many women worldwide, and to a lesser extent men, live in a state of marital bondage, and in many undeveloped nations there is no escape. Even in Western nations, despite the helps available to the needy, there are often circumstances that prevent leaving a difficult situation. It may be threat by the partner, lack of financial alternatives or pure ignorance of the options available.

For children, the problem is worse. Unless someone else is aware of a problem for children in a family or institution, the child will remain in the environment. Especially during the earlier years, he or she will probably think the situation is normal. The common denominator in all these situations is their apparent hopelessness. But the story of the Exodus is one that brought hope—although delayed—to the Israelites in their future experiences of bondage.

If you are currently in a situation like this, there are two thoughts that Israel's story suggests. Firstly, God was aware of their cries for deliverance long before his intervention. Deliverance delayed is not deliverance denied but a time for recognition that God is with his children during their distress and a period of strengthening faith.[1] Our faith under stress is as much a witness as his deliverance. But secondly, God is the deliverer and he will come to our aid in surprising ways and often at an unexpected time. His presence in distress and the anticipation of his deliverance are hopes all Christians share.

---

[1] James 1:2–3

Monday: Exodus 13:1–16

The Passover event, when the firstborn children of the Hebrews were spared, became an ongoing celebration that is still practised by Jews today. Of particular interest is the idea that the firstborn of both animals and humans belong to God, for they were the ones God spared when the Egyptian firstborn were slain. It is a Middle Eastern practice that if someone saves another's life, the one saved belongs to the saver. The saved life is now surrendered for the service and benefit of the one who saved it. It seems this idea is implicit in today's reading.

Thus, the life of the firstborn belongs to God. Firstborn animals were required to be sacrificed to him and firstborn humans were to be redeemed. This involved the sacrifice of animals in place of firstborn humans, and the continuing memorial to the Passover was to be a teaching tool to the children that followed. Jesus himself, being the firstborn, was redeemed in this way.[1] Later, Jesus identified the symbol of his shed blood in the memorial cup of wine with that of the lamb sacrificed for the firstborn at the original Passover.[2]

In a similar way, the blood that Jesus shed redeemed us and our children. Our regular remembrance of the Last Supper, celebrated as the Lord's Table or Communion, is not only a

---

[1] Luke 2:22–24
[2] Luke 22:20

constant reminder of our allegiance to him but also a teaching tool when children ask why we do it. It is a reminder that both children and his own people are precious to him, and he does not take the death of either lightly.[1] Those who take innocent life willingly—and especially those who counsel it—God will one day hold accountable.

Tuesday: Exodus 20:1–7

The Ten Commandments were composed of two "tables," the first four commandments dealing with our relationship to God, the remaining six dealing with our relationship to one another. While most people may give qualified agreement to much of the last six, many ignore the first four as irrelevant to their lives. Yet all history is largely built around religious concerns, indicating the desire implanted in all humans for a connection to their Creator.

These commandments have been the cornerstone of Western law for centuries. It is only in the last century or so that "enlightenment" has managed to dispose of God as necessary to life and develop the secularist view that religion is a superstitious fantasy of personal choice. It has left us with an affluent but empty existence. However, if God is as real and vital a part of life as the Bible reveals, then any life without him is based upon a lie. Without God, the foundation for decisions is unstable and life becomes precarious and devoid of any real meaning or direction.

Men once believed that the sun rotated around the earth, and we still tend to believe that life revolves around us. But it is God who is the real centre of our universe of life. This emphasizes the importance of the first four commandments, which define our relationship to God. If life is uncertain without God, our marriages without him are uncertain also. The decline in our culture as a result of omitting God from its thinking makes nonsense of the assertion that our families do not need him. It is

---

[1] Psalm 116:15, Matthew 18:2–6

God, not ourselves or our children, who needs to be the centre of our families if we are to have hope in the future of our marriages, children and society.

Wednesday: Exodus 20:4–6

Today we revisit and consider some verses from the Ten Commandments. This and parallel passages[1] have often been taken to mean that children will suffer punishment for their father's sins. This idea is not limited to our time, as Ezekiel had to do battle with it a thousand years later. He condemned the saying of the time: "The fathers eat sour grapes, and the children's teeth are set on edge."[2] In response, he made it clear that the soul that sins will be punished, not the son for the father or vice versa.

The reading of other Scriptures clarifies that it is children who continue in their father's sins that will be punished, for the fathers set patterns for the children to follow. This is illustrated convincingly in the stories of the kings of Israel, commencing with Jeroboam, son of Nebat. His sinful behaviour became the standard by which succeeding kings were measured. About a dozen successive kings of Israel were accused of following the sins of Jeroboam.[3]

However, the emphasis of our reading today is not the punishment that sinning generations receive, but rather, the blessing of God on a thousand generations that love him and obey his commandments. What is clear is that parents can exert an immense influence on the spiritual formation of following generations. Parental teaching is an important element in this process, but the demonstration of allegiance to God in every area of life is also essential. The greatest gift we can give to our children is our own consistent and faithful commitment to God and his Word.

---

[1] Exodus 34:7; Numbers 14:18; Deuteronomy 5:9–10
[2] Ezekiel 18:1–20
[3] 1 Kings 16:25–26; 22:51–52; 2 Kings 3:1–3; 10:28–29, etc.

Thursday: Exodus 20:12

While we have spent a considerable amount of time on parental responsibilities, the Bible also has instructions with regard to the responsibilities of children toward their parents. Today's instruction to children to honour their parents is the only one of the Ten Commandments that has a promise attached to it.[1] This promise is the reverse of the frequent assertion that faithful parents automatically pass God's blessing on to their children. Whether children take advantage of it is up to them, and their decision determines whether or not they benefit from it in the long run.

Thus, when children honour their parents, their likelihood of long and enjoyable life is increased. Most of those children who rebel against their parents' principles in early life come to an understanding of their parents' wisdom later in life. Of course, there are parents who are failures and their children suffer greatly as a result. But even those parents should be honoured with dignity and respect while their actions are rejected.

But how do parents cope in an age of so many rebellious children? Most parents maintain their love for their children even in the face of arrogant and cruel treatment from their children, whose poor behaviour will adversely affect the lives of their parents as well as themselves. In the final analysis, parents are not in the place of judge, but responsible parents will take necessary steps for the welfare of their children. Children also have their responsibility highlighted by the biblical requirement that a rebellious son could be put to death.[2]

Friday: Exodus 20:12–17

As we have already noted, the first four laws of the Ten Commandments are generally considered irrelevant by those

---

[1] See Deuteronomy 5:16, Ephesians 6:1–3
[2] Deuteronomy 21: 18–21

with a secular mindset. They reject God's involvement as unprovable and base the meaning of life only on what their five senses observe. Yet even secularists recognize humanity as transcendent, having a value beyond detection by the senses. There appears to be no reason to make this claim other than personal identification: what I desire all others must desire also.

This mindset has given rise to generally accepted basic human rights—life, liberty and property—which are advanced by all "civilised" nations as the basis for law, and these have become enshrined in the Canadian Charter of Rights and Freedoms. These rights closely mirror the last six commandments, demonstrating their universality, but with the exception of adultery.

Adultery is seen as the "soft underbelly" of the interpersonal commandments, as it is not considered a violation of the person. But the commandment against adultery was included by a God who was ultimately concerned with the welfare of his creation and who knew the havoc wreaked by indiscriminate sexual union. Although there is no Western law against adultery, it was once the only grounds for divorce according to Scriptural guidelines. It was enforced in the Israel of Bible times with severe penalties, indicating how serious God considered it. Do we consider it with the same gravity, or have we been influenced by the sexual laxity of our culture?

Weekend ~ Honouring Parents

Ann's parents failed to provide an adequate home for their children due to mental illnesses. The children were frequently taken from the home by the authorities and the family was well known in the neighbourhood for its critically dysfunctional nature. Ann's aunt often provided required clothing, and neighbours frequently brought food for the children. Inside the home there was barely enough disreputable furniture for needs; even that was often destroyed during the mother's worst periods of bipolar extremes. The children were often taken from the home for their own safety, and Ann's three brothers—all of different fathers—spent most of their childhood in institutions. Ann herself finally went to live with her grandmother during her teen years.

Yet even these appalling conditions did not lessen Ann's love for her parents. As a teenager, when her mother would return to the home after her frequent stays in the local mental hospital, Ann would attempt to restore normality in the home with donated furniture and equipment and spend time encouraging and supporting her. Even in the face of repetitive destructive behaviour, she determined to alleviate the home conditions— simply because they were her parents. During our early married years, items from our own growing home were used to rebuild Ann's shattered childhood home on several occasions.

Although Ann often feared for our own children's safety—for a period we lived close to the mental institution that often housed her mother—she kept up ongoing contact with her mother and father, ensuring as much as she could their wellbeing in spite of their destructive behaviour. She encouraged her brothers to remain faithful to their parents, although their homes would also show signs of inherited dysfunction. She honoured her parents in this way until their deaths, recognizing the greater imperative that God requires of us more than our natural responses often give.

Week Sixteen

Monday: Exodus 21:7–11

The Israelite community was not egalitarian, regardless of the assurance of rights under Mosaic Law: there were the poor and rich as well as masters and slaves. Slavery was not today's notion of total possession of one human being by another, but rather, similar to indentured servants with rights of their own. In particular, where a man needed to sell his daughter due to poverty, that daughter was protected from exploitation. Of course, she was probably not protected from physical and mental abuse any more than today's wives, but the conditions of sale were meant to provide some measure of social protection for her.

Should she not please her master, then she could be bought back by her father. If she was to be the wife for the master's son, she was given all the rights of a daughter in the family. If the son chose a second wife, all the needs of the first wife were to be met or she was allowed to go free. While this may fall short of the standards for women that we would espouse today, the degree of protection provided was probably advanced for societies that existed prior to 1000 BC, this passage being one of several that set out Hebrew women's rights.

As these passages give some indication of God's concern for women, particularly daughters, so we can be encouraged that God cares for our daughters. There is always concern that girls are more vulnerable than boys, despite feminist rhetoric. When it comes to their adult relationships, how are our daughters going to fare? When the fates of our beloved girls are out of our hands, we can be sure that they are never out of God's care.

Tuesday: Exodus 34:1–14, 28

The Law—the Ten Commandments—was carved into two tablets of stone. The first, Moses smashed in anger,[1] and in today's reading God commanded Moses to replace them. Significantly, during this time on the mountain, God appeared before Moses and revealed his nature to him. That nature consisted of seven characteristics: compassion, grace, patience, love, faithfulness, forgiveness and justice, revealed to Moses before inscribing the words of the covenant in stone again. God was juxtaposing his character against the Ten Commandments as an indication of how he would administer them. Of the seven characteristics, the first six could only work in Israel's favour; the last afforded judgment if the others did not keep Israel in fellowship with God.

That ratio—six to one in Israel's favour—is a ratio that also works in our favour. He is the kind of God I like, in fact, the kind of God I need. Those of us who have entered into the New Covenant desire to participate fully and respond to God's requirements of us so we may enjoy the benefits of that relationship. But we need to live in his covenant of grace and forgiveness because of our constant failure to live up to his standards.

You may also have noticed that those characteristics that God revealed to Moses are human as well—all of us experience them in our relationships. They are part of the image of God originally inscribed on our souls and should be evidence of our transformation to Christlikeness. And that evidence should show firstly in our closest relationships, expressing our compassion, grace, patience, love, faithfulness, forgiveness and justice to our partners and children.

---

[1] Exodus 32:19

Wednesday: Leviticus 10:1–20

At first reading, this passage appears confusing, mainly because it is part of the requirements of the priesthood for which Aaron was responsible. For our purposes, the details are relatively unimportant; it is the behaviour of Aaron and his children that is helpful to us. You will note that both pairs of sons, Nadab and Abihu, and also Eleazar and Ithamar, failed to perform their duties correctly. Yet the outcome for each pair was different.

It was the sons of Levi that were set apart for the priesthood, and Aaron—a descendant of Levi and the brother of Moses—became the chief priest of the emerging nation. All of Aaron's sons had previously been instructed in and consecrated for the special duties required of the priesthood.[1] However, Nadab and Abihu deliberately used their position to disregard the instruction they had been given. They took their duties lightly, perhaps fooling around and amusing themselves at the expense of those for whom they were to intercede. The judgment from God was immediate and swift; the arrogance and scorn exhibited by these two men could not be tolerated.

Yet Aaron's other two sons, Eleazar and Ithamar, were also faulted by Moses for not carrying out their duties correctly. But they were not judged like the first two. Following the disaster with their other brothers, it seems unlikely they would deliberately abuse the requirements of their office, and Aaron interceded for them when accused by Moses. Their blunder may well have been a mistake or an error in judgement, and even Aaron admitted he had made mistakes in the past. After Aaron's intervention, Moses, speaking for God, "was satisfied." While deliberate defiance of God may eventually bring judgment, we must always take the opportunity open to us during this period of grace to intercede for our family members.

---

[1] Leviticus 8:1–36

Thursday: Leviticus 18:6–21

The loosening of sexual mores since the 1960s has produced a spate of acceptable alternative lifestyles previously stigmatised in the West for centuries. Once the basic restriction of sexual relations to that between a man and wife has been breached, there is no specific point at which sex can be easily restricted. If sex outside of marriage is an acceptable recreation, why not sex between other relationships? The pornography industry demonstrates this as it has burgeoned to include a variety of sexual preferences, including pedophilia and incest, available on the web and for which there are few effective sanctions.

Our passage today sets out unacceptable sexual practices including homosexuality and bestiality. It also includes a prohibition of offering children to Molech—the sacrifice of children to appease the god. The use of children for sexual satisfaction is little different, and Jesus' clear teaching on the need to protect children places those who abuse children at the judgment of God. As we noted previously, the more defenceless the victim, the greater the sin.

The trafficking in children for sexual uses is common in many eastern countries, with children, especially girls, commonly sold into sexual slavery for the economic needs of the family. We are also reminded of the sin of Sodom, where all the men were eventually drawn into a violent gay lifestyle.[1] There is an infectious nature about alternative sexual lifestyles. For those involved in pornography there is the danger of a widening circle of preferences—even to the desire for children—which draws God's censure.

Friday: Leviticus 18:22–24

The subject of homosexuality continues to be hotly debated, and this passage quotes one of the Scripture passages

---

[1] Genesis 19:4

forbidding it. But it should be noted from our reading yesterday that homosexuality is only one of many forbidden sexual unions. However, disagreement with gay unions from the Christian community is broadcast in almost complete disregard for the practice of other sexual unions also forbidden in Scripture. Either we set a policy for all Scripturally unacceptable unions or lessen our criticism of illicit same-sex unions. Outcry against one and silence on others is seen as tacit approval of the latter.

Yesterday's reading prohibited sexual union with "any close relative."[1] Ingrown societies have experienced the likelihood of defective genes combining in close relatives and issuing in defective children, hence this prohibition is in the laws of most countries. This reveals the wisdom of Scripture in prohibiting sexual contact with close relatives so early in human history. But other prohibitions are not generally followed in modern Western culture, perhaps on the basis that they do not pose the same threat. But there are other threats from illicit sexual unions, for promiscuous sex—gay or straight—furthers the spread of sexually transmitted diseases (STDs), especially AIDS.

Those of us committed to our families are the first line of defence against the dangers of illicit sex. Living by the scriptural rule of one man and one woman for life provides the containment of our sexuality and avoids the possibility of infection from STDs. To berate gays without the same censure for illicit straight sex is hypocritical, but worse, may lead into other dangerous sexual liaisons because they seem acceptable. No relationship outside of marriage can ever be considered safe—from discredit and disease for ourselves, to transmission of disease to our marriage partners, to heartache and misery for our whole family.

Weekend ~ Sexuality

The Western culture in which we live is a highly sexualized society. Sex pervades TV, movies, advertising, the internet

---

[1] Leviticus 18:6

and most forms of communication. Methods of heightening sexual intercourse are frequently touted in magazines and a whole industry has arisen around attaining the perfect body. Variant sexual behaviours have become mainstream—much that was previously considered deviant has been normalized. Recreation has become the main function of sex, now even acceptable among teens. Pornography abounds, especially on the internet, including child sex and incest, which appears to have a widening audience. In general, there are no social limits on sexual behaviour—all varieties are considered legitimate and entitled choices.

Of course, little of this is news to you, especially if you were born late in the twentieth century. What you may not be aware of is that this has not always been the case. During the first half of the last century, social acceptance was generally restricted to heterosexuality, primarily within marriage. Other sexual preferences did exist but mostly in private and underground. Homosexuality was punishable under the law. The source of this morality was Christianity, which pervaded Western culture. The restrictions were not considered oppressive and society as a whole was safer and less traumatized and adrift than it is today.

In today's culture, these restrictions are considered archaic, bigoted and intolerable, but they still form the basis of biblical morality, even if Christians are a minority. But there are two advantages to the current situation. Firstly, Christian morality stands out in sharp contrast to the surrounding culture and, as such, is an important witness to our faith. Hence, we have to ask ourselves if our marriages are a faithful witness to our beliefs. Secondly, Christians must now view those the Bible considers aberrant differently. Whereas in the past we may have considered them a negligible fringe in society, now they face us as real people needing the grace and compassion God has bestowed upon us. Perhaps we can now identify with them—we all practise deviant behaviour; it is called sin and places all of us in need of a Saviour.

Week Seventeen

Monday: Leviticus 19:29–37

There is no doubt that there were as many unprincipled people in Israelite society as there are within our own. This passage in particular deals with those who would abuse people and laws without conscience. Several times in the passage, the commands are reinforced by denoting the author himself: "the LORD" or "the LORD your God." For our purposes, verse 29 is of particular concern, for it dealt with an alternate way in which a corrupt father could "sell" his daughter. While earlier readings provided an honourable way in which a father could provide for his family, today's reading clearly prohibits prostitution as a father's option.

Prostitution has generally been stigmatised in most civilised cultures and rightly so. Although in our present Western culture there has been an attempt to clean its image—"prostitute" is considered a pejorative term and is now substituted with "sex trade worker"—prostitution by any name dehumanises women, whose lives tend to be characterised by abuse and murder. Both in British Columbia and Alberta, major crimes against a number of prostitutes, including serial murder, are currently under investigation and indictment.

Unfortunately, many of the girls in the trade have little choice. Many are forced into it by modern day covert slavery across national boundaries; some nations allow daughters to be sold into prostitution, who are then abused by "sex tourists." Some are captivated by drugs and can only pay for their addiction by selling themselves; others are rebellious teens who have fallen afoul of the criminal elements of society. Thus, today's passage is concerned not only with the father's behaviour and the daughter's welfare but also recognizes the tendency for prostitution to be the leading edge of other evils.

Tuesday: Numbers 27:1–11

We have previously noted that, at first glance, the Bible appears to favour a patriarchal family system where the father is the autocratic head of the clan. Because the clans were large—they included servants, maidservants and herders—the need for some form of governance was necessary. This meant that someone needed to take responsibility for the safety and prosperity of the clan, and the patriarchal system supplied that need. When the father died, it passed to the eldest son. However, that did not necessarily mean that the women were chattels of the men, and this story demonstrates that they were given their own rights.

Earlier meditations provided examples of women asserting their rights in the early days of Scripture. Sarah had freedom to deal with her servants as she pleased, and in one case Abraham was encouraged to allow this by God himself.[1] The story of Leah's mandrakes is a classic. In return for Leah's mandrakes—which were reckoned to enhance fertility—Rachel allowed Leah to sleep with Jacob that night.[2] Jacob had little say in the matter.

Zelophehad's daughters had no brothers, and so needed inheritance laws to include them to continue the family line and property. Perhaps this was a new idea for Moses. He asked the Lord for guidance, and God gave clear instruction: "If a man dies and has no son, give his inheritance to his daughter." This meant that the eldest daughter also took the responsibility of leading her clan. The lesson for parents today is to give both girls and boys

---

[1] Genesis 16:6; 21:11–12
[2] Genesis 30:14–16

equal educational opportunity. This is one way in which we can instil the equality of the sexes made in the image of God.[1]

Wednesday: Numbers 30:1–16

This is a strongly paternalistic view of women if ever there was one. On the face of it, here is complete discretion for a father or husband to monitor and approve of any vow that a daughter or wife may make. The concept assumed that the woman in each case was unable to make an intelligent decision or that the man could force the woman's decision according to his own capricious desires. This would rightly not fly today, but I'm not sure that it would have been acceptable on those terms at that time either.

It has to be recalled that Israelite society was patriarchal—*not* a pejorative term—which meant that as the father was head of the household, he was also responsible for its welfare. In that sense, his oversight of his wife's decisions was to ensure that it was in keeping with the wellbeing of the household. But he could not make his decision on a whim, nor, as the passage asserts, change his mind whenever he wished. If a demand was perverse, women in that society were not voiceless in their demands as the patriarchs' wives made clear.

At the risk of stereotyping, most women today still enjoy the idea of security within the marriage bond. Where a husband's first desire is for his wife's wellbeing, a woman is foolish to step outside that safeguard, especially with children. This, of course, does not preclude her leaving an abusive situation. In fact, husbands will be called to account for their love and service to their wives, serving them "just as Christ does the church."[2] In the same way, women will be held accountable for frivolous rejection of the God-given support of a good husband.

---

[1] Genesis 1:27
[2] Ephesians 5:29

Thursday: Deuteronomy 5:1–21

We have discussed earlier the critical feature of the covenants that God made with men: they were without conditions. However, this list—the Ten Commandments—looks far too much like a list of contractual obligations. The problem of obedience is not limited to the Old Testament Law but is frequently queried by Christians. If we are saved by grace through faith leading to forgiveness of sin, then why keep standards set by the Bible? Even Paul faced the question that as we are no longer under the law, what's to prevent us from sinning?[1] Throughout the centuries, there have been groups that have lived without moral law on this basis. But almost instinctively, we realize that something is wrong with this outlook.

Although we live by grace, we still believe in keeping the Ten Commandments. Here are some suggestions why we do. Firstly, as God's people we are witnesses to a moral and just God and so should reflect who he is.[2] Further, to indulge in sin is to contradict the rebuilding of the lost image of God in us.[3] But probably of greatest importance for our purposes, obedience is a response of participation in God's covenant—whether it was Israel in the Old Testament or us under the New Testament. To continue in sin does not nullify God's covenant with us, but we lose out on the blessings and fellowship it provides.

Similarly, our response of faithfulness to our partner's promise of faithfulness is less about maintaining a pact and more about enjoying the relationship with each other. We can live under the same roof while ignoring or reneging on our covenant promises, consequently losing the companionship it affords. But that is hardly a marriage.

---

[1] Romans 6:15
[2] Deuteronomy 4:5–8
[3] Romans 8:29

Friday: Deuteronomy 5:8–10

God is a God of abundance. In the spring when blossoms and seeds appear on the trees, it is impossible not to notice there is far more than necessary to propagate the species. The same is true of animal life—if it is not interfered with by humans. When left to themselves, the waters teem with fish and insects would proliferate at an alarming pace if not for predators. And today's passage reminds us that while God judges three or four generations that follow in their father's sins, he blesses a thousand generations of those who love him.

These things are an example and a measure of the grace of God. He gives far more of what is needed than is necessary. Even those sinful generations that return to him can find acceptance, for grace is far more abundant than the sin it covers.[1] Here in the Ten Commandments, God's punishment is limited to four generations, but he is merciful to a thousand generations of those who show their love by obedience. How encouraging it is to note that the very document that reveals our sin is the one that contains this all-encompassing promise.

Today's passage also notes God's jealousy. Jealousy out of control can result in terrible things—violence and even murder. But jealousy is a God-given characteristic to maintain fidelity; anger at deception is a tool intended to bring the offender to repentance. It is God's jealousy that continually calls us to repentance and condemns rebelliousness. We have a right to jealously guard not only our marriages but also our children, that they, like us, may continue to enjoy the grace of God.

Weekend ~ God has no Grandchildren

A bumper sticker I once saw read: "If I'd known grandchildren were so much fun, I would have had them first." It's great to have fun with the grandchildren and then send them back home

---

[1] Romans 5:20

when we are tired. But when it comes to spiritual things, to be a grandchild of God is a vulnerable place. I made a commitment to God when I was ten years old and it was a meaningful decision. However, my assurance of faith was based on my father's conviction of *his* faith. His clear annunciation of what he believed and his ability to preach confidently convinced me of what I claimed to believe.

As long as our assurance of faith is based on our confidence in someone else, we are grandchildren of God. If we lose the security of reliance on someone else's belief, our own faith may falter and our confidence be undermined. Jacob is a prime example. For the early part of his life, his confidence was in the God of his father Isaac.[1] But it was later, when he met God at Bethel, that the Lord became his God. Then, for the rest of his life, his personal relationship with God—however tenuous at times—became his mainstay. Joseph came to that place much earlier in life, when he lost all contact with his family and those who knew God. His adversity drove him to seek God for himself as his later life shows.

There is nothing wrong with leaning on others during a time of incubation and maturing of our faith, but a systematic knowledge of God's Word and experience of God's involvement in our lives will make our faith our own. It is then that we can "give the reason for the hope that you have."[2] Where are you on this journey?

---

[1] Note his reference to "the Lord *your* God" in Genesis 27:20
[2] 1 Peter 3:15

Week Eighteen

Monday: Deuteronomy 6:1–9; 20–25

The setting for this passage follows the recital of Israel's history in the beginning chapters of Deuteronomy and the Ten Commandments we read last week. These were basic directives given by Moses prior to entering the Promised Land. That this instruction—to teach children—is the first to follow signifies its importance. Christianity is always one generation away from extinction, and our children's welfare and prosperity is dependent on our attitude to God; that attitude is the essence of our love to God.

Today's reading explains two things about teaching children. Firstly, teaching is done in everyday life settings: "when you sit at home and when you walk along the road, when you lie down and when you get up." Teaching is not confined to religious places or environments; faithfulness to God is all pervasive. In fact, to leave teaching to a purely religious experience implies a faith divorced from life and leads to compartmentalising it within life. But secondly, the latter verses provide for religious events to explain faith. By observing special times in our church calendar, we explain what God has done for us and why we believe.

Should we, in fact, "bind scriptures on our hands and foreheads and write them on our doorframes"? While ultra religious Jews might take this literally, it certainly means that what we do and think is to be conditioned by our relationship to God and our homes should be places where God is revered and honoured. It is not the observances that we fulfil, as important as these may be, but the way we live, the spiritual dynamic that we bring to every part of our lives and homes, that will influence our children the most.

Tuesday: Deuteronomy 7:1–11

God is a covenant-keeping God, but those who fail to participate in his covenant will miss the benefits of it. This passage must seem extreme in its judgement at the first reading, but it should be remembered that those inhabiting the land were at least four hundred years past Abraham's experience and response to God.[1] This was a time of judgment for the Canaanites and their allied nations, as verse 10 indicates. The warning for Israel to avoid contact with them was to ensure they were not ensnared by the same practices that brought judgement on Canaan. The discrimination was not racial but religious, to maintain Israel within the covenant God had made.

But it was not only Israel's obedience that would keep them in the covenant; it was also God's love that maintained the covenant with them despite their smallness as a nation and their disobedience.[2] The verses referenced from Deuteronomy chapter 9 indicate that the emerging and youthful nation of Israel was a "stiff-necked people," who continually rebelled against God and the requirements he set up for their benefit. It is a reminder of those fractious teen years when so many young people rebel against parents' instructions given for their benefit. Nevertheless, parents' love for their children never abates.

The sobering truth is that Israel would suffer the same consequences as the other nations if they did not abide in God's covenant with them. This is also true of teens who will reap the rewards of frequently rebellious lifestyles, either under the law or in growing health or addiction problems. As with God, it is this unruly behaviour that highlights a parent's love for the child. The

---

[1] Genesis 15:12–21
[2] Deuteronomy 9:4–6

child is not loved for achievement, good looks or even good behaviour but is simply loved for his or her sake. Love does not need a reason beyond itself.

Wednesday: Deuteronomy 10:17–22

Jesus recognized a variety of reasons for singleness. Some are born not to marry, some become single by the actions of others, and others choose not to marry.[1] Jesus was responding to the disciples' suggestion that maintaining a faithful marriage could be so difficult that singleness was a preferable option. The tragedy of our time is the number of persons that have become single because of that difficulty. A single mother—and in lesser numbers, a single father—is in the same state as a widow, and needs to be accorded the same care. In fact, as in today's reading, Scripture repeats God's concern for widows and orphans many times, providing instructions for their sustenance and accusing those who ignore their plight.[2]

Our current culture, which continues to devalue the family, has deceived many into believing that easy divorce means an easy way to terminate a marriage. While the tools for divorce may be easily accessible, it is rarely the predicted "easy way out." Quite apart from the pain of divorce, the drive for women's independence has led many women to a life of unnecessary hardship. While some marriages break up because of intolerable abuse, those that end due to simple dissatisfaction could have been saved to the benefit of both partners and the children.

Unfortunately, the pressures from society to take "the easy way out" have left many unmarried mothers to fend for themselves and their children without the benefit of married companionship and support. It is all too easy to pass blame upon those who fail in a relationship without reckoning with the false

---

[1] Matthew 19:11–12. Note that the word "eunuch" can include other types of singleness.

[2] Deuteronomy 27:19 is typical of several other charges.

messages that delude us—that moving in and out of relationships is as easy as getting in and out of various beds. The biblical mandate for faithful marriage may be demanding, and resolving marital conflict is challenging, but the rewards are incalculable.

Thursday: Deuteronomy 13:6–11

The punishments mandated in today's reading seem grossly overdone by today's standards. Many in Western society disagree with the death penalty even for murder, and as penalty for a religious disagreement it would be considered intolerable, even revolting, to execute that punishment on members of one's own family. So the question remains, how can we understand this passage in today's terms?

Firstly, there is a standard in this passage for staying faithful to the true God. To deny their Lord as the one and only true God was not only an offence against him but also a basic lie about the world Israel inhabited. The results of the same lie today can be seen in the gradual moral decay of our Western society and the uncertain philosophies that endeavour to take God's place. While we may not agree with the punishment of apostasy that this passage demands, we should not take lightly the seriousness of the sin that the punishments measure.

Secondly, we need to respond in the spirit of grace ushered in by Jesus Christ who was "full of grace and truth."[1] The grace extended to us is the grace that we are now required to extend to others, even those who deny the truth, and in particular, those of our own families.

A couple we know was concerned about visiting a daughter whose husband was an unbeliever. Our advice was that their presence there was probably sufficient intimidation for him, as he most certainly knew their stand for the truth. If he was willing to receive them, their responsibility was to love and enjoy him as part of their family and extend to him their Christian grace.

---

[1] John 1:14–17

Friday: Deuteronomy 22:13–29

Because the Israelites lived in a patriarchal society, many of the regulations concerning women were given for their protection. A woman who displeased her husband had to be given a divorce certificate to avoid later charges of adultery,[1] and Jesus later indicated that the reason for divorce could not be trivial.[2] Similarly in this passage, although adultery by either sex would not be supported, there was protection given for a woman who was raped.

While the regulations seem primitive compared with our laws today, there was an attempt to ascertain whether the union was consensual. If the union took place in the country, the law took the woman's word for rape, for there was no one to hear a cry of distress. But if she was in the city when the intercourse occurred and she did not cry out, the union was considered consensual. In cases where rape was confirmed, marriage was mandated and there was no possibility of divorce.

But the penalty for adultery was death. As previously discussed regarding apostasy,[3] the response seems totally out of all proportion to the offence—especially in today's social climate, which is accepting of all sexual liaisons. Yet as we have discussed elsewhere, adultery is a form of apostasy. The marriage bond is a picture of God's relationship to his people, therefore adultery is a lie that suggests that God is unfaithful to his people.

Weekend ~ Introducing Joshua

Next week our thoughts will dwell on passages from the book of Joshua. This book records the entry of the Israelites into the Promised Land and the wars that took place to conquer the land. These stories find their counterpart in the current situation

---

[1] Deuteronomy 24:1
[2] Matthew 19:8–9
[3] Deuteronomy 13:6–11

in Palestine, with Israel seeking to maintain its place in the land by military means and the constant threat from her neighbours to "push Israel into the sea." Thus, it is not possible to read Joshua without emotions evoked by the current crisis, both for and against Israel, colouring attitudes to Joshua's campaigns conducted some 3,500 years ago.

But whatever our feeling regarding Israel, few of us would not be repulsed by the methods of war reported in Joshua by today's standards of conduct. Nevertheless, that was a time when war formed the economy of many nations by the acquisition of fertile land and resources from elsewhere. In fact, an aside in the Old Testament sheds light on this: "In the spring, at the time when kings go off to war . . ."[1] The culture of the day was a response to the warlike ambitions of most nations—something we still face from nations today.

Part of the value of Joshua, as with much of the Bible, is the reporting of actual history, whatever our response to it. But the warfare that we read in Scripture is also symptomatic of individual lives and relationships. The attitudes and actions of nations can be repeated in family life, and the foolishness, deceptions and failures of the nation of Israel recorded in Joshua can be helpful in analyzing our own lives. After all, the dark side of our individual natures is no different in essence from that of nations and is, in fact, the motivating force behind all conflict— personal or worldwide.

---

[1] 2 Samuel 11:1

Week Nineteen

Monday: Deuteronomy 24:1–5

The first year of marriage is commonly known as the honeymoon period, and the last verse of our reading attests to this. But it also raises the issue of the wife's happiness. In Hebrew culture barrenness brought shame, so bringing children as a joy to one's wife was a requirement. Thus, spending a year at home before going to war would be important for the wife as well as to ensure a growing population.

But then, as now, not all marriages were happy. The first verses of chapter 24 indicate that divorce was permissible if a man's wife was "displeasing to him because he finds something indecent about her." This did not mean burning the toast, an interpretation favoured by the Pharisees, who reckoned a man could "divorce his wife for any and every reason."[1] The reason was only valid if he "finds something indecent about her." But there are two cases in our reading where a Hebrew man could not divorce his wife at all during his lifetime. These were in the case of the rape of a virgin, when the man was obliged to marry her, and when a man's claim that his new wife was not a virgin was disproved.

In these cases as well as divorce, the protection and status of the woman was the concern of the law. Without a bill of divorcement, the wife of a prior marriage could be charged with

---

[1] Matthew 19:3

adultery if she remarried. All this does not mean that adultery or some other form of sexual misconduct, although grounds for divorce, requires divorce. You may be experiencing the pain and loss of trust in a partner. It can be devastating, and recovery often needs a lengthy period of time. But if the option to reconcile is possible, it is a less destructive and more satisfying outcome in the long term.

Tuesday: Deuteronomy 30:1–20

When we buy a new car we read our instruction manuals to ensure we receive good service from it. Of similar importance is where we take the vehicle. Obviously, some vehicles are meant for rougher terrain than others, but most of us have vehicles that are built for highway use, not mountaineering. We sense a great freedom in taking to the highway if it is clear of traffic. In North America the places we can take our car are almost limitless, but there is one condition—we stay on the road. Try driving across a muddy field and we soon find our freedom strictly curtailed until someone pulls us out.

Our reading today sets out the importance of Israel keeping the covenant if they wanted to enjoy the benefits of it.[1] Enjoyment of the freedom that the covenant provided depended on Israel's continuing response to the terms of the covenant. Opting out did not nullify the covenant—it continued to remain in force—but to reject it meant living in a heathen wilderness and losing the freedom the covenant offered. Similarly, enjoying the fruits of our covenant with God means staying on the "highways" God has provided for us. If we wish to take off across a "muddy field," we will eventually bear the consequences of it.

Making a marriage work is not just a matter of common sense; it is a God-given covenant, and as such requires adherence to the rules of the covenant just as for any natural law. As many have found, a love-centred marriage is not only a source of

---

[1] Reading the previous two chapters will give fuller insight

companionship and personal dignity but also a place of great emotional freedom. Where a partner has transgressed the faithfulness of the covenant, conflict and bitterness will restrict that freedom, but a joyous response to the covenant our partner has made with us will only enhance it.

Wednesday: Joshua 1:1–9

Today's reading stands out as one of the great motivational passages of all time, particularly for the Christian community. While its basic message is real, it has often been distorted to mean that Christians will always be prosperous and successful, and most of us realize that is not so.[1] So how can God's encouragement to Joshua help us in our relational dilemmas?

Firstly, we must put the passage into context. It is a continuation of the promise of land for the Israelites contained in the covenant given to Abraham and his descendants. God is simply saying that his promise is certain and Joshua can have confidence in it. However, as we have pointed out previously, acceptance of the covenant required following its guidelines to obtain the benefits of it. In this case it required living out the "Book of the Law" —"Then you will be prosperous and successful." This would enable Joshua to be "strong and courageous," as stated three times in this passage, for it meant that Joshua could be assured of final conquest of the land. In practice, though, Joshua failed on some counts and the conquest was never completed. As a result, Israel experienced an unstable peace.

Secondly, we need to recognize that we are like Joshua: not able to fully maintain our faith in hazardous times. But there are two aids for life here that pertain directly to us as well as Joshua. One is the instruction to dwell in the "Book of the Law," or the Bible, and "meditate on it day and night."[2] Many Christians live

---

[1] See Hebrews 11:32–40
[2] See Psalm 1:1–3

mediocre lives because the Bible is not the foundation for their way of life. The other help for us is the promise that "the Lord your God will be with you wherever you go."[1] This reminds us that "success" is not totally up to us but that God has final control of our circumstances—often in spite of us.

If you are facing the prospect of marriage—joyfully, but perhaps with some trepidation—or are already in a marriage that you consider unsuccessful, the instruction and promise given to Joshua is the key to maintaining faith. After all, success is not necessarily measured by changing conditions but in remaining "strong and courageous" in our trust in God for all the situations of life.

Thursday: Joshua 8:30–35

Our reading today centres on the renewal of the covenant between God and Israel. Joshua was fulfilling the command given by Moses to state the terms of the covenant when they had reached the Promised Land.[2] We may ask the question: Why then was it necessary for Israel to repeat the covenant promises and curses? You may recall that the land Joshua and the people of Israel now occupied was one of the promises given to Abraham and his son and grandson. As part of the covenant, their continued enjoyment of this land depended on their response of trust in God's covenant. Thus, a reminder of the terms of the covenant as they began to conquer the land was appropriate.

This was not the last time that Israel renewed the covenant, and as we shall see later, they frequently rejected the covenant and lost fellowship with God as a result. This led to domination by oppressors, or in extreme cases, allying themselves with ungodly nations, even worshipping their gods. Thus, a reminder of the covenant was always a corrective measure. In addition, the people of Israel faced a daunting future. There were many battles

---

[1] See Matthew 28:20
[2] Deuteronomy 11:29

to be fought and city kingdoms to be taken. To remember the promises of God and his presence with them was an important encouragement to stay with him as they faced the uncertainties ahead. Equally important was the recitation of the curses, a reminder of the dangers of forsaking God.

When it comes to the marriage covenant, many couples renew their wedding vows at special anniversaries, reminding themselves of the blessings their marriages have brought and pledging to stay faithful to ensure those blessings continue. But continuing to enjoy that partnership means staying faithful to the terms of the marriage covenant just as Israel needed to stay faithful to God's covenant. Perhaps a remembrance of the pitfalls that face marriage and the wretchedness they could bring should also be added to the recalled marriage vows as a help towards maintaining them.

Friday: Joshua 9:1–16

This story is an occasion when Israel failed to maintain the covenant regarding their entry into Canaan, the so-called Promised Land. Israel had been clearly told to destroy the inhabitants of the land and not to make treaties with them[1] in conjunction with the promise of victory in Joshua's battles.[2] It is a great story of deception and the failure to perceive it, which has repercussions for our own lives. It was all too easy for Joshua to use deception as an excuse and claim innocence in his dealings with the Gibeonites. What went wrong, and how can we learn to avoid the same trap in our marriages?

Joshua knew the right question to ask; he wanted to know where they came from. Perhaps the first sign of deceit was the prevarication in the first answer — "We are your servants" — a veiled response. Joshua failed to be alerted by this evasion. In fact, both he and his men simply believed the Gibeonites' story on the

---

[1] Deuteronomy 7:2
[2] Joshua 1:4–5

basis of their provisions and failed to seek wisdom on the issue: they "did not enquire of the Lord." They also succumbed to pressure. Why was it necessary to sign a treaty immediately? The truth was out in three days and if they had waited for guidance, revealed truth would have given it to them.

But perhaps the underlying cause was a desire to be deceived. Joshua had already fought several battles and faced many more. This would be one less fight, with a readymade excuse to avoid it. We deceive ourselves more effectively than we deceive others, and when it comes to issues of fidelity our guard falters easily; a working or other legitimate liaison with the opposite sex can mask a hidden desire to be deceived. Seduction is a form of deception, rarely fulfilling its promise, almost always ending in misery. Because it is based on lies, misrepresentation and inconsistencies will accompany it. Seduction also brings pressure; there is a demand for immediate gratification. In contrast, a talk with God—that simple act of prayer—will often interfere with plans to respond to seduction. Or conversely, our desire may interfere with our prayer.

Weekend ~ Avoiding Pitfalls

Some of you may be old enough to remember drive-in movie theatres. It was a great place to take a girl and make out. Many a girl has been compromised in the back seat of a car in a situation like this. Of course, the act didn't just suddenly occur at the drive-in but had already been initiated when the decision to go there was made in the first place. You may recall news broadcasts about injuries and killings from fights late at night at bars and nightclubs. Part of the way to avoid vulnerability is to avoid risky situations in the first place. It is often a particular lifestyle that places one in jeopardy.

Scripture gives us guidance for receiving the best from life and lays out pitfalls to avoid. However, avoiding life's pitfalls is not always simply a matter of willpower. Often it can simply mean having a lifestyle that does not include those settings that are the most risky. Some jobs provide challenging settings: travel requiring overnight lodgings, lonely shift work or close working liaisons with the opposite sex. All these can provide potentially compromising situations, and some have even chosen to change their jobs in order to avoid them.

The problem with the above examples is that they are perfectly legitimate activities, frequently without suitable alternatives. But here are some suggestions for reducing the risk: attend church regularly, become involved in activities with numbers of people, increase the activities you do with your partner, avoid times that take you away from your partner and that provide contact with the opposite sex. Changes like this may require some sacrifice, particularly where the activity is legitimate, but the sacrifice will be worth more than the price paid if it avoids future infidelity and the resulting conflict and pain.

$$\mathcal{W}eek\ \mathcal{T}wenty$$

Monday: Joshua 20:1–9

What a great idea: cities of refuge. How many times in your life have you wished for a place of refuge from the storms of life? As we write this, the news is full of the after-effects of Hurricane Katrina that devastated New Orleans and much of Mississippi and Louisiana in 2005. For the first week there was no refuge for thousands of displaced persons until they could be transported out of the chaos to cities of refuge like Baton Rouge, Houston and others throughout the United States. For the Jews of Joshua's time, cities of refuge were designated for those who had committed crimes by accident, especially murder, until their case could be heard by an impartial court.

Much of life is complicated by misunderstandings. Communication is hampered by our own inability to state clearly the problem facing us. We may have poor communication skills, be too emotionally involved to see things rationally or even be fearful of expressing ourselves truthfully. There is also the dynamic of the emotional involvement of the listener, who has his or her personal agenda, personal fears or fixed ideas of the issues at hand. Further talk only seems to lead to greater confusion. I have noted on occasion that Ann and I have argued with each other on some issue only to finally realize we were both arguing for the same thing.

But where is our city of refuge in times of torment? Firstly, it is the Word of God, not as means of escape, but as a source of instruction for our distorted thinking resulting from sin. But as a complement to that, God has provided us with a community of faith to support us in times of need. To seek help is not to admit failure, but rather, to find objective thinking for our dilemma. A Christian counsellor who is familiar with the Bible and has experience with most marriage problems and good analytical skills can help us state our case plainly and correct our distorted thinking. Stating the problem clearly is half the battle to resolving it.

Tuesday: Joshua 24:14–27

Most of Joshua's campaign is bracketed by the two rehearsals of the covenant. An earlier reading noted the recall of the covenant at the early stages of the campaign, and today we read of Joshua's final review of the covenant before his death. Earlier we also noted the habit of some to renew wedding vows at special anniversaries. Perhaps the vow renewal should take place not only at times of celebration but also at the difficult times in the marriage as well. As suggested in a previous devotion, the vows could possibly include warnings of those actions that could lead to marriage failure. Even with its negative connotations, this latter idea should inject some realism into the relationship and help attain "happily ever after."

Joshua was a realist. He gave the Israelites the opportunity to opt out of the covenant while asserting his own determination to remain within it. Regardless of their agreement that God was their benefactor and their assertion to serve the Lord—repeated three times in verses 18, 21 and 24—Joshua knew that they would fail to do so; he had his own experience to go by. The greatest failure of modern philosophical thought is the notion that man is essentially good and will improve himself over time using new idealistic ideas. These ideas should lead to an enlightened view of humankind unfettered by religious—particularly Christian—dogma. The last hundred years of human history have resulted in disillusion with this belief; Joshua had it right all along.

We all aspire to the fairy tale romance, which is not a bad goal, provided we inject some of Joshua's realism into it. The story of Prince Charles and Princess Diana had all the makings of a fairy tale romance—royalty, beauty, riches and adulation—but it failed because of the fallen human nature of both partners. Their belief that happiness was to be found outside the marriage caused intense distress to themselves and others. Recognising moral frailty within our own marriages may be the first step to avoiding the failure it could bring.

Wednesday: Judges 2:6–19

Today's reading is a summary of the book of Judges, which records the cycles of rebellion against God. These brought oppression from surrounding nations, Israel's cry for deliverance and God's provision of judges to release them from bondage. Even with God's continual deliverances, these cycles still deteriorated into anarchy[1] because of the desires of the individuals that made up the nation. Judges clearly demonstrates the perversity of human nature and our repeated tendency to seek independence from God, much to our own detriment.

It is this tendency that Joshua recognized and warned against. Independence, from both God and our partner, threatens to undermine marriage and relationships. Restrictions placed on our relationship with our partner are to ensure ongoing companionship. They may often seem irksome, but they prevent us from responding to gratification from other sources that the relationship precludes. We can be seduced into thinking that we can eat our seed corn rather than planting it for a future crop. It is the investment in interdependence with our partner that will ensure future satisfaction.

It is our unnatural desire for independence from God that is the great threat to our marriages. Even those who are not Christians can gain marital stability from adherence to godly

---

[1] Judges 17:6; 21:25

requirements. Unfortunately, the reverse is also true; there are Christian couples that lose out because they seek security for their marriages in the wrong places: money, love, acquisitions and so on. The true security for marriage is found firstly in maintaining our covenant with God, which in turn leads us to maintain our covenant with each other.[1]

Thursday: Judges 11:29–40

This passage, often referred to as Jephthah's rash vow, highlights two important aspects of parenthood: the never-fading reality of our love for our children and the foolishness of decisions made during emotional turmoil.

Tonya was having major problems with her sixteen-year-old son, probably sparked by marital problems. After a weekend away with her husband in an endeavour to mend their marriage, she returned home to find her house ransacked, contents smashed and liquor consumed. Her son's wild weekend party caused the damage. It naturally resulted in a showdown.

She laid out all the heartache and costs he had created for the family, not only by this incident but also by previous abusive and destructive behaviour. She told him that this time he would be reported to the police and ordered him out of the house. But as the immediate emotional crisis subsided, she had time to think more clearly. At what she felt was God's urging, she drove out to follow her son and caught up with him as he dejectedly wandered the streets. His cockiness had evaporated and his misery showed. She kindly invited him into the car and he broke down in sorrowful repentance for his actions. He knew she still loved him.

Jephthah made his vow in a moment of emotional turmoil, but he never considered the possible outcomes and it ended in tragedy. Did Jephthah sacrifice his daughter? It is unlikely; human sacrifice was forbidden in Israel and redemption by animal sacrifice was the usual practice. However, as she bewailed her

---

[1] Malachi 2:10–15

virginity, it is likely that she remained in seclusion for her lifetime, probably for some religious duty but the text gives no detail. We, however, may still have the opportunity to use our love as a motivation to try to reunite with a wayward child.

Friday: Judges 14:1–18

If ever there was a stormy relationship it was between Samson and his chosen women—first his wife, and later, Delilah. It seems that Samson did everything wrong: ignoring his parents' advice, choosing Philistine women, consorting with Philistine prostitutes,[1] and always acting in angry and vicious revenge. Yet in the face of this, our reading tells us that God had a plan for Israel in all this confusion and that he was using Samson to confront the Philistines who were ruling Israel. This raises two questions.

Firstly, if God was using Samson in his violent and rebellious life, did this mean that God condoned, perhaps even precipitated Samson's actions? Certainly, we can see God's big picture behind the events related in the story as we read Samson's life, but did this justify Samson's actions? The answer to this question opens up for us God's amazing ability to control events in the most adverse of circumstances. God's foreknowledge of Samson's lifestyle enabled him to use it for his purposes without denying Samson's freedom of will or subsequent guilt. Compare the Bible's judgment of Judas, who betrayed Jesus: he fulfilled God's will but was responsible for his own actions.[2]

Secondly, how should his parents have reacted? The previous chapter shows their devotion to God and their early awareness of Samson's role for Israel. But Samson's wilfulness caused them to question that knowledge. Perhaps this was a case for his parents to trust God with the big picture; even in the most contrary of circumstances our commitment to God is usable by him.

---

[1] Judges 16:1–4
[2] Luke 22:22

Have you cause to question the purpose of your life because events are contrary to your expectations? Scripture makes it clear that you can trust God with your life, even when your closest relationships fail. He is able to "repay you for the years the locusts have eaten."[1] God can still work in the life of the most rebellious and angry of children.

Weekend ~ Anarchy

We have seen in this week's readings that anarchy is simply a result of everyone seeking his or her own way. It does not necessarily mean the rule of armed thugs, as experienced in New Orleans after the devastation by hurricane Katrina, although that is one form of anarchy. Anarchy can also be experienced when everyone conforms to their own set of rules within a "civilised" society. Western culture today has largely thrown off the restraints of Christian values and lives on a smorgasbord of religions and spirituality—including secularism—that provides a glut of conflicting lifestyles. Where these lifestyles are based primarily on the fulfilment of personal desires, the cohesiveness of society is undermined and friction increases within it.

In many ways the time of the judges after Joshua is similar to today's Western culture. As worship of God waned, so a variety of religions and religious experiences took its place. Even individual households maintained their own priest and religion,[2] clear examples of personally concocted spirituality. This process, then and now, provides religions of convenience and allows the practitioners to assume and validate any lifestyle of their choice. With so many options and the diverse advice that they offer, many people fall prey to a confusing array of values, often conflicting and rarely sustainable in the long run, and finish with a disruptive anarchy within themselves. If one or both partners

---

[1] Joel 2:25
[2] Judges 17:1–5

are in this dilemma, their marriage is built on a foundation of shifting sands and will not stand against the winds of change.

The answer to anarchy is truth. A stable society cannot survive without the cooperation of the individuals within it, reflecting the truth of God's personal inter-relationship within the Trinity. Similarly, recognizing and practising the truth revealed to us in Scripture will provide lasting stable guidance for all of life and beyond.

Week Twenty-One

Monday: Judges 16:4–21

In England, the country of our birth, there is a saying: "Don't make love at the garden gate. Love is blind but the neighbours ain't." Certainly, in the early stages of courtship, a level of infatuation conceals the faults in the other. Today's story of Samson recalls the story of Patrick, a Canadian who, on the rebound from a divorce, met a girl on the internet who lived in California and claimed to be a Christian. He fell for her, regardless of the fact that she had a criminal record and two children from previous relationships. She persuaded him to lease and pay for an apartment for herself and her children, pay several thousand dollars to fix her teeth and buy her a vehicle. He purchased a new car in Ontario, taxed and insured it and drove it down to California for her. It was a great example of blind love.

You may have guessed that he heard very little from her afterwards, except calls for money to support her children. It took a year for a good friend to help him realize the impossibility of the situation, and by then Patrick had met a local Christian girl prepared to marry him. He finally phoned the landlord, indicating he was no longer responsible for rent as the lease was up. He and his friend flew to California, "stole" the car back—he still had keys and proof of purchase—and drove it home. It still had Ontario plates on it.

But blindness in love is not always bad. Ann came from the "wrong side of the tracks" and lived in a totally dysfunctional home known throughout the neighbourhood. Some of her boyfriends had shied away when they knew where she lived. Ann was fearful of my visiting her home, fearing another runaway. She says she fell in love with me partly because I scarcely noticed her environment, her bizarre mother or the dilapidated condition of their house. But I can hardly take credit for looking past those things: my love for her had given me a convenient blindness.

Tuesday: Ruth 1:1–22

The story of Ruth is a different kind of love story; it is one of God's guidance in arranged marriage. Ruth was a remarkable woman with a quiet determination and devotion. In marrying Naomi's son, she clearly accepted his faith and adopted his family as her own. When all the men of Naomi's family died, Ruth could not be deterred from returning to Judah with her mother-in-law. Naomi assumed that Ruth's reason for following her was to obtain a new husband through the tradition of "levirate" marriage.

Levirate marriage played a big part in Ruth's story. This custom required the brother or other near male relative of a deceased, childless husband to marry the widow, raise children to the dead man and ensure his lineage. The sorry story of Judah's three sons and his daughter-in-law Tamar is based on this tradition.[1] But Ruth's reason for staying with Naomi was not for another husband but a natural outcome of faith in Naomi's God. Naomi's faith, people and God had become Ruth's.

In our current culture, which tends to despise mothers-in-law, it is refreshing to see Ruth's devotion to hers. To be fair, this relationship is a two-way street. A mother who believes her son-in-law or daughter-in-law is not good enough for her child is courting rejection for herself: a daughter may be torn between her parent and her husband. It also hinders the grandchild/grandparent relationship, often denying the grandparents the joy of being a part of their grandchildren's lives. Although not always recognized in

---

[1] Genesis 38:6–11

our Western culture, lineage is important to a child, and one with good extended family relationships forms a secure identity.

Wednesday: Ruth 2:1–3:6

The time of the judges[1] was not a good time to be alive, for "in those days Israel had no king, everyone did as he saw fit."[2] There are indications in our reading that these conditions were prevalent in Ruth's time: Boaz told his men not to touch her and Naomi warned Ruth not to go to someone else's field where she could be harmed. Boaz himself was a good man, devoted to God and appreciated by his employees. But there seem to be other dynamics at work. Boaz was curious about this new girl in his field and was further impressed by her care for Naomi. His interest showed itself further as he invited Ruth to share his water, bread and grain; ensured extra grain was left for her to glean; and asked her to remain in his fields until the end of harvest.

If Boaz was taken with this young woman, Naomi's interest was far more practical. Boaz was a relative who could marry Ruth and raise offspring to both Naomi's and Ruth's dead husbands, thus keeping their heritage alive. Naomi gave Ruth instructions to make contact with Boaz and seek his agreement to marry her and so maintain her husband's line. Her approach had cultural overtones that we may not fully understand, but her request to be covered with the corner of his garment was a symbolic request for him to fulfil his levirate marriage duty.

This was no Sadie Hawkins Day proposal of marriage. Rather, it was a request for Boaz to discharge a contractual duty even though under the social conditions of the time it could not be imposed. The initial contact between the two was by chance: "As it turned out, she found herself working in a field belonging to Boaz." Yet we know there is little left to chance for those who choose to live godly lives. Whether arranged or by choice, God

---

[1] Ruth 1:1
[2] Judges 17:6; 21:25

will provide a partner with whom both can fulfil God's desires for their lives.

Thursday: Ruth 3:7–18

The meeting taking place at the grain pile was open to allegations of impropriety, particularly when we look at it from our current Western culture. However, there is some scriptural indication that there was a cultural form behind Ruth's request to Boaz: "Spread the corner of your garment over me, since you are a kinsman-redeemer." The same terminology is used of God as he prepared to look after the emerging nation of Israel, eventually leading to their "marriage."[1] A later meditation will review that passage.

There is a sense that this was to be an arranged marriage, although not forced—Ruth had the choice whether or not to respond to the idea. It is clear from the book and this passage that Ruth's foremost concern was the family that she had adopted without reservation earlier. This was indicative of her nature and desires, obviously well suited to marriage and the demands that would be placed upon her by others: husband, children and those who might become dependent upon her.

The passage also reveals some characteristics of Boaz. He was obviously an older man and could certainly have been attracted to this younger woman. But his response was solicitous, considering her approach a kindness. He had been at pains earlier to ensure her safety in his fields, and now he didn't want her roaming dangerous streets at night. He was also concerned for her reputation. Staying the night to avoid danger could be misconstrued, so he advised an early return home to avoid scandal. He graciously agreed to her request for marriage and gave her some grain for the family. The attitudes of these two had the makings of a good marriage.

---

[1] Ezekiel 16:8

Friday: Ruth 4:1–22

Boaz's intention was clear—he was anxious to marry Ruth—but there was an obstacle: another man, a closer relative of Ruth than Boaz, had the prior right to "acquire" her along with Elimelech's land. We may speculate on Boaz's and Ruth's emotions during this wait. Was she in for a possible marriage to someone she had never met, and was Boaz fearful of losing this great woman? That wait must find an echo in most of our memories, if not a current situation, awaiting the answer of marriage from a proposal.

However, as the story tells us, this closer relative was more concerned with maintaining his own blood line than that of his relative Elimelech. Certainly, had he decided that there was enough personal advantage to inspire him to marry Ruth, that marriage would have been on a precarious footing, as it is any time personal gain is the basis for the relationship. But his negative response left Boaz free to marry Ruth, and together they become the ancestors of David and eventually of Jesus.

There are some interesting sidelights to this story. There are four women, apart from Mary, mentioned in the lineage of Jesus. Two are foreigners, Ruth and Rahab, Rahab being Boaz' mother, Ruth's second mother-in-law.[1] However, Rahab and David are separated by several hundred years, suggesting that there are several generations missing between Obed and Jesse, and it is unlikely that Rahab would have been included if she were not the Rahab from Jericho.[2] Even more surprising, the other women are Tamar[3] and Bathsheba,[4] both of whom were involved in adulterous relationships, and Tamar's produced a child included in Jesus' ancestry.[5] As Ruth became part of the lineage of Jesus, so we also enter God's family by a decision to commit our lives to

---

[1] Matthew 1:5
[2] Joshua 6:22–25
[3] Genesis 38:24
[4] 2 Samuel 11:2–4
[5] Matthew 1:3, 6

Naomi's God. This gives him the opportunity to guide our lives, including the provision of marriage partners.

Weekend ~ Stable Marriages

I recall a counselling professor once stating that there are three kinds of marriages: stable good marriages, unstable bad marriages and bad marriages that are stable. The first two seem obvious, but the last is perhaps surprising. Yet if we think of those we know, we can probably think of couples in the last category. The later years of Jacob and Rebekah are an example. Although it was a difficult relationship, the two needed each other—less for companionship than for maintaining identity even in a combative relationship. Unequal but complementary relationships will stay married, even if they are unhappy.

It was always a mystery to Ann and me why her parents stayed together. They were both identified as psychologically challenged by the head doctor of the local psychiatric hospital. Ann's mother, suffering from an extreme form of bipolar disorder, was frequently picked up for bizarre behaviour and returned to hospital for shock treatment and drug therapy. Men were frequent "visitors" to the home and Ann's three younger brothers all had different fathers. Ann's father was a paranoid schizophrenic, always grumbling at the authorities for injustices towards him or to his employers for short-changing him, but strangely, he remained faithful to his wife. It seems she needed someone to dominate and he required the level of acceptance he received within the relationship.

Ann, as the firstborn and only girl, became the mother of the family who desperately tried to bring order out of chaos and keep the boys out of trouble. She complained to her father for giving her mother his paycheque, which was immediately squandered in the pub. Ann often sat on the pub steps asking customers to tell her mother to come home. The children were frequently removed from the home due to its precarious nature and sent into children's homes where they received the luxury of clean clothes and three meals a day. Even so, the marriage survived until death parted them.

Week Twenty-Two

Monday: 1 Samuel 1:1–20

This is a story of both heartbreak and joy. As we have noted before with Jacob, having two wives is not a good idea. Friction between the two women seems to be the rule, as we have seen not only with Jacob's wives, but also with Abraham's dilemma in the dispute between Sarah and Hagar. It is true again with Elkanah and his two wives, Hannah and Peninnah. Childlessness was tragedy enough for Hannah in that culture, but doubly so when she was derided about it by her rival, Peninnah.

This passage is also about two women of opposite motives. Peninnah obviously had little time for the niceties of religious life, increasing her taunting of Hannah at the annual trip to Shiloh for sacrifice. But Hannah's attitude was in marked contrast. She could easily have been bitter towards God for her barrenness and the continual mocking from Peninnah. Rather, in her misery, she recognized that God was her only hope for change and drew closer to him instead. She prayed silently, knowing that God hears the prayers of the heart.

She left with the sense that God heard her prayers "and ate something, and her face was no longer downcast." Leaving our burdens at the foot of the cross will have that effect upon us. The inability to have children is not confined to biblical times and is a distress to many now. The knowledge that God is in control of our lives and that he will provide children or reasons for withholding them in his time can be a great comfort during a time of uncertainty. God does hear our prayers, and in Hannah's case, he gave her a son. But it is important to note that it was many years before God answered her prayers.

Tuesday: 1 Samuel 1:21–28

Hannah did an amazing thing. After giving birth to her longed-for son, she gave him up for service in the tabernacle. It was certainly within her character to give thanks for the son, but to give up that which was dearest to her heart was a major sacrifice. As a believing Jew, Hannah knew the firstborn belonged to God and was to be redeemed with an animal sacrifice according to the law. But in her case, she decided that she would perform closer to the letter of the law and give Samuel up for service to the Lord. She would see him once a year when making the pilgrimage for sacrifice.

For three or four years after his birth, Hannah weaned Samuel. But it was also a time of instruction for him. She would probably tell him about his birth as an answer to prayer and prepare him for his eventual service in the tabernacle. It is clear that her instruction included the knowledge of God and his requirements, for the last verse tells us that Samuel, still a child, worshipped God as he took up his duties.

Samuel grew to be one of the most devout and effective prophets of Israel's history. Little more is heard of Hannah, but her sacrifice gave Israel a period of stability unmatched in Israel's history. Parents are often required to sacrifice their children. Some die early; others are called into missionary service like Samuel and live in distant and often dangerous lands. The loss of a child is probably the greatest human tragedy, yet there are many that recognize God's call in this loss. You may be the one to make this supreme sacrifice—perhaps even unwillingly. Whatever your response to a call of this magnitude, it underlines for us the huge sacrifice of God's own Son made willingly for us too.

Wednesday: I Samuel 2:12–26

It is difficult for us in our Western lifestyle to imagine the way in which Samuel lived. There was no temple built until the time of Solomon, some 80 or so years later. The ministry of the priests was still carried out in the "Tent of Meeting," set up during the escape from Egypt 400 years earlier. Samuel probably also lived in a tent, sleeping on a mat, daily carrying out simple duties. To start with, he would probably open the tabernacle in the mornings, watch Eli and his sons performing their necessary rituals and serve them. Eventually, he would begin to perform these responsibilities himself, accepting and directing the sacrifices of those who came for cleansing.

In time, Hannah was also rewarded with more children: three boys and two girls. As Hannah came each year for the annual sacrifice, she visited Samuel and provided him with new clothes and ritual garments as he grew. Eli blessed her for her sacrifice of Samuel to the Lord. For Eli, not only was Samuel an obvious asset, he would be a replacement for his disappointing sons. These sons, in deep contrast to Samuel, exploited their position for personal benefits—forcing supplicants to give them unauthorized food from the sacrifices and sexually exploiting the serving women.

Eli asked his sons a rhetorical question: Who will intercede for you when you sin against the Lord? Eli's sons were, in fact, intercessors for the people before God, so when they themselves sinned against God there was no other intercessor for *them* before God. Eventually, Eli's sons died, as had been prophesied.[1] Samuel now became the intercessor for the people to replace Eli's sons. In this regard he prefigured Jesus Christ, who has since come and revealed himself to us. He is now the One who intercedes before the Father for us and for our children.

---

[1] 1 Samuel 4:17

Thursday: 1 Samuel 8:1–9

Samuel was a prophet, but he also acted as the last in a long line of judges that ruled Israel for about 400 years. As today's reading shows, the Israelites had reached a point where they were impatient with their differences from the surrounding nations. Like those nations, they wanted a king to rule over them. The differences were originally designed to make them *dissimilar* from the nations around them as a witness to the living God.[1] Samuel was displeased, for it meant that they wanted to replace his leadership in spite of his many years of loyal service to Israel. But God comforted Samuel, reminding him they were rejecting God as their King more than they were rejecting Samuel.

There is a tendency for novelty to wear off, which is why temporal things—which seem so attractive to begin with—never ultimately satisfy. This does not have to be true of relationships, which are not inanimate but formed by living creatures who constantly provide spontaneity and freshness in their interactions. However, this in itself does not avoid boredom; the relationship is deepened by constant and meaningful interaction. As Israel's fellowship with God lessened, God became less attractive to Israel and the "grass appeared greener next door."

This, of course, is one reason why many marriages fail. Maintaining mutual attraction requires participation in a partner's life and growing insight into the value of his or her abilities and differences. Lack of this interaction reduces the partner's apparent attractiveness and creates a void that outside attraction might fill. Unfortunately, the failure that created the loss of attraction in the first relationship will probably repeat itself in the next—the grass is not really greener next door.

---

[1] Deuteronomy. 4:5–8

Friday: I Samuel 8:10–21

Israel should have observed the old adage: "be careful what you ask for; you may get it!" Even though Samuel warned of the disadvantages of an earthly king, Israel clamoured for one and God obliged. What is of greater mystery is why God would agree to their request when it was not his original design. We can only speculate, as there is no answer given. Perhaps it was simply an accommodation to human sinfulness, similar to his permission for divorce. Maybe if God had not allowed it, Israel's insistence would have created a final, irreversible separation from God.

What we do know is that God's overall mastery of events meant that he was able to fulfill his desires, not only in spite of Israel's defection, but through it. God used Israel's desire for a king to provide for a lineage that would eventually return the kingship to God in the person of King Jesus upon his final (and still future) ascension to the throne of David. The provision of an earthly king for Israel would not provide for the essential needs of Israel any more than the surrounding nations found satisfaction in their kings.

It occurred to me one day that my employer was not the one who supplied my income so that I could provide for myself and my family. God was my ultimate provider; my employment was only the means of that provision. If my employment failed, God was still my provider and had other means of support for our family. Similarly, our partners are God's means of providing for our companionship and physical satisfaction. Thus, he directly participates in the companionship by serving us through it. But that relationship is finite, built on fallible people with limited abilities. To expect that relationship to fill all our needs is foolish and irresponsible. There are some needs only God can supply, and to lean on our partners for those is unreasonable—as was Israel's belief that a human king would bring them final satisfaction and security.

Weekend ~ Children Under Control

The way the child Samuel is described must seem too good to be true, although I'm sure he had his moments. My father put children and animals together in one category—he couldn't stand the disobedience of either. He was strict, and although I had bodily evidence of that quite rarely, he acted on the philosophical mantra of his era: "Children should be seen and not heard." This is a far cry from the attitude towards children today, when allowing children to "express themselves" results in spoiled brats who rule their households with their tantrums. A sensible balance between these two extremes is clearly the preferred approach.

My study window overlooks a busy intersection with crosswalks, no signals and lengthy sections of sidewalks with broad boulevards that approach it. Every school day, a mother with her own and other young children(usually five or six) comes to this intersection and needs to cross both streets to reach the elementary school. The older children, seven or eight years of age, ride bikes; younger ones walk or run and a preschool toddler furiously peddles his small plastic tricycle to keep up. In addition, the mother often pushes a stroller.

What intrigues me is that while she walks at a steady pace, the children happily range forward and backward on their bikes, sometimes a hundred yards ahead, with no apparent concern from the mother—but they always stop and wait short of the intersection. When she arrives, she shepherds them across the streets like a crossing guard, but once across, the children range ahead and behind freely again. Her control of the children is not by keeping them on a short leash, but by instilled obedience. As long as they live within her rules, the children are free to enjoy being themselves for the journey. Doesn't this give *us* some guidance about where to find *our* freedom?

Week Twenty-Three

Monday: 1 Samuel 10:1–27

Samuel looked for a king to rule Israel in response to the nation's desire, and God singled out a man for the job. This passage tells us a lot about Saul and his fitness for the job. He was appointed by God and anointed king by Samuel. He was filled with the power of God's Spirit and God promised to be behind his decisions. He was discreet, not passing on the news of his anointing, which was done in private.[1] Saul looked the part of king, being a head taller than all other contenders, yet he showed a remarkable humility, embarrassed at being chosen king and put on public view.[2] He was magnanimous to those who opposed his kingship[3] and later showed great prowess in battle as the one who "has slain his thousands."[4] All in all, he had the necessary qualifications to be the king God wanted and Israel needed.

Even so, the remaining chapters of 1 Samuel show Saul descending into an increasingly sour, despondent and violent disposition, erratic and vindictive. We will explore this change later, but it is sufficient to note that all the advantages we may have for success in life are no insurance against failure. Saul's later life suggests that he may have thought the gifts he had from God gave him unlimited freedom of action. Particularly, the gift of the

---

[1] 1 Samuel 10:14–16
[2] See also 1 Samuel 9:21
[3] 1 Samuel 11:12–13
[4] 1 Samuel 18:7

Holy Spirit he received probably gave him a sense of superiority—others were less favoured by God[1]—which in turn undermined his natural humility.

Personal spirituality can either make or break a marriage. If I entertain the notion that I am spiritually superior to my partner, it will engender personal arrogance, believing I have a God-given mandate to dictate the conduct of the relationship. This loss of humility between partners and before God can be as disastrous to a marriage as Saul's arrogance was to his kingship.

Tuesday: I Samuel 13:5–14

Saul had about 3,000 men with him as he faced the Philistines, who were "as numerous as the sand on the seashore"— certainly a battle for Saul to be concerned about. He has to be given credit for at least sensing the need to "[seek] the Lord's favour." In fact, it is easy for us to feel sorry for Saul. His men were "quaking with fear." He had waited the set time allotted by Samuel and many had already deserted his army to hide or even join the Philistines.[2] Samuel had still not appeared, so Saul felt he had to take matters into his own hands. He offered the required sacrifices in place of Samuel.

To accurately assess the situation, we need to be aware that the priestly and prophetic ministries were separate from the kingship. Samuel was responsible before God for these and Saul was responsible for the kingly duties. The voice of God, to which Saul was bound, came through the prophet. Saul was to wait for Samuel, who would come and make the required sacrifices. Saul's actions fell short on two counts: he deliberately disobeyed a direct command from God through the prophet Samuel, and worse, he showed a lack of trust in the promise of God to support him.[3]

---

[1] The gift of the Holy Spirit was not universal in the Old Testament as it was later in the New Testament church.

[2] 1 Samuel 14:21–22.

[3] 1 Samuel 10:7

Under the New Covenant, the Spirit of God indwells each Christian, giving assurance of God's promises.[1] Whether or not we trust those promises is up to us, and there are times of pressure when we may doubt God's control in our situation. It is then that we are likely to take matters into our own hands and increase our problems by failing to live according to the guidelines God offers us in his Word. Acting like this cost Saul and his children the kingdom. If we act like Saul, we opt out of God's covenant with us and in doing so we place not only ourselves at risk but our partner and children as well.

Wednesday: 1 Samuel 15:1–9

We learned yesterday of Saul's lack of trust and consequent disobedience and his loss of the kingdom as a result. In this incident, the instructions were clear: completely wipe out the Amalekite clan, both people and animals. Whatever Saul's reaction may have been, in our time we find these instructions horrific and are inclined to react against them. How can we reconcile requirements like this with the loving God the Bible maintains? This question has been debated for centuries, and we are unlikely to find a completely satisfactory solution within a few thoughts. But the Bible does give us some direction.

We need to ask ourselves the question: What would heaven be like if everyone made it there on their own terms? The answer is simple: it would be a copy of earth as it is now and no heaven. It only takes one cancer cell to destroy the body, and likewise, only one sin could destroy heaven. God's judgment is simply a separation of good and evil; the place of the former is heaven and the latter is hell. When humans refuse to be separated from their sin, they go to that latter place with it. That God will ultimately judge sinful people is seen in the flood, the destruction of Sodom and Jericho and also in today's passage. In relation to this passage, those who continue in their parents' sin will be judged with their

---

[1] Ephesians 1:13–14

parents. But there is escape from the wrath of God as we recognise our sinfulness and avail ourselves of the forgiveness in Jesus Christ.

The eventual judgment of God is an important concept—and one of comfort, knowing that injustice will be penalized. For those in a marriage relationship who have been abused, neglected or abandoned, there will be a day of reckoning for the abuser. We often cannot find justice for ourselves—and should not, even if we could, for God has told us that he will ensure justice is done.[1] We may not know how this will happen, but we can simply trust the One who will always judge perfectly.

Thursday: I Samuel 15:10–29

Today's reading shows that, even given another opportunity, Saul had not learned his lesson and confirmed his habit of giving excuses for his failure. In sparing the king and the animals he was certainly not driven by humanitarian concerns; he more likely wanted to keep the plunder for himself and his men. It was clearly his desire to keep the plunder a secret, claiming, "I have carried out the Lord's instructions." Unfortunately, the animals gave him away, as revealed by Samuel's sarcastic reply: "What then is this bleating of sheep in my ears? What is this lowing of cattle that I hear?"

At this point Saul compounded his deception, not simply by making an excuse for keeping the cattle but by giving a spiritual rationale for doing so—they had "spared the best of the sheep and cattle to sacrifice to the Lord your God." Jesus condemned the same rationalization used by the Pharisees and Teachers of the Law who deflected money to themselves that could have been used for needy parents by labelling it "a gift dedicated to the Lord."[2] The Christian man who leaves his non-believing wife for a Christian girl so they can be "one in the Lord" is no different.

---

[1] Deuteronomy 32:35; Romans 12:19
[2] Mark 7:10–12

Unfortunately, rationalization of our bad behaviour is so common as to be almost unnoticeable. Frequently, when our poor conduct is discovered, our first reaction is to find excuses. Often we simply blame someone or something else or point to some good that was in view. In particular, for a husband or wife to claim some spiritual reason for poor attitudes or actions to his or her partner is the most offensive. Fulfilling our obligations to our family is our first duty to God; if we fail our family, we oppose God. Saul found the nation torn from him even as he tore the hem of Samuel's robe. If we neglect our family—even for "spiritual" reasons—we deserve to lose them also.

Friday: 1 Samuel 16:14–23

The Holy Spirit filled all the followers of Jesus who were assembled together on the day of Pentecost[1] and so inaugurated the universal gift of the Spirit who is available to all Christians. Before that day, however, the Spirit of God was restricted to specific individuals that God had chosen for leadership in some capacity. It happened to Saul upon his anointing as king,[2] as it had with many of the leaders of Israel previously.[3] In today's reading, we see the Spirit of God coming upon David as he was anointed king but departing from Saul as a result of his earlier attempt to cover his sin.[4] What was worse was that "an evil spirit from the Lord tormented him."

This last phrase generally raises the question of whether evil comes from God. The Bible always maintains that God is not the creator of evil but the provider of choice. Evil comes into being when a choice is made to oppose God. This is true of angels[5] and men, as it was with Saul, but the phrase "from the LORD" also confirms God's mastery over the forces of evil—they operate only

---

[1] Acts 2:4
[2] 1 Samuel 10:9–10
[3] Numbers 11:24–25
[4] 1 Samuel 15:1–28
[5] Isaiah 14:12–15, generally considered as allusion to Satan.

with his permission, not from his weakness. The story also reminds us that our spiritual warfare is against live spiritual forces[1] and rebellion against God provides opportunity for spiritual evil to influence our lives. Conversely, we also see that the Spirit of God, through David's influence, could restrain the evil spirit in Saul.

We cannot be sure whether Saul's increasingly dark moods were spiritually influenced or just a deepening psychosis. Perhaps the former was the trigger for the latter. What we do know is that moodiness in a marriage will only escalate if not dealt with, and it is a potently destructive force. If it has a spiritual cause, as with Saul, it will require reconciliation—both with God and the partner and others that have suffered from it.

Weekend ~ A Story of Recovery

Saul's foolishness need not have been the end of his career, for the rebuke of Samuel could have led to repentance and restoration rather than rebellion. Todd's experience is an example. He followed in his father's footsteps and became a pastor. Married, with two children and a church to pastor, he seemed set for life. However, friction set in to the marriage and he became angry, and his wife left him. He took steps to deal with his anger, but his wife was unresponsive, denying any role she had in the break-up. When reconciliation was eventually deemed impossible, divorce followed. This is devastating for anyone, but for a minister it was a double blow, for it deprived him of his calling as well. It was the beginning of a long and painful process of restoration.

In addition to loss of family and job, of greater consequence was his possible loss of faith as well. His desired devotion to God had led him into adversity, not a sense of achievement. Did this mean that all his work for God was meaningless? Could he trust God to order his life in the future? Would he be able to work for

---

[1] Ephesians 6:12

him again? But there were redeeming features to his life. There were many who had benefited from their ministry during the better years. He had performed weddings for couples and followed their lives in the latter years, retaining many friendships. With his background, he was able to find work with handicapped people, a means of restoring his sense of worth as well as assisting others. But above all, with the help of good friends and partners in ministry, he was able to experience and receive the grace of God in restoration.

But he never lost his faith. He retained a sense that God was above it all, somehow fulfilling his will in what seemed senseless. As he found healing and renewal, he began finding places of assisting ministry in the church that had accepted him and recently found a great lady and remarried. For Todd, both the past and the future are in God's hands.

Week Twenty-Four

Monday: I Samuel 18:5–16

We mentioned previously the problems escalating negative emotions can create if they are not curbed. Today's reading shows that David's music, accompanied by the Holy Spirit, became insufficient to check Saul's increasingly black moods. Saul was fuelled by jealousy over David's successes, Israel's love for David and resentment of the Lord's presence with David. Saul spent the rest of his life trying to kill David, occasionally interspersed with brief periods of regret, although never sufficient to change his course of action.

What a tragedy that Saul, a man with such promise and potential, should waste a whole life on jealously and resentment. Yet this is not uncommon. Whole lives are often needlessly paralysed by bitterness, hatred, anger or guilt, leaving a legacy of broken lives and injured people in their wake. Even worse, this unnatural way of living can appear normal to its practitioners, as if living within this cloud of gloom is the best that life can offer, often accompanied by cynical pleasure derived from holding others in the same misery.

Are you going down this road yourself, and is this how you intend to finish your life? Life is short enough without wasting it on destructive emotions. But remember, it's not how we start out or even where we are now that is important. How we finish is far more vital. Our lives are fragile; death is always only a step away. Is it going to come before you are prepared?

Grieving the Lord is clearly the greatest sorrow, but what of the ones dependent on you: husband, wife, children that live in the misery of your shadow—or worse yet, carry on your legacy? Wouldn't you rather leave as Paul did, saying: "I have fought the good fight, I have finished the race, I have kept the faith"?[1] It is not too late.

Tuesday: I Samuel 18:20–27; 19:8–17

David, although still a youth and being recognized for his amazing prowess in battle, remained remarkably humble. At first he rejected the possibility of marrying the king's daughter because of his lowly background. Then the eventual arranged marriage to Michal appeared to be happy. Later, Saul gave Michal to another when David became an outcast,[2] but David demanded her back when he came to power.[3] Michal loved David, and in today's story, she willingly deceived her father to save David's life. The choice of saving David or deceiving Saul was not a difficult one for Michal, and it seems fairly clear to us why she would do so.

Michal's choice raises the possibility that there are circumstances where telling the exact truth may be against the interests of those in our care. This was clearly demonstrated during World War II. Those who were hiding Jews from the German Gestapo lied when asked if there were Jews in the house. You may also recall the lies of Rahab when she denied the presence of the Israelite spies she was hiding.[4]

Occasionally, simply telling the truth is not beneficial. There may be times when this is true in our family relationships. But how do we justify this as Christians? Is there a formula to help us arrive at that decision? Perhaps there is some guidance in the

---

[1] 2 Timothy 4:7
[2] 1 Samuel 25.44
[3] 2 Samuel 3:14
[4] Joshua 2:3–6

Hebrew understanding of truth. The Hebrew word *emet* used for truth has a wider meaning. It does not simply mean a mechanical recitation of the facts, but rather, carries the idea of faithfulness in much the same way as a lover promises to be "true" to his beloved. This means that truth is relational; we always communicate what is of the greatest benefit for the one we love. By withholding that which may be hurtful or harmful on occasion we express our faithfulness to them.

I recall one dear lady who was faced with the opportunity to gossip about someone. Her justification was: "It is the truth!" Truth it may have been, but it was hardly a faithful act toward her sister in Christ.

Wednesday: 1 Samuel 21:1–15

In this story David fled for his life from Saul and finished up among Philistines, the enemies of Israel. Here he sought refuge with king Achish of Gath. The story is marked by David's lies to the priest of God, subterfuge as a madman before Achish and eventual escape back to Judah. Later in David's life, he was in a similar position and in danger of fighting against his own countrymen.[1] In addition, he almost lost his family and the families of his men.[2] In both situations, David appears to have lost faith in God's protection and his promise of the throne as he fled from Saul.

Yet, if there is any grading of sin, it can be said of David that he chose the lesser evil. In his fear of Saul and temporary lapse of faith, he chose to flee rather than harm Saul. But in the second escapade, he came close to fighting against Saul in the battle that eventually caused Saul's death. In this case, the hand of God was in the Philistine commanders' fear that David might turn against them,[3] and thus, David avoided the battle.

---

[1] 1 Samuel 28:1–3
[2] 1 Samuel 30:1–6
[3] 1 Samuel 29:1–11

David's all too human story reminds us of our own weakness of faith and probable times of lapses from it altogether. For those of you facing a continually difficult home life, there are often times of disillusionment, which may lead to questioning God's involvement in your life and marriage. It is in these times of despair that you may fear loss of faith for a time, which adds guilt to the burden you already carry. The stories of David's failures of faith remind us of three things. Even in times of failure, God looks on the heart[1]—often stressed beyond limits—and remains faithful to us. Further, during those times God will often preserve us from mistakes that may cause greater distress later. And finally, there is always hope in God for a time when he will release us from our adversity.

Thursday: 1 Samuel 24:1–22

For about fifteen years after David was anointed as Israel's next king, he lived mostly in fear of Saul's ambition to kill him. Although early in this period he spent some time in Saul's court, the remainder was spent as a fugitive from Saul, living in desert strongholds or on the move, supported by some who favoured him. Saul's erratic behaviour drove others away, and they joined David and became loyal to him. It was during this time that David and his men had opportunity to kill Saul, which is recorded in today's reading and in a similar story in chapter 26.

The remarkable thing about David was his fierce loyalty to Saul in the face of Saul's threats. Notwithstanding his opportunity and his men's exhortation, David refused to kill Saul and even regretted cutting off part of his cloak. David remained loyal to Saul because Saul was anointed as king by God and God saw fit for Saul to remain king. It was clear in David's mind that God, who placed Saul on the throne, was the only one who had the authority to remove him. David would wait for God's timing for his turn as anointed king of Israel.

---

[1] 1 Samuel 16:7

If you believed that marriage to your partner was God's plan for you, then your partner still remains God's choice. If he or she has reneged on the covenant made with you, or worse, wandered away from allegiance to God, it doesn't change that relationship. Most know the real truth of their position even in denial, much the same way that Saul (at least temporarily) recognized the truth of David's claims. Eventual reconciliation depends mostly on maintaining faithfulness to the promises you made to your partner and to God, even if your partner has not. David endured many years of rejection until God brought David to the place of release—in this case through the death of Saul.

Friday: 1 Samuel 25:1–42

Abigail was both intelligent and beautiful—a great combination. And Abigail showed her intelligence at a time when David was angry and bent on revenge. Living with her "surly and mean" husband, Nabal, Abigail had probably developed strategies to get around Nabal's obstructive ways. These were put to good use when she faced the possibility of her men being slaughtered and her home being ruined by David's armed and angry men. Much of the terminology—master, lord—is common to the culture, and the idea of the gifts to pave the way is reminiscent of Jacob's conciliatory approach to Esau. With this in mind, let's explore Abigail's tactics.

Abigail was approachable, shown by her servant coming to her about impending danger, although it is also true that facing death may have emboldened his approach. Secondly, she was resourceful, taking charge of the situation rather than letting it develop. Thirdly, she acted bravely, probably fearing a meeting with a vindictive band of men.[1] Perhaps in womanly guile, she hoped her beauty would give her some reprieve. Although Nabal had placed them in this predicament, Abigail took blame upon herself, thereby saving her menfolk and her foolish husband. In

---

[1] Note vv. 21–22

seeking David's forgiveness, she presented him with the long view beyond the anger of the moment—always a good balancing outlook in times of stress.

Abigail appeared to be devoted to God, mentioning the Lord's name seven times in her plea to David. She probably knew of the hostility between David and Saul and saw in Saul some of Nabal's arrogance. On this basis she believed that God would eventually vindicate David and give him the throne. She warned him not to jeopardize his future peace of mind by senseless slaughter or any wrongdoing. As David conceded to her wisdom, he became aware of Abigail's virtues as well as her beauty, and when Nabal died a few days later, David asked her to marry him—which she did.

Weekend ~ Finding God's Will

I once met a young Christian man who worked for a local concrete company. His zeal was not in question as he relayed his desire to find a place of service to God. His work with the concrete company was simply a parking spot while awaiting a call to "ministry." What he failed to realize was that his work at that moment *was* his place of ministry. God may well have called him to a specific place of service later; we never knew as we lost touch with him. Once we become Christians, our whole life is a place of service to God, wherever we may be.

We also knew a young lady who came to our church, having moved west from Montreal. She was zealous to ensure God's will for her life but she had a dilemma. She had prayed for God to guide her decision to move but did not feel that she had received a specific answer. So she packed her bags and moved, later fearing she had missed or ignored God's will for her. I suggested to her that perhaps God sometimes leaves the decision to us and that he could use her equally in Montreal or any other city she chose to move to.

The more mature in the faith we become, the less likely God is to direct every decision we make. We are no longer children; we should be able to know God's will in most situations.[1] He still has the prerogative to intervene if he desires to give us specific direction.[2] What is critical is that we commit ourselves to God's direction. From then on, God's will for us is in whatever situation we find ourselves—including our particular marriage and family, in spite of, or perhaps because of, its difficulties. But remember, being in God's will does not necessarily mean hardship. He will more often call us to those things we enjoy because he has gifted us for them—including the joy of marriage.

---

[1] Romans 12:1–2

[2] Compare Paul's experience Acts 16:6–10

Monday: 2 Samuel 1:1–18

David's love for Saul, and particularly David's love for Saul's son Jonathan even with Saul's persecution of David, is clearly depicted in this chapter. David not only refused to raise his hand against Saul but held to account the man who claimed to have killed him. In actual fact, Saul had committed suicide when critically wounded rather than falling into the hands of the Philistines,[1] but David was not to know this until later. David found no pleasure in the deaths of Saul and his sons, even though this gave him access to the throne of Israel. The remainder of this chapter is taken up with David's lament over the death of Saul and his sons and the defeat of the Israelite army.

It defied human logic for David to act this way. Most people would consider it normal to be thankful for Saul's death and God fulfilling his promise to David. Saul got his just desserts and David would have been vindicated to regard Saul as his enemy. Some would even have tried to persuade David to rejoice at these events. Although David was an ordinary person, he had an extraordinary understanding of God's character, sensing the way God thinks and seeking to be like him. These qualities made him a man after God's own heart.

Enduring difficult relationships is not easy. It can make or break us, but whether it does or not depends on our choice. And

---

[1] 1 Samuel 30:2–4

that choice is not so much necessary personal determination, but to find our resources in God to see the relationship through. Our own strength will fail us; enduring strength is only found in dependence upon God—increasing our knowledge of him through his Word, enabling us to trust him better and prayerfully cling to him.

Tuesday: 2 Samuel 2:1–11; 5:1–5

The split of Judah from Israel had its roots long before David. While there does not appear to be animosity between the two prior to David's time, they were frequently referred to separately. Judah was always known as the one that would provide royalty.[1] Even in Joshua's time and during the anarchic period of the Judges, the two were listed separately in the battles to subdue the land.[2] During the reign of Saul, the fighting men were numbered and fought separately,[3] but both Judah and Israel were united behind their new commander-in-chief, David.[4]

Still, our readings record that after the death of Saul the split began to show itself. Judah claimed David as King in Hebron and Israel placed a son of Saul, Ish-Bosheth, on the throne of Israel, and war between the two erupted. Yet the history of Israel was—and we believe still is—overseen by God himself. As David was anointed and promised the throne of Israel by God, so eventually David succeeded to the kingship of the whole country. Israel and Judah remained united until the death of David's son Solomon, and the division that followed was due to Solomon's waywardness.

Marriage is God's idea and plan for most of us. The break-up of a marriage can have two causes: the wrong choice of partner before marriage or failure to understand or follow God's working

---

[1] Genesis 49:8–10
[2] Joshua 11:21
[3] 1 Samuel 11:8; 17:52
[4] 1 Samuel 18:16

plan for marriage. We identified earlier the foundation of servanthood for marriage, ensuring our priority is our partner's wellbeing, desires and growth. For those who are not Christians, the possibility of marriage failure increases, especially during a time of declining Christian influence in Western culture. Both the choice of a marriage partner and the subsequent success of the marriage depend on knowing God's will for it, just as David knew God's will for Israel and Judah.

Wednesday: 2 Samuel 6:1–23

Once David was secure on the throne, he wished to honour God by placing the Ark of the Covenant in a place of prominence. He would thus signify the Lord's kingship and rule over himself and the people. But David's first experience in returning the Ark was a fearful one. Even though Uzziah was trying to save the Ark from damage, he violated God's directions for managing it.[1] The price paid—the death of Uzziah—was a dreadful reminder to David of the gravity with which God viewed the honour to be accorded him and a reminder to us of the awesomeness of the God we serve.

Michal's behaviour is harder to assess. Why was she not by his side, rejoicing in the return of the Ark? Perhaps the procession was for men only, or maybe her abstention from the ceremonies, viewing them from the seclusion of a nearby building, implied her scepticism of the whole affair. Certainly her outburst at David for his perceived frivolity appeared to signify a deeper resentment. Perhaps she resented David's succession to her father or begrudged the adulation being accorded to the Lord (see verse 21). Either way, her attitude had changed considerably from the early days of their marriage, where she protected him,[2] and the barrenness that followed today's incident implies God's displeasure.

---

[1] Numbers 4:5–6, 15
[2] 1 Samuel 18:20; 19:11–13

This passage reminds us of two things. Firstly, status and comfort can undermine our sense of our need of God. Power easily corrupts, and perhaps Michal's attitude was affected by her prominence as queen; her manner was condescending and judgmental, which hindered their relationship and earned David's rebuke. Secondly, David reminds us of the seriousness of our personal responsibilities to God; marriage must be maintained by allegiance to God—even if one partner disagrees. But that partner deserves respect. David's response to Michal was equitable, as he was careful to state the truth and referred only to himself and his conduct with no censure of his wife. We need to treat our partners with love and respect; it is God who is eventually the judge.

Thursday: 2 Samuel 7:1–17

The covenant that God made with Abraham and his descendants was timeless: it did not die with Abraham, Isaac and Jacob.[1] Today's reading is a reminder of the permanence of the covenant, for it was renewed to King David a full millennium after Abraham. The promise made to David reiterated both the greatness of the nation—in this case through their king—and a secure dwelling place for Israel. In this passage there is a play on the word "house." David was anxious to build a "house" for God—the temple that Solomon would eventually build. But the promise to David was that God would build David's "house"—that is, his lineage—and his throne would be established forever through a son born to him.

The son born to David who continued the monarchy was Solomon. Despite Solomon's sin, it was through him that the throne would eventually be established. Although the monarchy ceased after the nation's exile some 500 years later, the lineage continued to the time of Christ, the Son of David, the One who will eventually return to claim his throne. In the intervening time between Solomon and the exile, the nation of Israel "divorced"

---

[1] Romans 11:26–29

into two separate kingdoms. David's descendents reigned over the southern portion known as Judah, which included Benjamin, while usurpers reigned over the northern ten tribes called Israel. Ezekiel, living through the exile, forecast the reuniting of Israel into one kingdom.[1]

Some of you who read this will have been through the misery of divorce. By this time the opportunity of reconciliation is over, the damage done to any children of the marriage irreversible and there is no apparent source of healing. While our faith may bring comfort, remorse and guilt may remain. Yet although there is no marriage in heaven,[2] it is a place where not only our sin but the effects of our sin will be erased. Somehow, God will bring to completion all those things that we have left undone or broken, and we will rejoice in God's solution to our failures.

Friday: 2 Samuel 11:2–13

To this point David's experience with wives was generally positive. The stories we have looked at so far took place while David was estranged from Saul, both his marriage to Michal and, while on the run, his encounter with Abigail. By the time we reach today's story of David's adultery with Bathsheba, David is well secured on the throne of Israel. This gave David several disadvantages when tempted by sexual seduction. While his armies were away he had more time to be distracted by temptation, and as the saying goes, the devil finds work for idle hands. Also, neither he nor Bathsheba could ever keep their actions secret, for they both communicated through messengers.

As king, David's word was final; he could command Bathsheba to come to him. Perhaps here is a power play similar to Potiphar's wife—it would be dangerous to defy the king. However, unlike Joseph, she did not refuse to go to the king, and there is no evidence of protest from her. Although this cannot be

---

[1] Ezekiel 37:15–22
[2] Matthew 22:30

certain, her bathing in full view of the palace suggests her interest in the relationship; she might well have known of David's occasional walks in the cool evening air. But if her behaviour was seductive, it did not absolve David of his responsibility—as king, he had the greater influence.

The meeting had consequences. These could have been foreseen, but the heat of passion rarely sees the big picture. The fact that Bathsheba had just purified herself from her period[1] indicates that she was not pregnant when she slept with David. Since Uriah, her husband, was away with the army, they were assured that the baby was David's. This forced David into further deception to cover up his sin; he tried to get Uriah to sleep with Bathsheba and so claim the child as his, but Uriah's devotion to his duty foiled that plan. As with all deception, David entrenched himself more deeply with each move.

Weekend ~ Adultery: Pleasure or Misery?

What are the reasons for adultery? Frequently it is an escape from the challenges of home life—pleasure without the accompanying worries. It may be a targeted seduction or simple adventurism. Certainly, there is always a sense of pleasure from sexual fulfilment and release. But as the writer to the Proverbs suggests: what is sweet to the taste can often become sour in the stomach.[2] David's moments of pleasure led to a lifetime of distress, both for himself and for others. The Bible is clear that David's woes were consequences of his sin, even though the events that followed his marriage to Bathsheba do not seem to be directly related to his adultery with her.

While it may not be possible to follow the causes and effects in David's case, it is easy to forecast friction as a result of infidelity— by either the husband or wife—in any marriage. The sense of betrayal, anger and loss of trust by the wife of a philanderer is

---

[1] Leviticus 12:2
[2] Proverbs 5:3

alone sufficient to cause tension. The variety of attitudes expressed by the husband, from outright denial or excuses to utter remorse and self-reproach, can only add to the conflict. Further, the affair might still drag on after discovery, and even if it doesn't, the wife's loss can trigger a prolonged period of mourning countered by the impatience of the husband. Often there is no reconciliation and the marriage breaks up, or it continues in an uneasy co-existence while the wife uses guilt to hold the husband hostage.

While it is clear that infidelity creates a near-death experience for the marriage, it is remarkable that so many relationships survive and become meaningful for both partners again. Most of David's life is a remarkable record of his source of survival; we find that he never lost his confidence in God, and his psalms are a legacy to us of his victories in times of difficulty. David found contentment in the fact that, although he had to face the consequences of his sin, he found God's grace toward him in the forgiveness he received. David's example can bring both comfort and strength to continue in times of adversity.

Week Twenty-Six

Monday: 2 Samuel 11:14–27

If trickery did not work to mask David's adultery, perhaps murder would. In arranging for Uriah to be placed in harm's way, he also made others complicit to his actions. This says little for those around David—particularly Joab, who was entrusted with this task. Joab was violent and self serving, and during his service to David he killed Abner[1] and Amasa,[2] two rivals to his desire for commander-in-chief of David's army. He eventually killed David's son Absalom against David's wishes.[3] In today's reading it is clear that David used what he knew of Joab's violent nature, their connivance evident in the veiled messages between them regarding Uriah's death. This left Bathsheba free to marry David, bringing her pregnancy into the marriage and hopefully saving David's reputation.

As the saying goes: O what a tangled web we weave, when first we practise to deceive.[4] David's position as king gave him the opportunity to stoop to murder in order to conceal his adultery, but most adultery is unlikely to lead to such drastic escalation. I'm sure, when entering an affair, most feel they can manage the risks. Unfortunately, we can rarely predict the outcome because unknown complications are always a threat. Neither can we ever

---

[1] 2 Samuel 3:26–27
[2] 2 Samuel 20:8–10
[3] 2 Samuel 18:9–15
[4] Sir Walter Scott, *Marmion, Canto vi. Stanza 17.*

assume, when discovered, that our marriage will endure the threat of divorce, for adultery strikes at the heart of the marriage bond.

Uriah was an innocent victim in today's story, paying the price for David's sin. There are always those who will pay for our infidelity, particularly children, who frequently suffer the consequences of adultery and the often resulting marriage failure. As I write this, news reports tell of a Toronto man who threw his five-year-old daughter from a highway overpass so his wife would not get custody of her. Miraculously the child survived. In actual fact, the results of a failed marriage that we *can* imagine are serious enough without the *unforeseen* costs of our folly.

Tuesday: 2 Samuel 12:1–14

It is difficult while reading this passage to see why God considered David a man after his own heart.[1] By our judgment, his sin was greater than Saul's and, like Saul, he did all he could to cover it up until it was revealed to him by the prophet Nathan. What was the difference between Saul and David that condemned Saul but commended David to God? We have seen how Saul not only attempted to cover up his sin but also tried to rationalize it away. In addition, Saul's confession was not one of true penitence but regret at discovery, further marred by excuses[2] and an underlying concern for his reputation.[3] David, in contrast, admitted his sin, gave no excuses and showed true repentance.[4] It is this honesty in the face of factual accusation that draws God's response of mercy and forgiveness.[5]

Although David did not know what the outcome of admitting his sin might be—he could have been facing his own death—he did not flinch from frankness in his confession. True honesty

---

[1] 1 Samuel 13:14; Acts 13:22
[2] 1 Samuel 15:24
[3] 1 Samuel 15:30
[4] See Psalm 51 for his prayer of repentance.
[5] Psalm 51:17

requires courage. What his honesty did do was to legitimize Bathsheba—both she and her next son, Solomon, were part of the lineage of Jesus. However, unlike the child thrown from an overpass referred to yesterday, the child of their illegitimate union did *not* survive—a further victim of David's adultery.

Honesty about who we are and what we have done always requires courage—especially when the outcome may be harmful to us. How many public figures come out courageously and honestly admit their wrongdoing when it is revealed? Too often, dishonesty is easiest in our marriage relationships because we can manipulate the facts, confuse the details and often force our opinions upon our partners. This makes cowardice easier, courage unnecessary and, we hope, avoids unpleasant consequences. But it also makes for an uneasy and distrustful co-existence.

Wednesday: 2 Samuel 13:1–21

Although yesterday's reading tells us that the Lord took away David's sin, he did not absolve him from further consequences. David's household, especially, would be the centre of strife, not peace, which they experienced until his death. In this reading, Amnon raped his half sister Tamar, Absalom's full sister, and later in the chapter, Absalom killed him in revenge. From then on, the rest of David's life recorded in 2 Samuel is a litany of the struggles David faced, mostly stirred up by Absalom—even after Absalom's death. Thus, forgiveness did not mean that David "got away with it." We have already seen that he lost a son through his adultery; now it created friction in his household.

The prophecies of Nathan[1] were coming true. The child born to Bathsheba had already died. David's wives and concubines were ravished in full view of the people by his son Absalom when he rebelled.[2] David found himself fleeing from Israel as Absalom increased his following among the people; even David's throne

[1] 2 Samuel 12:11–12
[2] 2 Samuel 16:20–22

was in jeopardy. Later, Absalom himself was killed as a result of his rebellion. David had now lost three sons. As David lay dying, even while he appointed Solomon as his successor, another son, Adonijah, tried to usurp the throne and died for his trouble.

But as destructive as adultery is to the lives around us, the greater damage is our sin against God. Part of Nathan's rebuke to David was that in his sin he *despised* God.[1] As Christians, our first concern should be what our sin does to God. As his representatives, our shortcomings sully his reputation, fostering lies about him to those around us. For instance, if we are unfaithful to our partners, then it follows that perhaps God is not to be trusted either. Always remember that a sin against another— above all, a partner—is a sin against God.

Thursday: 2 Samuel 15:1–16

Relationships with adult children have their challenges, none more so than those experienced by David with his sons. We have already noted the strife that accompanied David's reign after his adultery with Bathsheba. It began as Amnon raped his half-sister Tamar and Absalom had him killed in revenge. David longed for Absalom[2] during the five years he was banished from the court, so he finally reinstated him.[3] But in spite of his re-acceptance by David, Absalom continued to oppose his father for the rest of his life.

Scripture records Absalom was a very attractive man with a vigorous head of hair. Early in his life, he married and had three sons and a daughter.[4] Upon his reception back into court after his banishment, he began to solicit support from those coming to Jerusalem with complaints. He obviously used his appearance and became a charmer who offered better time and compensation to

[1] 2 Samuel 12:10
[2] 2 Samuel 13:39
[3] 2 Samuel 14:33
[4] 2 Samuel 14:25–27

the complainants than David did. Over a period of four years, Absalom seduced the people of Israel away from his father. This put him in a position to set himself up as a rival king to his father.

However, one wonders what David was doing all that time. It is impossible that he did not know what was going on in his own city. Most likely, his love for Absalom blinded him to his son's current deception, regardless of his previous murder of Amnon. Eventually, David fled from Absalom to avoid bloodshed rather than fight to save his throne, but that gave rise to a period of confrontation and war anyway. It is a reminder that we are susceptible to letting our love for our children blind us to their faults. Particularly as they grow older, those faults will have increasing impact and more grievous results.

Friday: 2 Samuel 16:22–33

Absalom returned to Israel from Hebron, where he had proclaimed himself king. He had neither any sense of repentance for the slaying of Amnon nor respect for David's forgiveness and reinstatement. David had foresight enough to plant Hushai within Absalom's court as a spy. Ahithophel, until then a trusted advisor to David, turned himself over completely to Absalom's plans, probably hoping to finish on the winning side. We do not know whether Absalom or Ahithophel knew of Nathan's prophecy regarding David's punishment,[1] but Ahithophel did know that Absalom sleeping publicly with David's concubines would be obnoxious to the Israelites. In turn, they would consider enmity sufficiently firmly entrenched between Absalom and David to reduce the possibility of reconciliation, which to that point had always been possible from David's previous history.

Thus Absalom fulfilled the prophecy of Nathan against David, sending his father the most aggressively rebellious message yet. David, unwilling to fight against Absalom, nonetheless realized

---

[1] 2 Samuel 12:10–12

he needed to muster his troops for defence. Hushai's subversive advice to Absalom gave David time to recover from the flight, hear about Absalom's plans and prepare for battle.[1]

This reading brings up the old problem of responsibility for fulfilling prophecy. Surely to do so is fulfilment of God's will, but is any behaviour that brings it about acceptable? There is no doubt that David was totally responsible for his sins of adultery with Bathsheba and the murder of her husband. But at the same time, Absalom was also responsible for his actions, just as Judas was held responsible for his betrayal of Jesus.[2] While our children can hold us accountable for our failures as parents, they cannot eventually hold us responsible for their actions once they reach the age of understanding.

Weekend ~ Politics and Cinderella

David had to balance politics and love; he was king and husband, and both positions had their challenges. The history of politics, after all, is a sordid tale of the power-hungry manipulating nations for their own benefit and adulation, of dictators forcing ruthless rule over exploited people, of conquest and war as a means of extending rulers' influence. But in contrast to this, the first love Michal had for David and their remarkable relationship with God[3] is closer to the love story of Cinderella and seems a far cry from the politics David needed to practise.

Yet there may be more of a common thread to both politics and our favourite love stories than it appears. Behind those stories and books like *Utopia*[4] and *Erewhon*[5] lurks the idea that "Once upon a time . . . happily ever after," reflects a perfection of love and living that our hearts yearn for and our best experiences imply. Political theorist John von Heyking has written a book

---

[1] 2 Samuel 17:14–16
[2] Luke 22:22
[3] 1 Samuel 18:28
[4] *Utopia* by Sir Thomas More, 1516.
[5] *Erewhon* ("Nowhere" backwards!) by Samuel Butler, 1872

entitled *Augustine and Politics as Longing in the World*.[1] The title invokes a sense that, even with its excesses, politics arises from the notion that there is an ideal to strive for beyond the ravages of earthly life—a thirsty longing that wrenches our hearts but is never fully satisfied. And as maidens dream of perfect love, so men envision the ideal society and strive for it.

I'm sure most politicians start off with the desire to better their communities, but they easily get caught up in the subterfuge, manipulation and compromise that ambition seems to require, which undermines their good intentions. If we could read the rest of the story of Cinderella and her prince, it seems probable we might find a degeneration of their love into self-serving manipulation. But neither of these evidences of fallen human nature should blind us to the desire God has placed in our hearts for the perfection that is only to be found in him. If the yearning of the human soul is only to be completed in God, then the best that marriage can provide is to be found in him also.

---

[1] Columbia, MO: University of Missouri Press, 2001.

Monday: 2 Samuel 18:31–19:4

David must have been aware that Joab was a violent man who took whatever actions he needed to advance his own ends. Not infrequently, leaders continue to employ such men because those very faults support the leaders in their duties. It may well be that David kept Joab for the same reasons—Joab had no scruples; he was an asset in war—but there was always the possibility that Joab would betray David with the same faults. Against David's unmistakable instructions that Absalom was not to be killed in the final battle, Joab took his revenge and killed him in cold blood.[1]

The effect on David was devastating. His cries: "O my son Absalom! My son, my son Absalom! If only I had died instead of you—O Absalom, my son, my son!" ring with the pain that anyone losing a loved one can feel. David's misery and grief were so intense that his army, which had won against the insurgents, returned subdued, as if ashamed of defeat. It was Joab, the one responsible for David's distress and now impatient with David, who with typical coldness, berated him for his grieving and called him to celebrate with the army.

While we could fault David for his obvious favouritism of Absalom, we can sympathize with his loss of a child—even in adulthood. But the loss of a child to drugs, crime or general antisocial or destructive behaviour can be just as profound,

---

[1] 2 Samuel 18:5, 14

especially as the grief is ongoing and may last for years. In his distress, David remained faithful to God and even showed magnanimity to some who had berated him during his flight from Absalom.[1] However great our loss and grief, it can only be worsened by a flight from God instead of drawing closer to him.

Tuesday: 2 Samuel 21:1–10

This is a rather complex story of retribution for Saul's sin in attempting to destroy the Gibeonites after Joshua had promised to spare them.[2] This caused the three-year famine recorded in this chapter, for which the subsequent death of seven sons of Saul was considered sufficient judgement. However, our interest here is with Rizpah, the mother of two of Saul's sons. After the sons were slain and laid out on a hillside, she defended the bodies from bird and animal predators. She stayed there from the "first days of the harvest" until "the rain poured down from the heavens on the bodies."

We do not know how long that may have been, but it was certainly as long as it took for God's anger to be appeased for Saul's sin, for the rain signalled the end of the famine and the satisfaction of God's judgement. For Rizpah, the task was daunting—she was unable to sleep day or night, continually fighting wild animals and birds that would seek to devour the flesh of her sons. In her eyes, although her sons were slain in judgment, their bodies were not part of the bargain. We note that when the rain fell and justice was fulfilled the bodies were given a decent burial.[3]

It is significant that the love of God for his people is typified by the love of a mother for her children. In answer to Israel's complaint that God has forsaken them, God replies that it is less likely for him to forget them than for a mother to forget the child

---

[1] 2 Samuel 19:21–23
[2] See Joshua chapter 9
[3] 2 Samuel 21:13–14

at her breast.[1] When we are tempted to feel that God has ceased to hear us, the story of Rizpah and the example of our own love for our children are there to remind us that God's faithfulness is greater than ours. He will be faithful to us even in our darkest times.

Wednesday: I Kings 2:1–12

As we have seen with the patriarchs, David followed the custom of giving final advice to the son who was to succeed him, which Solomon also gave to his son extensively in the book of Proverbs. This passage is clearly divided into two sections, the first a general instruction to Solomon regarding the importance of devotion to God. The second part deals with unfinished business, particularly the need for judgment on Joab. Because David had failed to deal with Joab's crimes during his reign, Joab had contributed to David's difficulties with Absalom. Perhaps now, on his deathbed, these issues had become clearer and David realized the folly of not dealing justly with the violence at the time.

But of greater importance was the urging of David for Solomon to remain committed to God. Whatever else needed attention, David's first concern was that Solomon should ensure the nation's future by observing God's requirements. The promise of future prosperity and generations of kings in David's line depended on the obedience of David's descendants. We know that, although Solomon started well, he failed to live up to David's advice and the kingdom was split for 500 years after his death.

The advice given by David to Solomon is not only good but also the primary advice for us to give to our children, youth or adults. Many of us have children that have started badly, the opposite of Solomon, who started well and finished badly. But our children who start badly have the opportunity to finish well. Franklin Graham rebelled against his father, Billy Graham, for many years until, as he said: "I became sick and tired of being sick

---

[1] Isaiah 49:15

and tired." He became a leading proponent for the faith. As Solomon himself said, "Train a child in the way he should go, and when he is old he will not turn from it."[1]

Thursday: 1 Kings 3:4–15

Solomon had many advantages as he followed the faith of his father. Not only did he have David's example to follow and the power to ensure his nation would follow it, he also had an extraordinary gift of wisdom granted to him. His admission of his inability to fulfill his duties apart from God's direction gained for him this gift of God's grace. But his greatest asset—as it was for the succeeding kings of Israel—was the faith of his father, David. God promised Solomon control of the kingdom throughout his lifetime specifically on the basis of the faith of his father.[2]

But Solomon had weaknesses as well. In particular, he had absolute power, subduing the nations around him and ushering in the longest time of peace in Israel's history. It was all too easy to come to a place of assuming that he had accomplished this himself, thus reducing his reliance upon God. The corruption of power is the belief in personal invincibility and flawless decision making—a sort of divine right to rule. Many political leaders, including Adolph Hitler and Margaret Thatcher, have succumbed to this delusion. Solomon's ease of victory in war and treaty making with other nations provided him with the same persuasion.

If Solomon's greatest asset was the faith of his father, his greatest downfall was not following his father's advice. Solomon had moments of great spiritual awareness,[3] yet he finally succumbed to his desire for women, ending up with a thousand wives and concubines.[4] These women brought their pagan ideas

---

[1] Proverbs 22:6
[2] 1 Kings 11:11–13
[3] 1 Kings 8:25–27
[4] 1 Kings 11:1–4

into his kingdom, and Solomon's tolerance and support of their practices watered down his own faithfulness to God. If you are a believer, beware of marriage to a non-Christian, for statistics suggest that a relationship between a Christian and an unsaved partner usually favours the latter.

Friday: I Kings 11:1–13

Solomon can be likened to Saul; he had a lot "going for him." His early life showed great devotion to the Lord and he was given great wisdom. Both were seduced away from their devotion: Saul by pride and plunder, Solomon by his wives. Yet Solomon continued to be blessed by God "for the sake of David your father." Solomon's downfall was not simply marrying the wrong wives. Marrying the daughter of a rival king was a common way of forming an alliance to avoid war, but doing so exhibited a lack of trust in God, who had promised to preserve Israel. Of course, these foreign wives brought their gods with them, and Solomon, in true liberal tolerance, simply added them to what became a pantheon of gods that included the Lord, the God of Israel.

Acceptance of these gods led Solomon to worship them, and as Saul experienced before him, God warned that the kingdom would be torn away from him. But there was a difference: Solomon would retain part of the kingdom and the separation would not take place until Solomon's death. Why the difference? It was simply that the devotion of David, despite his failures, was so unwavering that his legacy was passed to Solomon and the promise of a continuous lineage was passed to Solomon's descendants. The promise of a permanent lineage[1] was given to David well before his adultery with Bathsheba; God foreknew both David's future faithfulness and future failures.

We can find immense encouragement in knowing that God looks on the heart, even in our times of relapse. It is also

[1] 2 Samuel 7:1–17

important to note that our faithfulness or lack of it can have significant impact upon our families, including our partners, our children and our later descendants. It's not just a matter of setting an example for our children who know and see us, as important as that is, but our devotion to God can directly affect those generations that follow after us. For God shows his "love to a thousand generations of those who love me and keep my commandments."[1]

Weekend ~ The Real Gift

We frequently give gifts as evidence of our love or concern for others. But really, these offerings are only substitutes for the real gift. The true gift is a gift of ourselves, and things make a poor substitute. That is not to say that gifts given as remembrances at Christmas, birthdays and other anniversaries are not meaningful, but the presence of the giver has greater worth. Two of our daughters live a distance away from us, and they send us cards on our birthdays with wonderful and welcome sentiments, but it is the phone call, the desire to speak with us or to be with us for a while, that we appreciate most.

Material gifts as substitutes for love are probably most destructive in the relationship between parents and children. The absent father, whose work precludes sufficient time with his children but who showers them with gifts and money, may well leave his children empty and rebellious. Too often they become the "spoiled brats" that plague our society, much to the astonishment of their parents, who "gave them everything they wanted." Everything, that is, except a gift of themselves—time with their children.

The real gift is time: time to listen or play; time to give advice, rejoice in accomplishment or complete a task together; time just to "hang out" and simply be together. Our time is a real gift because it is limited, and thus, our most precious commodity. The minutes

---

[1] Exodus 20:6

or hours we spend with and for others are moments we will never have again and cannot be replaced. The years that our children are with us, difficult and interminable though they may seem at the time, eventually pass all too quickly, and it is the time we failed to be with them that may haunt us the most.

Week Twenty-Eight

Monday: 1 Kings 11:26–40

Jeroboam, son of Nebat (there is another Jeroboam), was chosen by God to lead the part of the nation of Israel that would be taken away from Solomon's son. God would be with Jeroboam to the extent that he would be given a lineage similar to David's but not outlasting it. There were conditions: Jeroboam must walk in God's ways and be obedient to God's laws and commands. Subsequent chapters of 1 Kings show that Jeroboam did not do so, and his name became synonymous with disobedience to God as future kings of the northern ten tribes of Israel followed in his ways.[1] It seems significant that God chose someone who rebelled against his anointed, Solomon, in the first place and so was also likely to rebel against God himself.

The question arises: Why would God choose a rebellious individual to rule Israel (the northern ten tribes)? As a man of standing and an official in Solomon's court, Jeroboam would have had knowledge of the requirements for kingship as well as the requirements of godly rule—at least from the earlier years of Solomon's reign. That makes sense so far, but surely God's foreknowledge of Jeroboam's future should have precluded his selection for king. Similarly, we could say that Jesus should have avoided choosing Judas Iscariot as a disciple—yet we know that selection fulfilled a greater will of God for our salvation. We only

---

[1] 1 Kings 16:25–26; 2 Kings 3:1–3; 13:2; 15:9, for example.

know that God's plans are more far reaching than our limited vision, for Israel's future as well as our personal lives.

There are two principles that follow from this. The obvious one is that in the bleakest of times—as Israel had yet to go through—we are still in God's hands, and his plans, though obscured for a time, are still in progress and under his control. Of greater importance for us in this book is the notion that being called into marriage is not a carte blanche for our desires. If we fail to follow God's requirements for maintaining our devotion to him and serving our partner, we place our union in jeopardy.

Tuesday: I Kings 12:1–24

We have already read about Ahijah's prophecy to Jeroboam— that he would inherit ten tribes of Israel—and now Jeroboam sought to fulfill it. Yet there was consultation between Rehoboam, Solomon's son and heir, and the rebellious Jeroboam. Jeroboam was probably looking for an excuse to take over the ten northern tribes, and Rehoboam foolishly gave him one. Clearly, the impetuosity of youth meant more to Rehoboam than the wisdom of the elders. Especially noteworthy was the advice of the elders to make his reign one of service to his people, but he preferred to rule as a tyrant and lost the northern kingdoms as a result.

This episode raises the question of the relationship of prophecy to the actions that fulfill it. If the prophecy fixes the actions, then the perpetrators of the actions are not accountable— they simply fulfill a predetermined role. The answer to this paradox lies in God's foreknowledge. As we look back to choices made freely but now fixed in history, so God sees choices freely made in the future and uses them to accomplish his plans. This does not discount but takes into account the influence that prophecy may have on those free choices.

The hidden factors behind divorce are frequently wrong assumptions about how marriage works. Rehoboam assumed the people were there to serve him and not vice versa, while Jeroboam assumed a right dealt him by prophecy. Thus, the separation was all but inevitable. What are your expectations of your marriage? Are they based on what you expect to receive or to ensure your rights within the marriage? Unless you reckon to give more than fifty percent to your marriage, it is probably in jeopardy already.

Wednesday: 1 Kings 21:1–16

No review of the women of the Bible would be complete without a look at the woman Jezebel. Her name has become synonymous with seductive behaviour.[1] Her claim to fame was the idolatry she brought to Israel. She was from Tyre in modern day Lebanon and married to Ahab, King of Israel, in a treaty to secure his northern borders. As with Solomon's similar marriages, this direct defiance of God, who promised to be Israel's protector, wrought havoc within Israel.

Although given away by her father to accomplish this treaty, Jezebel was not a woman to be taken lightly. She was strong-willed, bringing with her 450 prophets of Baal and another 400 prophets of the goddess Ashtoreth. She claimed worship of these gods equal to the Lord, which brought her into conflict with Elijah.[2] She was forceful and fanatical for her gods, killing the Lord's prophets when they opposed her.[3] Our reading today shows how ruthless she was in gaining her own ends as well as those of Ahab.

But of particular note in today's reading is the relationship between Ahab and Jezebel. She considered him weak and indecisive. Clearly, she took charge in Ahab's dealings, literally acting as the power behind the throne—she could be the self-directed female model of some feminists. But although much of Ahab's rule was dictated by Jezebel, Scripture indicates that he was still responsible for his decisions.[4] God will still hold us

---

[1] Revelation 2:20–23
[2] 1 Kings 16:30–33; 18:19
[3] 1 Kings 18:13–14
[4] 1 Kings 21:25

responsible for our actions if we allow the duress of a dictatorial partner to coerce us.

Thursday: 2 Kings 4:1–7

The readings for the next three days are about Elisha's care for the state of two mothers and their children. Today's story is known as the Widow's Oil, and it displays the nature of God in looking after his own people. In particular, this woman was the widow of a former priest whom Elisha knew had "revered the Lord." Now her husband was dead, she was destitute and the only way of paying her creditors was to sell her two sons into slavery. This meant that it could be up to fifty years before her sons were eligible for release in the year of Jubilee.[1] So she pleaded with Elisha to help her.

I wonder what help she could have expected. Perhaps she thought Elisha could find the money to pay her creditors or persuade her creditors to forgo her debt. Yet God often supplies in ways we cannot foresee. The solution is one that few would have imagined—pouring oil from a bottomless jug into containers to sell and pay off her debt.

It is not uncommon for people in fulltime Christian ministry to suffer financial loss as a result of their labour. Those who pastor small churches, missionaries with inadequate support or indigenous pastors of poor countries called into ministry are constantly anxious about providing food, shelter, clothing and education for their children. Yet all of them can tell of ways in which God has provided—often in simple ways but sometimes by extraordinary and quite remarkable sources. This weekend's commentary provides an example of the way in which God provided for our family during a time of inadequate income.

---

[1] See Leviticus 25:47–55 for an Israelite's right of redemption in the year of Jubilee.

Friday: 2 Kings 4:8–17

It seems the writer of 1 Kings grouped together these two stories of Elisha's encounters with women and their concerns for their children. Today's story also illustrates the way in which God supplied Elisha's needs. The woman and her husband were wealthy, and they provided room and board for Elisha when his journeys took him their way. These people were God fearing and wanted to use their resources for their Lord's service. Elisha's tenure was during a time of apostasy, and some income was probably a luxury.

Elisha wondered aloud to Gehazi, his servant, what he could do for the woman in gratitude for her generosity. Finding she was childless, he sought God for a child for her and promised a son would be born to her in the spring. However, the woman's response showed she had doubts about the possibility and was worried that Elisha was raising dubious hopes. Little did she know the later tragedy that awaited her.

In Old Testament times large families were considered a sign of the Lord's blessing, and absence of children suggested God's displeasure. As we now know—and as Scripture often suggests—childlessness was frequently an accident of nature that God reversed out of compassion for the affected women. While there are many resources to assist in overcoming barrenness, we recognize that God alone is the author of life. Thus, it is important that we pray to God for children for ourselves and for others who may fail to have children.

Weekend ~ In Time of Need

Ann and I felt a call of God into full time ministry, which eventually culminated in pastoring two churches in Burnaby, British Columbia. But to do that, we also felt the need to take some full time training, so I attended Regent College in Vancouver for over two years to achieve a Master of Divinity degree while Ann provided indispensable support and assistance.

But with a small child beginning school and the need to provide for a home, it wasn't long before we ran short of money.

God provided for us in two surprising ways. One of the instructors at the college was moving out of a house he had rented for some time and suggested we might rent it. The owners were Christians and were willing to rent it to us for a generously low figure. We had a house for sale in Alberta, and Ann was led to a buyer who bought it privately, sight unseen, just as our funds dried up.

We placed the money we obtained from the sale in guaranteed investment certificates for two years. What was remarkable about this was the timing of that investment. Interest rates in 1980 had climbed to record highs, mortgage rates reaching 20% and higher. We received interest of over 16%, but the day after that investment rates began a free fall to much lower levels; we had received a peak yield from our investment. With the money Ann was able to make by running her own small secretarial business and over $600 per month return on our investment, we had sufficient funds to see us through our time at college. God provided for us for our entire period of financial need.

Week Twenty-Nine

Monday: 2 Kings 4:18–37

A son was born to the Shunammite woman as predicted by Elisha, but the boy later died as a result of a brain disease, perhaps a tumour or aneurism. It is one thing to mourn childlessness but another to grieve the loss of a long-awaited child. The passage reveals the mother's great distress, as she refused to talk to Gehazi and wept at the feet of Elisha. She felt that Elisha's intercession for a son was a bitter hoax, bringing her only greater misery, and she said so to Elisha.

Elisha's response was immediate. Gehazi was instructed to tuck his cloak in his belt—a sign that he was to run—and take immediate action for the boy until Elisha's arrival. Elisha pleaded with God on behalf of the woman a second time, this time for the boy's life. Elisha took what action he could, seeking to revive the boy by breathing mouth to mouth and warming the small body with his own. But life, whether in the womb or on a deathbed, belongs to God, and God restored the child's life in response to Elisha's earnest prayer and out of compassion for the mother.

Many can relate memories of children that have been healed from disease and restored to the family. But it is not always so. A child's grave is the most tragic place in a graveyard. We remember the words on one tombstone: "For a while in our arms, forever in our hearts." The loss of a child will remain for a lifetime. The one consoling fact in the midst of grief for a Christian is that the child, whether miscarried or dying, will forever be in the arms of God.

Tuesday: 2 Kings 14:1–15

Today's reading gives details of one of the battles typically fought between Judah and Israel. In fact, during the 200 years following Solomon's death, the two nations continued in an uneasy co-existence, frequently fighting each other as well as occasionally banding together to fight common enemies. This was aggravated by a general decline in the spiritual condition of each side, even though a few kings attempted to return the nations to God. Eventually, in 722 BC, Israel was deported to Assyria, and in 586 BC, Judah was exiled to Babylon.

Both Israel and Judah continued to live in the same land, but the one nation had separated and the two sides constantly squabbled with each other. While the two nations could with some reason point to Solomon as the original cause of their misery, they had within themselves the ability to change their course of history. Ahijah the prophet told Jeroboam that his problems stemmed from his own actions.[1] His problems began when he provided alternate, idolatrous worship in Samaria instead of allowing his people to worship at the temple in Jerusalem. Those problems continued as long as Jeroboam continued to act in accordance with that decision. It prolonged the separation.

Like Israel, a fractious marriage, in which two originally became one, now becomes two individuals again living separate lives. They may live under the same roof but now exist in various degrees of tension with one another. Divorce rarely happens all at once; rather, it is the culmination of a series of disagreements over a period of time. Even small things during this time loom larger because of their incremental effect on already strained relations. But these conflicts probably have at their core a fundamental

---

[1] 1 Kings 14:9–10

difference regarding the expectations of marriage as well as possible ignorance of what God requires. A review and adjustment of what we might expect may provide direction for reconciliation if there is desire for it by both partners.

Wednesday: 2 Kings 17:1–13; 24–28

The northern nation of Israel was the first to go into captivity; the inhabitants of the land were transported away and the land resettled with exiles from other lands. The purpose of resettlement was to ensure there would be no further rebellion, as happened under Israel's last king, Hoshea. The capital of Israel at that time was the city of Samaria. In addition, the entire northern region was also known as Samaria, an alternate name for the northern kingdom of Israel. Because of the resettlement that took place in Samaria, the races became mixed and the resulting people were not considered true Israelites. When Judah later returned to the land, the residents of Samaria became the hated Samaritans.

The separation of Israel and Judah happened because of the sin of Solomon and Israel under his reign. The separation, continuing because both nations continued to practice the same sins, became final with the ultimate disconnection of each nation from their Lord. This is in total contrast to the state of the nation of Israel under David and the way it could have been if both nations had sought the mind of God and obedience to his desires. But in seeking freedom from the rule of God, Israel and Judah found themselves enslaved by the nations around them.

Marital problems are firstly spiritual. A loss of faithfulness to God undermines the understanding of marriage that Scripture portrays as service. Once that has been lost by one or both partners, all that is left is the demand for personal fulfillment. If self-fulfilment is not found in the marriage—either sexual or otherwise—it will be sought from outside sources, compounding the separation. The marriage then becomes a fight for possessions and children. This was Israel's experience: a loss of their spiritual roots and then continual skirmishing for possession of the land.

Eventually the forces they unleashed became their masters and the choice was no longer theirs.

Thursday: 2 Kings 24:18–25:12

It was the year 586 BC when Jerusalem fell to Nebuchadnezzar, king of Babylon, the most powerful nation on earth at the time. The leaders of Judah were executed and most of the people were taken captive and transported to Babylon. The poorest were left behind to till the ground and harvest the crops. As our reading shows, the city, including the temple, was burned and destroyed, and it was 50 years before any Jews returned to Jerusalem. Today, no temple stands on the site, only the Muslim Dome of the Rock.

As you can imagine, this was a time of utmost misery for the Jews, the displaced inhabitants of Judah. Jeremiah records much of this part of Judah's history in detail, and his Lamentations record the desolation and despair of the time. Everything that expressed the meaning and direction of life was destroyed—no familiar landmarks or faces, no meaningful work left, all desire for life crushed—only grief, pain and hopelessness were left to fill the void.

The desperation experienced by Judah reflects the grief and pain of marital conflict, and in particular, the feeling of powerlessness when it becomes apparent that separation and divorce are inevitable. Everything that is meaningful in life appears in doubt, the present is intolerable and the future looks empty. It evokes inexpressible anguish for any children of the marriage as they try to make sense of the collapse of their only known world. Are you going through similar trials now, thinking that a separation is the only answer? If intolerable conditions give you no option, separation may be inevitable and only you can make that decision. But there is wisdom in seeking advice,[1] for if there are any options for reconciliation, the results are worth it.

---

[1] Proverbs 15:22

Friday: 2 Chronicles 36:15–23

Today's reading covers the same events as our last reading. This time, however, we are given a summary of the reasons for the exile and also some hope of return. There is a period of 70 years from verses 20 to 22. There were three deportations to Babylon. The first, in 606 BC, included Daniel; the third and last deportation, in 586 BC, included Ezekiel and was marked by the destruction of Jerusalem. Jeremiah was left in Jerusalem but was subsequently taken by the Jews who finally fled to Egypt. These three prophets and their extensive writings were the mainstay of the Jewish people through the difficult years of exile. Any understanding of these prophets must be seen in the context of Judah's exile from their homeland.

The final editor of the two books of Chronicles was unable to leave the depressing story of the kings of Israel and Judah and their final exile without hope. Possibly added sometime later, verses 20 to 23 indicate that there was an end to the exile and many Jews were able to return to Israel after seventy years. The writer clearly expresses the reasons for the exile. God had exhausted the possibility of Judah's return to him from their idolatry "and there was no remedy." The decline had led to a point of no return.

There is usually a point of no return in all disputes. It is in the early stages of a dispute that reconciliation is possible, but there comes a point where all talk and action has been completed and will have no further effect on the situation. The problem is that we cannot always determine the point before which reconciliation is possible and after which it is not. Indefinitely maintaining our position, however justified we feel, is the greatest barrier to settlement. It is too easy in our anger and sense of injustice to refuse to back off until it is too late. Don't let that happen to you.

Weekend ~ Responding to Rebellion

Perhaps the greatest challenge for parents during their children's teen years is figuring out how to discipline a wayward child. Where is the balance between punishment that provokes antagonism and leniency that encourages the behaviour? The former risks an escalating confrontation that increases the problem; the latter leaves the problem unresolved. Making matters worse, while some of us seem born to be natural parents, most of us clearly are not. Today we will discuss the three basic approaches to discipline that can be found in Scripture.

There must be a sense of justice if resentment is not to be added to the problem. This means that the punishment must fit the crime, and the three "R"s of justice give some guidance: retribution, restitution and rehabilitation. Often, correcting a wrong where possible is the simplest and most effective form of justice. Secondly, the practice of mercy upon genuine repentance reflects a merciful God. This may mean forgoing disciplinary action when forgiveness is the correct response to remorse.

The final response to defiance is release—both physically and emotionally. This is the most difficult, for it separates us from the child we love and places him or her beyond our control. But we must remember that God has already treated us this way and returning to him is our choice. The story of the prodigal son is Jesus' example of the definitive act of love. One of our daughters had a plaque on her wall that read: "If you love something, let it go. If it returns it's yours. If it doesn't, it never was!" The return of a child at their own initiative will provide an enjoyable and lasting relationship that will span the later years. In the final analysis, the ultimate source of protection for our teenagers is total commitment of ourselves to Jesus Christ and regular commitment of our children into his care.

Week Thirty

Monday: Nehemiah 1:1–11

Nehemiah had great sorrow at the state of the homeland that he loved, even though the end of the exile was now some 90 years previous and he had probably never lived there. Like many Jews, he had stayed in the land to which his fathers had been exiled, finding employment in the palace of Artaxerxes in Persia and rising to a place of prominence. Although some time had elapsed since the first exiles returned, much of the city of Jerusalem remained in ruins.

However justified the resentment of the Jews towards their captors may have been, Nehemiah expressed sorrow to God, recognizing that the reason for their exile was their estrangement from him. His prayer is remarkable in that he identifies with the sins of his forefathers even though he had no personal responsibility. Thus, his prayer is one of confession, recognizing the wickedness of the sin the nation had committed and justifying God's actions as consistent with the covenant he had made with Israel. But Nehemiah also reminded God of the promise to restore Israel if they returned to him and sought God's grace for his efforts to assist in their recovery.

It is doubtful that any marital dispute is the fault of only one partner; all of us carry some responsibility for the difficulties we experience in marriage, regardless of if it ends in break-up or not. Whether we consider ourselves innocent or not begs the question of our own sinfulness, which contributes to the shortcomings of earthly experience. To pray, justifiably, for God to avenge injustice towards us is only half the prayer; to seek God's forgiveness for our sinfulness that makes us complicit in our distress is the other necessary half.

Tuesday: Esther 2:1–18

The book of Esther reads like a novel, with turns and twists in the plot sufficient to engage any reader. What is unusual is that there is no mention of God in the story. Yet the devotion of Mordecai and Esther to their faith and God's influence behind the scenes is clear to the perceptive reader. Our main concern here is the relationship between Esther and her cousin Mordecai— presumably much older than Esther—who became her guardian. He was her guardian, not only in the parenting sense, but also in whatever protection he was able to give in that despotic regime, enquiring about her welfare daily as she prepared to meet the king.

Mordecai evidently raised Esther well. While beauty was her obvious asset, it was complemented by an openness and innocent charm that "won the favour of everyone that saw her." There may have been other women of equal or greater beauty brought to the king, but Esther found the greatest favour with the king and became his queen. Of greatest value to her was her willingness to accept advice from those in authority or with expertise. She had evidently listened well to Mordecai's tutelage, for she took his advice to keep her Jewish blood secret and later took Hegai's advice when sent to the king.

You probably wish all your children were like that. Most children learn from their parents, but some learn the hard way. Esther learned that Mordecai had total concern for her welfare and she had implicit trust in him. This, in turn, led her to trust others the same way and prepared her to learn from others. While there is danger in indiscriminate trust, parents who set an example of respect for those in legitimate authority pass on to their children the ability to learn from others.

Wednesday: Esther 4:6–17

It is not difficult to think of Mordecai as a somewhat eccentric man with little to commend him to those in high office. Haman, who turned out to be the Jews' arch enemy, was particularly incensed at Mordecai's indifference to him, as the full story relates. When Mordecai learned of Haman's edict against the Jews,[1] he openly mourned in sackcloth. Esther, even with her luxurious life at court, retained a continuing concern for her cousin and guardian and sent him clothing to wear. But Mordecai refused them, sending back to Esther the news of Haman's edict and requesting her to use her position to influence the king.

Mordecai's message to Esther pulled no punches. It was probably given in the same vein as instructions he gave her during her growing up years that inspired her to trust his advice. Despite the danger, she agreed to petition the king for the Jews, including herself. The continuing story relates her courage in facing the king, his favour toward her and the instructions he gave to help the Jews. The Jews still celebrate their victory over their enemies at that time in their yearly feast of Purim.

Our children will always remain our children, even into late adulthood. For that reason we often worry for them. As they face difficult circumstances or decisions, we still feel a responsibility for their pain and subsequent actions. Too often we give advice when they know themselves what the solutions are if we have instructed them well. In this sense they are usually just as capable as we are to deal with the challenging situations of life; indeed, they may be more so.

Thursday: Job 2:1–10

The book of Job is rarely taught and even more rarely understood, but it states many of the problems that believers in an all-powerful God face. What we do know is that Job's trials

---

[1] Esther 3:8–9

were a test of faith, probably beyond anything most of us will face. In the first chapter, Job lost his sons and daughters and all his wealth. In this chapter, he now also loses his health and is reduced to sitting on an ash heap, scraping his painful oozing sores with broken pottery.

The main lesson of these chapters is that beliefs are not necessarily validated by results. It highlights the fallacy of pragmatism—that truth is confirmed by results. If this were true, then Job's wife was right in telling Job that his trust in God was pointless and that he should "curse God and die." Job lost everything, including his wife, and was left with only an apparently miserable, meaningless existence. But Job had wisdom enough to know that there was nowhere else to go but to God.

Bruce Waltke, an Old Testament professor and translator, tells the story of taking his son to the doctor for vaccination. The little boy was terrified of the needle and cried on his father's shoulder. But rather than running away from his father and the needle, he clung all the tighter to his father as he was carried to it. This lad illustrated the difference between faith and denial. His trust in his father was greater than the pain he faced. So it was with Job: he believed he could simply trust God with raw faith when all the evidence seemed to point in the opposite direction.

Friday: Job 24:1–24

In this passage, Job asks a lot of questions that are commonly raised today, such as: Why does God let evil continue if he is all-powerful? Job is troubled at the violent treatment of the defenceless. In a previous reading of the story of the Widow's Oil, we read of the practice of selling children into slavery in order to pay debts, and Job lists this as one of his complaints. In fact, the problem of children caught up in the cycle of violence that engulfed Job's world is an ongoing tragedy even today.

In present times, news coverage of exploited children brings the problem into our living rooms daily. Television advertisements by humanitarian organizations regularly highlight the plight of children in poor countries. Child slavery is rampant in Sudan and Westerners make the child prostitutes of Thailand a tourist stop. Anti-personnel land mines left in war zones kill and maim hundreds of unsuspecting children. AIDS in Africa has orphaned millions of children, some of whom become parents to siblings while still children themselves. I'm sure you can add other atrocities to the list.

It is too easy to feel impotent in the face of so vast a problem. Yet children suffer as individuals. Don't let the impossibility of doing everything blind us to the ability to do something for one child at a time. Christian organizations are in the forefront of assisting children the world over with the help of individuals like ourselves. The importance of helping one is illustrated by the story of a little boy who noticed hundreds of starfish left on the beach by the receding tide. As he started throwing them back into the sea, a passer-by commented that he was making little difference to the vast numbers. The boy threw another starfish into the foam as he replied: "It made a difference to that one."

Weekend ~ Depravity

When I first learned to ride a bicycle, I was let loose on the streets of my neighbourhood and almost immediately came into conflict with a car driver. My problem was a very simple one; I was riding on the wrong side of the road, as the driver testily informed me. My father had not taught me the first rule of the road—to ride or drive on the left (that was in England, of course). A moment's thought reveals to us the chaos produced without this one simple and basic rule.

When it comes to human nature, most are poorly informed of the one simple rule that governs all human behaviour and must be taken into account in any process of governing: our total depravity. This very definitely goes against the grain, especially as it suggests that we have nothing good in us. But it simply means that everything we do is somehow infected with sin; we act with mixed motives and engage in undesirable fantasies. Society assumes the ultimate good in all, a mistaken notion that contributes as much to society's ills as sin itself by applying incorrect notions. Sin is regarded as a correctable defect rather than a terminal disease.

In contrast, the Bible teaches that we are all infected by sin and need inward cleansing by our Creator. The first line of defence for our children is a commitment to Jesus Christ, responding to their recognised need of cleansing and forgiveness, first as an initial experience of salvation and then as an ongoing need in daily life. Unfortunately, these concepts are so basic that we take them for granted and forget to clearly instruct our children in them—as my father forgot to inform me of the first rule of the road.

Week Thirty-One

Monday: Psalm 2:1–12

This is a messianic psalm, one that forecasts the coming of the Messiah and here specifically points to him as a Son. The ludicrous ranting of the nations against God is set against the awesome power of the coming Son of God, King of the Earth. The ease of final victory for God's appointed King makes a mockery of the power of world rulers, however great it may seem during their brief rule. The psalm ends with a warning to all rulers to "kiss the Son," a reference to giving allegiance to him before it is too late.

I'm reminded of my childhood days when "I'll tell my dad on you" was the threat of retaliation for some perceived wrong. I assumed that my father had the capability to put down any other child who harmed me. I recall one boy who made no secret of his resentment when my father reprimanded him—especially as he wasn't totally to blame! Most children see their parents as their protectors and run to them for shelter in times of distress. This psalm is a reminder that Jesus will be *given* his power; it is an "inheritance" granted as a "possession."

The child who operates under his parents' protection and authority and God's Son, who has his Father's protection and power, both remind us that we also live under the authority of our heavenly Father. Not that he is our protection for our selfish desires or deceptive actions, but he can be counted on to support us as we dedicate our lives to him. Whatever mockery or persecution we or our family may sustain from others will be addressed when they give an account before the final judgment seat of the Son.

Tuesday: Psalm 37:25–28

Today's reading seems to fly in the face of what we consider to be true. While we see perpetual violence against the defenceless, David sees God's continual provision for the children of the faithful. Not only that, but David also contends that this has been true for his whole life—and he lived to "a good old age."[1] So we have to consider that not all children suffer disastrous fates throughout the world. Many, perhaps most, although with great differences in affluence, live enjoyable lives marred only by the inevitable quirks of life. Note that David qualified his remarks by referring to those who "are always generous and lend freely" and that his life was lived during a time of relative prosperity, winning most of the wars he fought and maintaining peace in his country.

David also stated the general belief of the Old Testament that to "dwell in the land forever" was subject to following God's requirements for his people; the history of Israel recorded in Scripture bears this out. Successive kings following David and Solomon led the nation in such sin that eventually the nation was exiled to Assyria and Babylon. Much later, blame for the crucifixion of Jesus was taken by his contemporaries: "Let His blood be on us and on our children."[2] And within forty years after that, Jerusalem was destroyed by the Roman army and the Jews scattered throughout the earth until the mid-twentieth century.

On a personal basis, if we are to avoid our "children begging bread" in the future, we must ensure that our current affluence is not seen as the status quo. Tomorrow's thoughts illustrate the danger in more detail. For ourselves, if we do not live with a clear expression of the importance of our faith and recognition of God

---

[1] 1 Chronicles 29:28
[2] Matthew 27:25

as our provider, our children may consider a prosperous life their right and not a privilege.

Wednesday: Psalm 78:1–8

Asaph, one of David's lead musicians, also penned many of the psalms. In this passage he gives a warning that is a counterpoint to David's encouragement of yesterday. Not only was it imperative that parents lived according to God's covenant, but they also needed to teach their children to do the same. In fact, Asaph saw the need for the teaching to be carried on through succeeding generations if they were not to suffer the fate of their forefathers—"a stubborn and rebellious generation whose hearts were not loyal to God." Perhaps Asaph was thinking of the period of the Judges when another generation grew up, "who knew neither the Lord nor what He had done for Israel."[1]

We have encountered this idea so many times already in relation to children it must seem like a broken record: it is necessary to teach our children the importance of faith as we ourselves live as examples by practicing that faith. There can only be one reason for this repetition—these requirements are so often neglected. We must ask ourselves why this is so when the need for them is so vital.

We tend to realize the necessity of seeking God during the difficult times of life, at which point it is natural to also teach our children to seek God and remain faithful to him. The paradox is that faithfulness leads to greater prosperity until the connection between the two is lost, particularly by children who never face adversity. Perhaps we are seeing this with a current generation of younger people. They have a sense that the prosperity we share now is either natural or the result of their own labours, presuming that a godly lifestyle has little to do with maintaining it. Eventually this must lead to a loss of prosperity and the need to

---

[1] Judges. 2:10

seek God begins the cycle again. We must be vigilant so that our children do not get on this treadmill.

Thursday: Psalm 80:8–11

The ideal marriage that most of us desire is rarely attained. Many relationships are quite the reverse, spelling disaster not only for the marriage partners but also for the prospects of the children. Yet in the same way that delinquent children often come from good homes, so children from dysfunctional homes may also become highly effective adults. Ann developed a strong survival instinct from her home life and was cared for by a godly grandmother who eventually took her into her home. Annie, as her grandmother was called, took Ann to church, where she found the love of God a compelling antidote to her childhood experiences. Both Ann and I were baptised together at the ages of 14 and 15 and have been committed Christians ever since.

Ann's experience reminds us that we are never destined to be conditioned by our environment. No one has perfect parents, and in learning to cope with parents' faults, children learn to cope with an imperfect world when they become adults. Ensuring that they do not repeat their parents' mistakes is often an important part of children's lives as adults. Ann was determined that her own home would never be the chaotic setting she had experienced. However, too many blame their upbringing for their inadequacies and failures, living as victims all their lives and not recognizing that their parents had imperfect parents too, which simply passes the blame back to Adam and Eve.

Our reading tells us that God brought Israel from the slavery of Egypt and planted her in a fruitful land where she might flourish. Israel's faith would provide a protective environment for its inhabitants. It is a reminder that placing our lives in God's hands allows him the opportunity to bring healing to us. But of greater significance, we now have the resources to provide a healthy environment for our family, whatever our previous home life might have been like.

Friday: Psalm 103:8–18

If you are currently having difficulties raising your children, then this psalm should give you encouragement (and we need all the encouragement we can get at times). While we can often see the problems and solutions in other families, our own can seem intractable. Exasperation and despair follow. We tend to forget we are dealing with children who are individuals that make their own decisions, not simply clones of ourselves. And for children and youths, those decisions are often made on a superficial understanding of life and not with the insight we have gained.

There are two ideas in this passage that may give us some help. Firstly, the passage sets God himself as our example. We know how stubborn and rebellious Israel was, confirmed by our own waywardness at times. He uses our love for our own children to reflect his love for us, not treating us "as our sins deserve," for he has compassion on us "as a father has compassion on his children." As we are all too aware of our children's shortcomings, he is aware of ours—in his eyes we may not be much better than our children.

Secondly, contrary to our brief tenure on earth, God's love for us is eternal, reaching to the generations that follow us even to our "children's children." As God knows how to deal with us, so he is our helper in dealing with our children, for he loves them as he loves us. We are not alone, and as long as our hearts are right with him, our children will also be under his care. We may fail on occasion as our children do, but God remains faithful to us. That is why we are invited to "cast all your anxiety on him because he cares for you."[1]

---

[1] 1 Peter 5:7

Weekend ~ An Adoption

Ann and I adopted a boy when our first two girls were in their teens. We both felt we had something to give and we had space in our home and hearts for a child in need. His history was one of a broken family, living with his father and a series of women that were brought into the home. The boy had developed a pattern of undermining the women and driving them out of the home because they interfered with his relationship with his father. When he was six, the boy's behaviour towards the father's women caused his father to give him up to the children's services. We first met him in a Salvation Army children's home—his permanent home apart from adoption.

After a year of visits with him, we adopted him into our family at ten years of age. His disturbing background had taught him to survive by using the system and manipulating those he came in contact with. This became our greatest challenge, one to which we did not respond well. Although he was with us for about three years, his increasing antisocial behaviour and bouts of trouble with the law eventually landed him in juvenile detention. We kept contact with him for a while longer during his stints in detention until later jail terms, and lost contact in later years.

We are still not sure where he is, although we know that he served most of his life in prison until into his thirties, when he later managed to hold down work in the oil fields. It has naturally left us with questions. Did we make a mistake in taking him in, and if it was God's leading at the time, why did it turn out so badly? We have to trust that there was some redeeming value in his time with us that perhaps only eternity will reveal. In the meantime, he continues to be the subject of our prayers that God's Spirit will persist in dogging his footsteps and draw him into his kingdom.

Week Thirty-Two

Monday: Psalm 127:1–5

Our children's behaviour may often remind us that they are infected with the cancer of sin like ourselves. But that makes them no less valuable than any other human being. In fact, far from being a curse, our reading states that children are a blessing from God—apparently the more of them, the greater the blessing. Certainly in the Old Testament, barrenness was often a punishment from God, as exemplified by Michal's contempt of David's vigorous worship and her subsequent barrenness.[1]

Today's attitudes towards children are different. In spite of protest about how important children are to us and the severe public censure and penalties for pedophiles, Western culture practices a great ambivalence in its care of the most vulnerable. Children are frequently considered an imposition, interfering with our right to enjoyment. Daycares proliferate as "childparks," allowing parents to pursue their own agendas or singles to work after separation from their partners. Some children are still unwanted, abused and neglected even after decades of abortion rights. Child pornography has grown exponentially as the internet has brought the world's proclivity for it into our homes. Parental rights become restricted as governments seek to protect children from their parents.

---

[1] 2 Samuel 6:23

Globally, the picture is the same. Children are deemed an aggravation of the population explosion, richer countries attempting to impose birth restrictions and encouraging abortions in poorer countries. It's easy for us to fall into similar traps. Do we consider large families anti-social or population control a necessary evil? Jesus had nothing but support and protection for children and considered them worthy of his blessing as they are his blessing to us.[1]

Tuesday: Psalm 128:1–6

Ann and I celebrate our birthdays in the spring, which is also the time for Mothers' Day and Father's Day. This means that we receive all sorts of cards and booklets from our children extolling the qualities of motherhood and fatherhood they see in us. While we appreciate their thoughts, it also raises a level of guilt that we have not really lived up to the standards they express. The senior years are a time for regretting some of the things done or undone during our parenting years. But we receive their sentiments of appreciation with great pleasure, thankful that they overlook our shortcomings at this time of our lives— although they often expressed them forcefully in their youth.

The desire and commitment Ann and I made to God when we were baptised was real and determined but often less so in practice, particularly during the difficult times of life. We believe it was because God saw our hearts and graciously overlooked our failures that we have experienced his protection, guidance and blessing throughout our lives. We can concur heartily with the content of this psalm, particularly rejoicing in our children and our "children's children."

But it is still with amazement that we see two things: the way God has blessed and continues to bless our children and grandchildren and the joy that Ann and I find in our companionship together in these latter years. We still wonder at

---

[1] Mark 10:13–16

the extent of God's grace to our family but also the unexpected level of joy that it has brought us. Ann grabbed my hand the other day—not unusual—but this time added that if I was taken, she did not want to regret missing any opportunity to express her love, a sentiment we should express at all times of life.

Wednesday: Psalm 131:1–3

This is probably a good psalm for the morning rush. How can one remain calm during the hustle to get the family out of the door for school, work and errands? It's a reminder that it's during the turbulent times of life that we sense that there should be answers beyond ourselves to the dilemmas we face. This psalm reflects David's decision to set aside his quest for answers: "not to concern myself with great matters or things too wonderful for me." He makes a decision to calm himself and to seek contentment in his current status. This is not an easy thing to do, yet there is no peace without some assurance that there is meaning in the instability of life.

I'm sure you have watched the sense of peace present in a child taking an afternoon nap. There's nothing like a full stomach of solid food to provide that child a contented sleep. David pointedly notes that it is the *weaned* child that is done with milk and seeks solid food that has a satisfied stomach and sleep. Too often we seek simple answers to complex questions, particularly those that may have no immediate answer. The writer to the Hebrews suggests that his readers needed milksop teaching, not solid food, due to their lack of maturity.[1] Just as we know that our children need solid food as they grow out of babyhood, so we need to advance in our understanding of the faith and wisdom that is found in God's Word if we are to find a measure of contentment in life.

Paul himself knew how to find contentment—in plenty or in want—for God could complete his work in Paul under all

---

[1] Hebrews 5:11–14

conditions.[1] Both Paul and David found that maturity didn't necessarily bring answers that gave hope, but it generated trust in God that granted peace when no answers were forthcoming. As David simply said: "Israel, put your hope in the Lord both now and evermore."

Thursday: Psalm 137:1–9

Today's reading expresses the suffering that the Jews were going through in their captivity, expressing their sorrow, humiliation and anger. Those who had dragged them from their homeland were now their tormentors, wanting perhaps to mock their display of love for the land they had been forced to leave. The miseries of both captivity and homesickness haunted them and they could not bear to sing the songs that reminded them of their life left behind. They remembered not only the joys of the city now destroyed but also the taunts of those who had rejoiced in its downfall and scorned them in their distress.

They expressed their anger as they sought God for justice for the brutality practised upon them, seeking the same cruelties for their attackers that they themselves endured at their oppressors' hands. In honest fashion, they did not play down their feelings or their desire for vengeance. But their cry was to God, knowing that he would avenge them in his own time and in his own way.[2] And of particular importance, because they called on God for justice, they denied themselves the possibility of exacting it.

It is true that divorce raises many highly charged emotions, not the least of which is anger—anger at the injustice perpetrated against us and those dependent on us. Irrespective of our own contribution to the break-up, the injustices practiced against us are real and the anger, reasonable. Like the displaced Jews, the expression of that anger in some harmless way is justified. But to express it outwardly simply spreads that venom to others; to

---

[1] Philippians 4:12–13
[2] Deuteronomy 32:35

suppress it turns it inwards and harms us. Our psalmist found a third way—confessing it to God, who understands our hurt and anger and is big enough to both absorb and avenge it.

Friday: Psalm 139:1–18

The impossibility of escaping from God is the overriding theme in this psalm. Whether we are with him or against him, neither distance nor darkness is beyond his reach. While this may be a fearful thought for those who rebel against him, it is the most comforting to those of us who honour and revere him. What is even more astounding is his knowledge of our inmost thoughts, many of which we may be ashamed to divulge to anyone, yet he loves us just the same. In fact, this Psalm notes he has known us from conception.

He "knit me together in my mother's womb." Even there "you created my inmost being." Who we would become and the plans for our life—if we were willing to abide by them—were already established in our unformed body. Even in the "secret place" and "in the depths of the earth"—here a euphemism for the womb— we could not escape God. The often used phrase "cradle to the grave" does not do justice to our lives. The Bible is clear: in the eyes of God human life begins at conception.

The sacredness of life has always been a cornerstone of Christian faith. Whether it is within the womb or on a deathbed, life is God's creation and our desire to end it for any reason must be weighed against that knowledge. This does not mean that everyone who takes a life is to be condemned. Perhaps few of us know the agony that may precede abortion or euthanasia. But the flippant ending of life for convenience or gain can never be condoned. That life is God's and we will have to give an account for how we have dealt with it.

Weekend ~ A Couple that Made It

We first met Darcy the day he entered our small congregation, dressed in his motorcycle leathers. We invited him for lunch and he tried to impress us with his spirituality, predominantly of a new age variety. He continued to attend, mainly—as he told us later—to find babysitters for his young son from a previous relationship. His son began to come with him, and he was poorly behaved, quite frequently disrupting our services. Darcy was connected to the drug fraternity, selling drugs on the street and managing an apartment building which frequently housed drug users. Over a period of a few weeks, however, Darcy became a Christian, leaving his drug connections and starting life over.

Josie came into our congregation supported by a cane. She had been involved in a car accident in her teens and was a certified quadriplegic, predicted never to walk again, but her slight build belied her fierce determination and she regained the use of her legs. She subsequently attended university—in a wheelchair—obtained a degree in social work and became gainfully employed. Darcy and Josie were an unlikely combination but they were attracted to each other. This relationship was tested when Darcy suddenly disappeared and we tracked him to an open jail—his past life had suddenly caught up with him.

Eventually I married them and Darcy was accepted into university to study law as a mature student, and even with his background, he was eventually accepted by the Law Society. Today, he is a successful lawyer, and although handicapped, Josie has given birth to two boys. They are an example of God's work in rehabilitation—Josie from her accident and Darcy from his old life. As they put their trust in God, he has provided what both of them may never otherwise have gained.

Week Thirty-Three

Monday: Proverbs 5:1–23

No one can be unaware of the sexual permissiveness that pervades our Western culture. This is not a product of this generation; it has been the practice of all generations to a greater or lesser degree. In his day, Solomon, the wisest of men, complained about it and its attendant dangers.[1] What is of interest in this passage is that it does not dwell on the immorality of promiscuous behaviour. Rather, it lists the considerable disadvantages of the practice and enumerates a variety of reasons for men to avoid sexual relations with women other than their wives.

Solomon does not deny that an affair might bring temporary pleasure,[2] but there is no love lost by an adulterous woman; her actions are purely mercenary or selfish and in the end bring misery. Most of us would agree that an affair, however pleasurable for a period, usually ends in wretchedness for all affected. Yet there are other dangers. Solomon believed that adulterous behaviour can end in death. It is most likely that sexually transmitted diseases were as prevalent then as now and many would die of the diseases. Certainly the ravages of disease are implied in verse 11 and death in verses 5 and 23.

---

[1] Proverbs chapters 6 and 7 continue with the same theme.
[2] Proverbs 6:25; 7:18

Not only are there physical dangers, but in verse 14 we are warned of loss of status as well. Even allowing for loose morality in current Western culture, standards of moral behaviour are still expected of high profile people. President Clinton came close to impeachment for his sexual behaviour and Jimmy Swaggart, the television evangelist, lost credibility and brought the gospel into disrepute by consorting with a prostitute. It must be recognized, however, that adultery is not wrong just because of the drawbacks against it. There is a command against it,[1] and failing to observe it on our part distorts the image of God—the ultimate faithful One—within us.

Tuesday: Proverbs 11:22; 14:1; 21:9

The word "house" in chapter 14 is better translated "household." It does not refer to a wife building the structure in which her family lives but rather the home that she provides for them. In contrast to the passage at the end of Proverbs referring to the virtuous woman, these Proverbs warn against women who are destructive. There are women of loose morals who break other homes, but today's readings are of a wife whose actions tear down her own home. No woman deliberately sets out to destroy her home, but some conduct tends to do just that.

While we can think of several ways in which a wife can be damaging to her family, the latter two verses suggest two ways in particular. Firstly, there is the quarrelsome wife. This word means "contentious, one who stirs up strife." In our culture it can be the nagging wife whose constant harping on faults makes a "corner of the roof" a welcome retreat. Nagging—mostly referring to women but can also refer to men—is always counterproductive, for it alienates the target. Believing wives are often driven to this in a desperate effort to convert their husbands. Jesus made his point clear but left people to their own decisions. Wives should take heed and comfort from his example, stating their positions and

---

[1] Exodus 20:14, Deuteronomy 5:18

needs and giving opportunity for their husbands to respond—or not. If the subject is critical, find a compromise or a way for viewpoints to co-exist peacefully as you enjoy each other anew.

Secondly, there is the wife who lacks discretion, someone who "turns aside" from discernment, resulting in poor taste and judgment. This usually refers to moral issues, for it is the "wayward wife" that lacks judgment.[1] It also refers to one who is spiritually obtuse, for it is "the fool [who] says in his heart, 'There is no God.'"[2] Her foolishness makes her beauty purely ornamental and of no value to the family. But there is nothing wrong with beauty; every man wants a beautiful wife. It is outward allure and inner virtue together that provide the unique combination that contributes to a secure, comfortable home, however poor.

Wednesday: Proverbs 13:22; 14:26; 20:7

These three verses indicate benefits that children receive from godly parents. Inheritance does not only mean a lump sum on the parents' death but includes support from parents during a child's lifetime. Having a secure refuge in the home is the greater benefit. Those of you from good homes know the comfort there is in a safe home during childhood setbacks. Security is derived from the bond between husband and wife, and the fracturing of that bond breaks the cocoon that produces joyful and strong development in growing children. This is the inheritance that godly parents give their children.

For those of us who are familiar with the common run of TV shows, it is noticeable how few shows are built around a normal family life. For TV writers, it appears that their impressions of normal are desperate housewives, the partner-swapping of the soaps or a hilarious round of sexual encounters without meaning. Even shows depicting persons engaged in professional activities—detectives, doctors and nurses, for example—are usually cast as

---

[1] Proverbs 6:23–24
[2] Psalm 14:1

swingers, divorced, single parents or struggling with marital problems. It seems the media have given us a negative confirmation of the message of today's verses by depicting the results of an ungodly lifestyle.

Unfortunately, the breakdown of Christian families also denies the truth of these verses. But it must be remembered that no family is immune from the difficulties of life and that proverbs are a general rule. Families that model godliness, not those that only pay lip service to it, are the most likely to pass their blessings on to their children. This is even true whether or not the parents profess to be Christians.

Thursday: Proverbs 13:24; 22:15

Several readings from Proverbs are isolated verses, and today's readings follow that pattern. Much of the book of Proverbs is a collection of sayings that have stood the test of time, and they are not set in any obvious order. In this way, every verse is a sermon in itself, demanding deeper thought. The second of today's proverbs suggests that a child can be foolish—not very acceptable in a culture that dotes on its children—and which even appears to oppose Jesus' teaching to become like little children.

We need to recognize imitable child*like* qualities that are easily lost in adulthood: innocence, trust and simplicity, to name a few. But that does not mean that we should become child*ish*. The self-centred nature of the newborn to ensure its survival is not a trait to be fostered as the child grows. Our instinct for self preservation is strong enough that the quality of self sacrifice needs to be taught. Jesus taught that we should love our neighbours as ourselves—a direct allusion to our propensity to care for our own needs first.

Solomon reckoned that childish and foolish ideas need to be opposed by discipline. In fact, the first proverb indicates that a lack of discipline displays a lack of love for the child. Thus, the motivation for opposing childish actions is not from anger or for the personal convenience of the parents; it is for the eventual wellbeing of the child and his or her ultimate acceptance into an interrelated community. No society can survive without sacrificial curtailment of the individual's unfettered freedom to fulfill his or her desires. That training begins in childhood.

Friday: Proverbs 20:11; 29:15

While example is critical in raising a child, this alone will not impart wisdom. The first of today's verses questions the innocence of a child. The idea that a child is born an empty moral package to be filled is foreign to Scripture. The temperament given at birth reveals itself in the way a child behaves, with both the negative and positive side of that temperament being expressed. While temperaments are diverse, they all have one thing in common: they are God-given characteristics as much as hair and eye colour are.

This raises the question why God would create temperaments that produce corrupt qualities. To ask this question reveals a misunderstanding of temperament. All elements of temperament are created perfectly; it is the use of them that is good or bad. For instance, an ignorant stubbornness is simply the flipside of steadfastness; superficiality is a symptom of the ability to see the big picture, and attention to detail often precludes depth of vision. An interesting exercise is to view the characteristics of your family and note the positive values of those qualities you dislike.

The second verse indicates the need for training. Our youngest daughter was the ultimate strong-willed child. Early on we realized that it is strength of will that produces results in a world that is hard to change. Our challenge was to retain that persevering nature while ensuring it was channelled in positive directions. Wisdom imparted by example is established by careful discipline. Our calling was not to break her will but to mould it.

Weekend ~ Children are a Joy

Children are a blessing to us, and despite their occasional bursts of bad behaviour, we wouldn't part with them. Frequent advice from older people is for parents to enjoy their children while they are young, as those years pass so quickly. Ann and I had two families, two girls born early in life when making a living and setting up a home was an arduous time. Our youngest girl was born sixteen years later, during the time the older girls were leaving home. I had treated the older girls quite seriously, missing much of the enjoyment I should have had with them and probably making their childhood harder than necessary. But with the youngest, I decided this was one for fun and enjoyment, leading to the accusation from her sisters and mother that she was being spoilt.

Life stretches endlessly before us in our youth, but looking back from old age, it seems to have passed in a moment—"Where did the years go?" This was David's understanding, having that sudden inspiration from God on the brevity of life.[1] It is also a common experience that life seems to pass more quickly the older we get—the end of life is shorter than the beginning and we have to run faster to catch up on those things we neglected earlier in life.

However, none of this suggests that old age is only a time for mourning missed opportunities. This is a time for rejoicing in our children and grandchildren. Ann and I take a considerable interest in the growth and education of our grandchildren, watching them develop into impressive adults and choose marriage partners. It is with the greatest joy that we frequently hang out with them and our children. In return, we regularly receive complimentary cards and notes from them—more than we deserve but which "are a crown"[2] to our lives in our later years. Those unable or unwilling to have children will miss out on one of the greatest blessings life has to offer.

---

[1] Psalm 39:4–5
[2] Proverbs 17:6

Week Thirty-Four

Monday: Proverbs 31:10–31

When we receive unsolicited advice regarding our relationships, how can we know what is good or bad? Let me suggest two approaches. Firstly, is the advice we are being offered really for our own good? We are always told that it is, but frequently it is from people who do not have a real interest in our welfare or who have an agenda of their own. When it comes to a lifetime partner, we should listen more readily to those whom we know *really* care about us. Secondly, does our lover stand up to the scrutiny of Scripture? Love for a woman of the qualities described in this passage is a good foundation for marriage.

Ann and I met when we were young teenagers, and we considered ourselves meant for each other. After four years of courtship, we found out our first daughter Heather was on the way. We were married when Ann was 18 and I was 19, with the blessing—perhaps apprehensive blessing—of our families. Ann came from an unsavoury neighbourhood and a severely dysfunctional family. I still had several years left to complete my architectural degree and we had no place to live. We received messages about how foolish we were, destined for break-up due to a forced marriage.

In addition to my overriding adoration for Ann, I saw in her the qualities that are listed in our reading today. I had no doubts about her ability to provide the partnership that marriage required, and we both had an unwavering commitment to our faith in Jesus Christ. Her home environment had provided her with great strength and resolve in addition to the qualities God had given her. Needless to say, our families' reservations—if they had any—were unfounded.   And those who predicted the impending disaster of our marriage are still waiting for it.

Tuesday: Ecclesiastes 3:1–8

The slogan "make love not war" appears to hit the high moral ground, but it fails on two counts. The sort of love the slogan evokes tends to be enjoyment of sexual pleasure, not reconciliation with enemies. But of greater dispute is the idea that war can always be avoided. Today's reading is disturbing because it outlines both good and bad activities that will always infringe on our time. It is almost as if we are being counselled to make room for those things that are distasteful rather than avoiding them and concentrating on the agreeable. We do tend to switch television channels if pictures of distress occur, and we certainly try to avoid looking at our own faults.

Yet we are all aware that evil invades our relationships as well as the world at large. There is a time for war as well as peace—a time to confront one another rather than act in toleration or appeasement. Even more surprising is the assertion that there is also a time to hate as well as love. What could we possibly be exhorted to hate? Surely we cannot be expected to hate people! Perhaps the answer can be found in defining hate as the Bible defines love: not a feeling but an action. There are times when we can act "hatefully," not in the common idea of a vindictive response, but in creative, positive, even fierce opposition to falsehood, stupidity and cruelty.

It is said that anger always has a reason but seldom a good one. Yet there are times when anger is justified, such as when one is deceived, betrayed or undervalued. Similarly, courts can be described as hateful and angry when convicting a felon, even though they are practising justice, not revenge. God expresses anger frequently, but it is always just, even as at one point he hated Esau.[1] Perhaps there is an issue that you need to confront your partner about. Maybe this is a time, not for love, but—in its redefined sense—a time for "hate."

Wednesday: Ecclesiastes 3:9–14

There's nothing like a day of accomplishment, a time when everything goes according to plan and when intended work has been done. But we have also had days when all we did was redo, repair or fail and nothing of significance was achieved. In reflection we realize that there must be times for preparation, planning and evaluation; times for correcting what has been previously done or adapting to changing circumstances; times for rethinking and renewing the way we live. It is almost as if we could add another verse to yesterday's reading: a time to advance and a time to retreat.

In the big picture, both the times of advance and seeming retreat are part of the same process. To advance again tomorrow as we did yesterday, we may need to retrench today. Today's reading helps give some rationale to this process. We see the beauty of God's creation around us and we have a sense of a bigger picture than just this life, but there are questions unanswered—"a burden upon us." Perhaps this is true of the process, particularly the setbacks of life, and we are baffled by the futility of it all. At these times the writer of Ecclesiastes exhorts us to find satisfaction in the daily routine, recognizing that every day has meaning in God's big picture beyond our grasp.

The process of relationship in marriage is much the same. We can easily be discouraged by the conflict and abrasion between partners, feeling at times that it may never be overcome. Stopping and dealing with interpersonal relations seems an unnecessary disruption to other important areas of life. But in the big picture, it is part of the process, as necessary as the happy times of joy and companionship together—and in the long run enhancing them. It

---

[1] Malachi 1:2–5

is often necessary to leave the big picture to God and trust him with what we can't figure out.

Thursday: Ecclesiastes 4:9–12

It is a common misconception that marriage is a union between two people. In fact, there are four parties to a marriage. Weddings are public for one reason: they are announcing to the community the couple's union and their responsibility to each other and to the children that may come from it. This is why marriages are registered and witnesses sign the register. A common introduction to a wedding ceremony states that "we are gathered here to witness . . ." Thus, the community has a place at the table as a partner to the union.

Obviously the other witness to the union of any church ceremony is God himself, as he is invoked at all religious weddings. But he is also a witness at every wedding ceremony, religious or not, for marriage was his idea. His register records the union too, and he is a witness to any action of a partner that breaks the relationship.[1] It goes without saying that God is far more interested in the outcome of the relationship than any earthly authority, for he is the protector of any orphan and widow that may be left from the break-up of that relationship. As husband or wife, we will be held accountable before God for the treatment of our partners and children.

God is also interested in maintaining the marriage. Our reading promotes a partnership because of its synergy—the work of two together is greater than the sum of each working alone. It recognises the help, comfort and protection two can bring to each other. But the last verse reminds us that it is the third strand in the cord that maintains a strong relationship that "is not quickly broken." After the wedding the state is no longer interested unless there is a problem. God, on the other hand, has a vital interest in

---

[1] Matthew 19:4–6

being with us throughout our marriage, rejoicing in the good times and supporting us through the bad—if we will let him.

Friday: Song of Solomon 4:8–5:1

There have been those through the centuries that have tried to ban sex on the basis that it was inherently sinful, even forbidding marriage.[1] But all that God has created is good—and that includes sex. Today's reading is selected from the Song of Solomon, King Solomon's love song to his bride. Although there are difficulties in identifying characters in the dialogue, it is clear that the subject matter is the celebration of sexuality, sometimes dressed in symbolic language, at other times explicit.

In opposition to those who would disparage sex, this short book makes it clear that sexuality is a gift of great beauty and wonder to be lavished upon each partner by the other. It describes in delicate song the intenseness of longing, the inexpressible beauty of the loved one, the exquisite sense of the other's presence. Today's reading finishes up with joy at the consummation of the relationship, expressed as final entry into the garden of his beloved while the background chorus urges them to "drink your fill of love." But it is not an arrangement based totally on sexual obsession; the book expresses a depth of passion and care that can withstand the rigours of life—a love story equal to the greatest love stories on earth.

Does this sound like your marriage? Perhaps not, yet there is an echo in most of us that yearns for that level of companionship. It is a reminder that under the stress and reversals of wedded life, there remains an experience of vitality ready to be awakened again. Don't be discouraged to the point of despair in a difficult marriage. If it is possible to fall out of love, it is also possible to fall in love again. There is renewal for the most jaded of marriages; the deepest joy is still to be found in the most vital relationship that God has provided for us.

---

[1] 1 Timothy 4:3–4

Weekend ~ Love and Marriage

An old song says: "Love and marriage go together like a horse and carriage." Unfortunately, too many think that idea went out with the horse and buggy days. Sex is now perceived as a recreational activity, generally divorced from the idea of marriage or children. Even a cursory knowledge of Scripture will reveal its message of sexual satisfaction only within marriage, and this is well confirmed, for marriage and family are the bedrock of civilisation across the world. At the risk of being legalistic, the restriction of sex to between marriage partners must be the basis, not only of a stable society, but also of secure and happy family life—for husband and wife as well as children.

However, this ideal requires certain fundamental features to be practised, the foremost of which is fidelity. Infidelity carries its own consequences beyond emotional trauma, particularly the prevalence of venereal disease and its possible transmission to the family. It is no coincidence that AIDS has blossomed with the sexual revolution and is only sustained by indiscriminate sexual union.

But infidelity, while inexcusable, often has its reasons. Sexual availability is a reason for and a promise of marriage,[1] and for it to be withheld or used as a weapon is a primary departure from the covenant and may foster infidelity. Secondary requirements for a happy marriage hinge on Christian servanthood and submission to the other, as discussed earlier. Simply put, and as Ann is fond of saying: "Be good to each other!" Lack of these practices can be just as harmful to marriage as infidelity.

---

[1] 1 Corinthians 7:5

Week Thirty-Five

Monday: Song of Solomon 5:2–6

The previous Scripture passage may have given a rapturous look at the joys of the marriage union, but a study of the book also describes some of the disruptions found in marriage—interruptions in companionship, denial of contact—and the patience and strength of love evoked at these times. Today particularly, there is a warning that boredom or apathy may set in to the relationship. The bride hears her beloved at the door calling to enter but she has settled for the night: "I have taken off my robe—must I put it on again? I have washed my feet—must I soil them again?"

His call was clearly inconvenient, not necessarily inappropriate or demanding. Her situation was not one of inability but of disinterest. Yet her desire for him was not lost, and as he tried the door, the old fervour reappeared. But by the time she had reconsidered her initial denial and dressed, he had left. The longings of yesterday had dissipated into indifference on her part and impatience on his. But the story goes on to record her change of heart, her search for him and their final love for each other.

The critical factor in any personal disruption is time. Perhaps this is why Paul exhorts us not to "let the sun go down while you are still angry."[1] The longer we put off reconciliation, the more

---

[1] Ephesians 4:26

entrenched each position becomes and patching up becomes harder. Each time it occurs it becomes easier not to reconcile at all. We've all heard of couples who don't speak to each other anymore. Love cannot bear the pain of separation; it is *this* pain we need to embrace and allow to provoke us into making up before the day is done.

Tuesday: Song of Solomon 8:6–12

Reading the Song of Solomon may well put together a great case for marriage, but is the joy of fulfilled love and the pleasure of closeness sufficient to hold a marriage together in the tough times? Our reading today reminds us that there are two sides to maintaining a secure marriage: consummation and discipline. The first is desirable, the second, unpleasant. In school, biology gave us a series of differences between humans and animals, but one difference was never raised. Animals grow, mature and propagate by simply following their instincts. However, humans degrade themselves if their instincts are not controlled and disciplined. The conscious choice of discipline over instinct is a distinctive and ennobling mark of humanity based on our freedom of choice.

Verse 6 raises the issue of commitment. Not only does this involve a pledge of allegiance for life, "a seal over your heart," but there is also a "jealousy unyielding as the grave," a God-given emotion that will endeavour to protect the relationship. Faithfulness in the marriage is compared to a vineyard. While Solomon had a natural vineyard to let out to tenants, the fruit of his lover's vineyard—her sexuality—was for him alone. Both lifetime commitment and sexual faithfulness are the key disciplines that guard the continuing joy inherent in the relationship.

But a further issue is raised, that of virginity, evidenced by a concern for a younger sister. Will she be a wall that shuts out intruders and maintains her virginity or a door that will let all come in? If the latter, her siblings will guard her with "panels of cedar." Virginity today is scorned on the basis that experimentation will provide better sexual adjustment later. In fact, the reverse is true. Sexual discipline *before* marriage is the same discipline that is required *in* marriage. To play loosely with sex prior to marriage is to enter into marriage with the ease of sexual adventurism and a correspondingly greater risk of infidelity and break-up.

Wednesday: Isaiah 9:1–7

Most of you will recall this passage of Scripture from Christmas programs predicting the birth of Christ. We recall each Christmas the amazing fact that God himself, Creator of all things, became a created being for a while. Our natural expectation for him, even as a created being, would be to come in some sort of majesty and power, yet he chose to come as a child. That he chose to come that way has several implications.

Firstly, he gave meaning and dignity to every life. By becoming a baby he identified with the poorest and weakest of humanity. Thus, the life of any child, but also the poor, disabled, oppressed or disadvantaged person—none of whom have less power than a baby—becomes significant to him and therefore should to us. Secondly, and of probably greater relevance for these studies, he determined to experience firsthand the trauma of life, especially that of childhood and the erratic events of family life. He had brothers who did not appreciate who he was and mocked him.[1] He was rejected, tortured and killed by the nation he considered his family. Jesus experienced the same range of emotions that you may have experienced in your own family.

We cannot imagine the depth of sacrifice necessary for the Lord of All to become a child, but a sacrifice it certainly was. Apart from the choice of a marriage partner, we have few options in our family experience. Jesus made his choice, not for marriage, but to become the child of a poor family. In doing so, he placed

[1] John 7:3–5

himself in the most vulnerable place of human experience, identifying with the weakest human state and becoming a victim of our fallen world. As a result, this same One, now exalted to the pinnacle of power, understands and provides strength and support to those who trust him in the uncertainties of earthly existence.

Thursday: Isaiah 11:1–9

In contrast to yesterday's reading, this passage takes us forward to the coming of Christ to earth a second time. This time he appears, not as a weak human being, but as the judge of all the earth. He will have all the human characteristics of compassion and justice and his judgment will be based on righteousness. In part, his mission will be to bring deliverance to children from the dangers that threaten them: children will be released from the fears of life, certainly from wild beasts, but by implication from other sources also.

It is within this perspective that we must view the suffering of our own children. While we often cannot reduce or dispel the pain of a child's suffering, we need to know it is of temporal duration. The Bible sees this life as a breath; our "days are like a fleeting shadow."[1] It is the stories of children killed or molested, those with incurable or terminal diseases and the vicarious pain the parents experience for their children that draw our heartstrings the tightest. But to forget the coming of the One who will bring final healing and justice to the earth is to live without hope.

It is a forceful reminder that no child suffers without Christ himself enduring their pain. As he suffered the barbs of childhood and later the pain of rejection and the shame of the cross, so he knows and records the suffering of children now and reserves judgment for those who inflict it.[2] We are reminded that his judgment is not based on hearsay or perception (verse 3) but by

---

[1] Psalm 144:4
[2] Matthew 18:6

the Spirit of knowledge based on truth. No one will be able to gainsay his judgments, "for the earth will be filled with the knowledge of the Lord as the waters cover the sea."

Friday: Jeremiah 1:4–10

We generally consider that two periods of life are the most vulnerable and the least productive. We have already discussed childhood; lack of strength and experience are a disadvantage when competing in the world. Certainly, we get this impression from Jeremiah as he responds to the call of God to prophesy to his people. You may recall Moses taking a similar approach when called by God to lead the people of Israel out of Egypt.[1] The approaches of both Moses and Jeremiah have the merit of humility. However, humility can be motivated by fear, resulting in a refusal to cooperate with God's call. On the other hand, a sense of inadequacy is essential if we are to recognize our dependence upon God and his ability to use us.

As Ann and I approach old age, it is tempting to revert to the excuse of childhood—that we now lack the strength needed to continue to work for God. That, of course, is tempered with a lifetime of experience that tempts us to think we have all the answers. It is critical for us to realize that knowledge—a simple library of facts—is useless without the wisdom to use it, and the source of wisdom is God: we are still dependent on him.

What Jeremiah, like us, failed to grasp was that strength and ability are not inherent in any age, particularly youth. Jeremiah denied his ability before he even had the job description. Perhaps he had an inkling of the life of persecution he would face as God's representative. He should have consulted Isaiah, who reminds us that: "Even youths grow tired and weary, and young men stumble and fall." But it is trust in God that provides strength for any task

---

[1] Exodus 3:11

he gives us, and that is available at any age.[1] No wonder Jesus taught us not to despise childhood.

Weekend ~ Maintaining Fidelity

Although women predators are in the minority, there is record of them in Scripture. The Bible frequently pictured the nation of Israel this way in her unfaithfulness to God, Proverbs speaks of the seductive adulteress[2] and we can recall Potiphar's wife.[3] But in the relationship between the sexes, men are generally the initiators to whom women respond. The continuing presence of prostitution is generally a response to the demands of men, not the desires of women. Men generally propose, and women—where women have this freedom—choose to accept or reject the proposal.

While this is true mainly of marriage, it is also true of most sexual encounters. Women's ability to say "no" becomes the final line of defence in a culture's morality. When the liberation of women to personal freedom leads them to instigate sexual encounters, the culture begins its descent into moral anarchy. You may allege that this places all the burden and blame on women for a society's moral stance, but in fact, men have the initial responsibility. Although Eve committed the first sin, Adam's acceptance and participation in it made him complicit. In an ironic reversal of fortunes, while men are responsible for entry into illicit sexuality, women become equally responsible when they consent to it.

This discussion of male and female infidelity reminds us of the partnership that God has provided. As a couple, both are in this together and neither is totally innocent or totally guilty. Each is a guardian of the other—in faith and fidelity. Jealousy is a tool given to us by God to rein in unfaithful partners. It is a natural and required response when a promise of faithfulness is broken,

---

[1] Isaiah 40:30-31
[2] Proverbs 5:3-6
[3] Genesis 39:6-12

as it expresses the pain of betrayal. God himself is a jealous God, requiring our continued commitment to him. It is our crucial service to God that we each protect our loyalty to the other and the devotion of each other to God.

Monday: Jeremiah 31:20

Following the reign of Solomon, Israel was split into two kingdoms: the northern kingdom, known as Israel, and the southern kingdom, called Judah. The southern kingdom comprised the tribe of Judah and eventually included Benjamin while the northern kingdom contained the remaining ten tribes of Israel. This was originally prophesied to Solomon, and also to his opponent Jeroboam, following Solomon's fall from faith.[1] At the time of Jeremiah's call, the people of the northern nation of Israel were in captivity in Assyria. It is clear from this passage that the people of Israel had realized that their sinfulness resulted in slavery in exile and they determined to repent of their sin.

We have alluded previously to the fact that God's relationship to his people is often likened to the relationship between parent and child, and this passage uses that comparison to show God's love for Israel, sometimes called Ephraim. The question arises: How can God claim love for his people when they are subjected to such privation? The answer is a long one, not in space but in time. For four hundred years, God time and again rebuked and chastised his people for their continuing sin, which often resulted in a behaviour change but rarely in lasting repentance. It is a story of escalating penalties culminating in their exile.

---

[1] 1 Kings 11:11–13; 34–36

I am reminded of the Cuban missile crisis, when Kruschev of the Soviet Union was planting nuclear missiles in Cuba and was opposed by President Kennedy of the United States. Kennedy's response was to raise the stakes for Kruschev in an incremental manner until Kruschev eventually backed down and removed the missiles. Similarly, punishment of our children should be matched not only to the severity of the behaviour that occasioned it but also to any escalating level of rebellion exhibited.

Tuesday: Jeremiah 31:31–37

Previous readings reminded us of our need to fulfill our covenant with God. This raises a question: What is *our* covenant with him? The reading today reminds Israel that God will eventually establish a New Covenant (New Testament) with Israel. The Old Covenant (Old Testament) had its limitations— primarily because Israel was unable to abide by its terms and so repeatedly lost the benefits of the covenant. The New Covenant would be written on their hearts, not on tablets of stone. It specifically speaks of a time when "they will all know me," a time when the knowledge of God would be universal.[1]

Clearly, much of this is still to come in the future, but the New Covenant was introduced by the coming of Jesus Christ and is already available, awaiting its full consummation at the return of Christ to earth. In the meantime, although the New Covenant is available to both Jews and Gentiles, this age has been provided for the Gentiles to enter the New Covenant, with the proviso that "all Israel will be saved" as they also finally participate in it.[2] God's commitment to his covenant toward Israel is guaranteed as long as his creation continues, stated unequivocally in verses 36 and 37, with no provisions required on Israel's part.

I am sure that making a similar level of commitment of love to our partners would be intimidating for most of us, even if our

---

[1] Isaiah 11:9
[2] Romans 11:25–29, referring back to this Jeremiah passage

desire is the same. But Israel's Lord is as faithful to us in our personal lives as he is toward Israel as a nation. We can bring that same God into our lives as we commit to trusting him, not only for our salvation, but also for his investment in our marriages to strengthen our ability to be faithful to our partners.

Wednesday: Jeremiah 32:1–15

Two of Ann's great-uncles lived in England just before the Second World War. They bought a row of cottages at a time when property values were at their lowest. Who would want to buy houses or property that might not be standing at the end of the war or valueless because of possible Nazi occupation? They picked them up for a song. As it happened, the cottages were still standing as the war ended—at a time when property values were at their highest. Housing shortages caused by bombing and lack of construction for five years had created a pent-up demand for property, especially houses. After some expense in upgrading the cottages, they sold them for enough money to retire on.

In our reading today, Jeremiah was faced with a similar dilemma—he was told to buy land when it was already occupied by the army that was besieging Jerusalem. It was worthless. The land was owned by Jeremiah's uncle, who wanted Jeremiah to buy it, perhaps thinking that the prophet was a little dense and would jump at the chance to buy it cheap. Jeremiah did buy it, but unlike his uncle and Ann's great-uncles, his interest was not in financial investment but to provide a practical illustration of God's promise that the exile was not permanent and God would bring Judah back to the land. "For this is what the LORD Almighty, the God of Israel says: Houses, fields and vineyards will again be bought in this land."

Whatever the outcome of any marital conflict we may be involved in, whether it results in break-up or reconciliation, our status with God will never change. Even during Israel's deserved exile, God remained their covenant Lord, committed to watching over them and eventually restoring them to the land and to himself. This is the same God that *we* worship and who keeps his covenant with us. The difficulties we face in relationships, often not of our own making, are temporary. The promise to us, as to Jeremiah, is that there will be a time of release. It may be in response to our prayers within this lifetime and certainly in an eternity with him.

Thursday: Ezekiel 16:1–14

The rather unsavoury passages for today and the next couple of days draw a distinct parallel between adultery and idolatry. These two words even sound similar, and there is a remarkable bond between the two in Scripture. Regularly in the Old Testament, as with this chapter, idolatry is considered a form of adultery against God, and in the New Testament the relationship between Jesus Christ and his church is seen as a marriage union.[1] Today's passage illustrates the mercy of God in rescuing the infant nation from its forbears and implies the establishment of Abraham as the original forebear of Israel, rescued from his pagan ancestors.

Later, when this despised one—as Israel is depicted—became marriageable, God became her husband and protector, lavishing his love upon her. This image is of the nation of Israel, born as a slave to Egypt, ill treated, persecuted until the Exodus and eventually under the reign of Solomon becoming a sovereign nation controlling her own destiny and at peace with her neighbours. For our purposes, the picture of the love of God for his bride is depicted in the love of a husband for his wife.

Some women reading this may justifiably bristle at the depiction of the infant Israel representing them—it hardly illustrates today's independent woman. Nevertheless, in much of the world's population women suffer exploitation by men rather than flourishing under men's protection. Thus, what is more to the point is the pattern shown by God's nurture of the weaker

---

[1] Matthew 22:1–2, Ephesians 5:22–27, Revelation 19:7–8

(and in this story, oppressed) sex to today's men, particularly husbands. The care and concern lavished by God on his selected bride demonstrates the nature of my part as a husband to ensure that my wife's independence and giftings are advanced for the benefit of the family and the community beyond.

Friday: Ezekiel 16:15–29

When I was a teenager, someone explained to me that every privilege carries a responsibility. The privileges afforded to Israel by God gave her the responsibility to respond wisely. But in today's reading, Israel is pictured as an unfaithful bride. She fell under the seductive power of affluence, which alone is insufficient to fill the longings in our hearts. It leads to boredom and a search for some form of entertainment to fill the void. This is the picture of Israel seen here: God has led her to a place of prosperity and she is now bored with him.

The charge of prostitution was not totally symbolic. The sexual activity of the Canaanite gods was believed to provide fertility to the earth, but they had to be encouraged and shown how. This was done by ritual prostitution within the religion, with prostitutes at shrines in public squares and streets. God charged Israel with participation that "degraded your beauty."[1] The charges of prostitution with the Egyptians, Assyrians and Babylonians was symbolic of military alliances sought for protection. Both the religious and military "prostitution" was a rejection of God's promise to provide fertile crops and protection from Israel's enemies.

Reading this chapter so far leads us to the philosophical question of whether fulfilling our responsibilities is right when it leads to a bad outcome. Would it not have been better for God to ignore the discarded baby if she eventually turned out so immoral? While the answer appears to be a rhetorical "yes," God

---

[1] Compare Judah's adultery with what he believed was a shrine prostitute, Genesis 38:21–22.

always allows freedom of choice, both in our response to him and within our earthly relationships. It reminds us that each partner, husband and wife, has equal responsibility—for him to discharge his duties to his wife and for her to respond faithfully to the advantages she receives. If earlier readings exposed the folly of male adultery, this passage is no less severe on women. As Israel's idolatry was a symbol of adultery against God and rejection of his promise, so women who seek fulfilment outside of marriage also deny God's faithfulness.

Weekend ~ Marriage Made in Heaven

It is a truism that we have to make the greatest choices in life when we are the least prepared for them. Surely, the best time to choose a marriage partner would be in old age, when life experience and wisdom would ensure the best decision—although even that could be suspect. But God did not create us this way, so how can we ensure our children and grandchildren make the right choices? We do not have the option of arranging marriages as some cultures do. But parents and grandparents can still be influential and provide guidance for later generations to achieve sustainable marriages.

Ann and I had three girls, and it wasn't until their later years that we began to think seriously about who they would marry. After a little experimentation, each girl brought home the one they had in mind to marry, and despite our lack of attention and prayer concerning these major decisions, God was very gracious to us and provided three special sons-in-law. But as our grandchildren were born, we felt constrained to pray for them. This was probably because they lived major distances away for the most part, and so we had less hands-on influence with them. Our prayers were that they would come into fellowship with God through accepting Jesus Christ as Saviour. But we also prayed for the ones they would marry, that those our grandchildren chose to marry would be God's provision. So we began to pray for those children also, although we did not know who they were.

To date, we have had the privilege of seeing two grandchildren marry and of welcoming into the family a terrific grandson-in-law and a beautiful granddaughter-in-law. It was a special joy for us to tell our granddaughter-in-law that we had been praying for her since her husband was born and then to hear her say that *her* grandfather had be praying for *our* grandson for the same length of time!

Monday: Ezekiel 16:30–42

Following the last passage, this reading shows us how Israel's increasing adultery led to loss of dignity. In fact, this outcome was similar to Israel's condition when God first found her. The process of her decline is paralleled to the decline of a prostitute as she gets older. No longer able to attract payment from her lovers, she must bribe them for favours and even, as depicted of Israel, pay others to obtain the fulfilment she still desires. Here is an allusion to the decline of Israel from the reign of Solomon, when Israel's influence was at its highest and other nations would want to make alliances with her— by the time of Ezekiel they had come to despise and exploit her.

The punishment described for Israel is only partly symbolic. The action of stripping her bare and naked is certainly suggestive of the pillage of the land by the Assyrians and Babylonians shortly after Ezekiel's writing. These armies invaded Israel and carried most of the inhabitants away into exile. But the destruction of the mounds and shrines is a real, no-nonsense description of the particular items that were the centre of Israel's disobedience.

Frequently, the result of immoral or addictive behaviour is not a punishment inflicted from outside. The decline and final defeat of Israel was an inevitable result of seeking solutions to her needs independent of God. The same is true in our lives; after failing to obtain enduring satisfaction, we frequently engage more deeply in the practice that has failed us. This is demonstrably true of dangerous drugs, which are themselves a representation of sin, and although less clear, it is also true in the practice of illicit sexuality. Until we find our fulfilment in God and the provision he has made for us, we will always be disappointed, however deeply we engage in independent pursuits.

For both men and women, there will be lasting satisfaction in a marriage where each is pre-eminently concerned for the other's welfare. Seeking to guard this relationship—however hard at times—can bring us unparalleled contentment. In the face of the large record of broken marriages, the vast numbers of couples portraying the truth of this passage attest to the wisdom of Scripture and the merit of following God's plan for the sexes.

Tuesday: Hosea 1:1–11; 3:1–3

From a Christian viewpoint, the story of Hosea and Gomer is surprising. Hosea is called by God to marry a prostitute. It is difficult to know from the story whether Gomer was a prostitute before Hosea married her or God just knew she would become one later. Either way, the story is an extraordinary tale of reconciliation under the most adverse circumstances. After she had borne Hosea's children, Gomer went into a life of prostitution, which led to her slavery. She became available in a slave market, and on condition of her restored faithfulness to him, Hosea purchased her back as his wife.

It is clear from the reading that this was an acted parable, frequent in prophetic writing. The behaviour of Hosea and Gomer reflected the relationship of God and his people, Israel. You will recall the passages in Ezekiel chapter 16 that told a similar story of Israel's unfaithfulness and God's determination to restore her to himself. Both of these stories were meant to remind Israel of God's enduring love that would not turn away from her.[1]

What is not so obvious is that our lives are also acted parables. As God's children, our lives tell others about God. Our

---

[1] Hosea 11:8–9

faithfulness reflects his; our unfaithfulness suggests we can't trust him. Faithfulness, especially reconciliation, reflects his love for us. But reconciliation is not the same as simple acceptance. Gomer was accepted back as she repented of and forsook her past life. It is the same with our relationship to God; his offer of forgiveness is available upon our repentance. But what especially characterizes the love of God is his fortitude to await that change. While some partners completely revoke their responsibility to a marriage, there is often opportunity to repair a relationship—but it requires patience, dedication and love for the other, and above all, a reliance on God, who has perfectly demonstrated these characteristics.

Wednesday: Hosea 11:1–11

Hosea prophesied to the northern nation of Israel (also called Ephraim), reminding them of the sinfulness that caused their exile and separation from God. Recall yesterday's poignant story of Hosea and his wife, Gomer, used as an illustration of the relationship between God and Israel. In this reading, the comparison is gone and the language is straightforward. In past readings we noted the severity of Israel's exile and the suffering it created. Today, we see God's love for his people in spite of their continuing waywardness. Particularly, he speaks of their "childhood" and his care and compassion for them after rescuing them from slavery in Egypt.

A recent news story related the abduction at gunpoint of a 23-year-old son of a millionaire in Vancouver. After the abduction, the parents appeared on television to plead for their son's safe return. Their distress was agonising and as difficult to watch as the many humanitarian agencies' depictions of the poverty of children in various parts of the world. Both of these pictures illustrate to some extent the heartbreak of God at his people's suffering, his yearning for their return to him and his promise of eventual restoration. He cannot treat them like Admah and

Zeboiim, the cities of the plain destroyed with Sodom and Gomorrah.[1]

While Israel is the son referred to in the phrase "out of Egypt I have called my son," the phrase is later used in relation to Jesus' return from Egypt after his parents fled there to avoid Herod's threats.[2] The love God had for his "son" Israel is the same as he displayed for his Son Jesus; the protection he accorded to the infant Jesus is the same as he provided for the emerging nation of Israel in Egypt. These examples indicate God's great care and concern for our children. We who are created in God's image can identify with the love that God has for the children that we are privileged to bear.

Thursday: Haggai 1:1–14

Probably the greatest source of friction in marriage is the use of money. Perhaps the wife likes to ensure a plentiful wardrobe and the husband has drinking and gambling buddies to help empty his pockets. The basic problem, even for frugal couples, is frequently insufficient funds to cover necessary expenses. Often, some alleviation of the problem can be gained by the advice of a good consultant. Certainly, we can all spend our money wisely and still have sufficient for some pleasure. A wise man once said that each of us is entitled to keep something of what we earn— indicating that a percentage should always be put aside.

While this passage can be used to suggest that Christians should provide a percentage of their income to support their local church, there is a more general application. Our spirituality may directly affect our ability to assure the provisions of life. The prophet Haggai made a direct connection between Israel's neglect of God's honour in their midst and their lack of prosperity. It may well be that the prosperity enjoyed by the Western world is a direct result of the Christian roots of that civilization, however

[1] Deuteronomy 29:23
[2] Matthew 2:14–15

erratic, meagre and poorly understood this faith has become. If this is so, then as God becomes increasingly irrelevant to Western culture, its prosperity will decline.

However, culture starts with the individual. How do we stack up to the need to honour God in our everyday life? How do we divide up our time and resources? Answering these questions may be the key to our personal prosperity and freedom from economic friction in our marriages. A happy home is a healthy home, and money is one area that may be eliminated from the dangers to marriage if we protect a God-honouring attitude.

Friday: Malachi 2:10–16

Adultery and divorce can never be undertaken lightly; adultery in the Old Testament required the death penalty, as did murder. In fact, sexual immorality has the power to destroy marriage in the same way as death, for it splits in two those who have become "one flesh." Our reading today infers that Jewish women were being divorced to make way for foreign wives, with the assertion that these divorces were violence against the Jewish wives. The idea that divorce is a form of violence, particularly against women, has profound implications. No wonder it provoked God's formidable statement, "I hate divorce," which puts into perspective the seriousness of divorce.

If this is true, why did the Law and Jesus provide for divorce?[1] Fortunately for us and for society as a whole, Jesus recognized that in our fallen state there would be occasions when marriage would fail—and for a variety of reasons. In Scripture, that failure was presumed to be a sexual violation of the marriage, and divorce could provide release from intolerable conditions. Thus, while the break-up of a marriage can be classified as a sin, it is sometimes unavoidable and certainly not the unforgivable sin.

---

[1] Deuteronomy 24:1–4; Matthew 5:32; 19:9. Note that Mark 10:11 and Luke 16:8 are abbreviated and do not include the exception clause; their concern is primarily with the permanence of marriage.

It is sobering to remind ourselves that most, if not all of us, have engaged in activity—sexual or otherwise—that could have broken our marriages. If, by God's grace, our marriage has remained intact, it does not make us less guilty than those whose marriages have failed. In this we are all in the same boat, equally needing God's forgiveness for the abuse of our marriages. Our reading encourages us: "guard yourself in your spirit, and do not break faith." Certainly this relates to breaking faith with our partners, but the wider implication is to not break faith with God. For if a Christian is unfaithful to a wife or husband, the example is a lie about God himself, for he is never unfaithful.

Weekend ~ For Us or For Him?

The Bible says little regarding marriage directly. As we consider marriage to be the cornerstone of society, this seems to be a strange omission. Today there is a thriving industry devoted to marriage and family guidance—even this book could be included in that—much of it inspired by Christian belief. But it seems out of all proportion to the extent it is treated in Scripture. For Christians, at least, perhaps the basis for maintaining marriage has been misplaced.

While there is little written specifically on the marriage relationship in Scripture, there is a great deal on interpersonal relationships, which in turn are based on the relationship between God and his people. Of even greater significance, our service to one another is considered in Scripture to be service to God himself.[1] Finally, our personal relationships are a witness to the faithfulness of God in his relationship to us, his people.[2]

However, it must be conceded that these ideas are strictly Christian. For someone with a totally secular outlook on life, the marriage relationship is based purely on what each partner needs or desires. On this level, love can do great things, but without an

---

[1] Matthew 25:40
[2] Ephesians 5:25, Philippians 2:5

outside referent only each individual's care for the other can be relied upon to continue the relationship. As our culture has moved away from its historical Christian roots—even worse, as Christians have adopted much of the culture's philosophy— marriage has become less secure. This is evident in the number of broken marriages, single family parents and displaced children. Marriages are a barometer of our cultural commitment to God. If we are serious about our Christian faith and its impact on life, we will lean less on interpersonal requirements and look more to our relationship with God to guide us in our commitment to one another.

Week Thirty-Eight

Monday: Matthew 1:18–25

Mary may have been filled with awe and wonder at her pregnancy, but it must have been a source of great anguish for Joseph. In their culture, to be engaged was equivalent to marriage but without the sexual union. Pregnancy out of wedlock was a source of great shame and stigma. Once Joseph was aware of it, he must have discussed it with Mary; only our imagination can discern the tenor of that meeting. Joseph was unhappy about the pregnancy, and initially he did not believe her story. After all, what she described was hardly a common occurrence.

However, for Mary, the situation must have been just as distressing, knowing her own innocence yet also knowing she would be under suspicion from everyone. Certainly her family and neighbours would have turned against her, but to be misunderstood by Joseph would have been the hardest to take, even if expected. But Joseph was a compassionate and devout man. Even though he could not accept her story at the outset, he wanted to provide the least grief for her and "divorce her quietly." Under the circumstances, God intervened, and Joseph learned the truth through his dream. Despite the possible scorn and stigma, he responded to the angel's instructions and stood by Mary.

A daughter's pregnancy is a common occurrence, and the questions are many: How will she cope with a child and no income? Will the father accept responsibility? How will the parents respond—with rejection or compassion? What will family and friends think? Is an abortion the answer? It is certainly a life-changing experience, but whether it will be for better or worse largely depends on the girl's parents. If their love for their daughter is greater than their fear for their reputation, they can steer her through the turbulent waters she has entered and eventually find great joy in the grandchild God has given.

Tuesday: Matthew 2:13–18

The concern over a pregnant child is natural, but it often overshadows the welfare of the unborn child. Herod saw the child Jesus as a threat to his throne, so he did all he could to destroy the newborn child. Again, it was God's intervention that saved the child's life. The worldwide tragedy today is that the young, even the unborn, are under immense threat from a variety of sources. In this story, Herod, in his attempt to destroy the Giver of Life, is the archetype of all who place young lives in jeopardy.

The threat to life is ubiquitous, from the parents, boyfriends and husbands of pregnant girls to systematic abortion by decree in nations like China and Western pressure for abortions in developing nations. Infanticide is widely practised in India and China, where daughters are considered a liability. Currently in northern Uganda, the young are forcefully conscripted into the "Lord's Resistance Army," a brutal rebellion that kills and maims at will, forcing children to commit these atrocious acts. In the West, the inconvenience of children is the major threat to the unborn, abortions numbering millions every year.

The trauma of an unwanted and inconvenient pregnancy is no excuse for taking the unborn child's life. Whatever the reason for the pregnancy, the life is still given by God. We may assume that sin is the cause of the pregnancy, but the child's life should not be sacrificed for the sin of the parents. As it is, there are often unintended consequences, beyond those imposed by family and society, that the unborn child may have to endure due to its inconvenient entry into a mother's womb.

Wednesday: Matthew 5:17–20

Too many people assume that the Old Testament in some way was superseded by the New Testament, and therefore, has no further relevance for Christians. Today's reading opposes that view, for Jesus indicated that the whole law remains in effect. Not only that, but the punishments associated with the law also continue in force. Throughout his earthly ministry Jesus never disallowed judgments under Moses' law, but he did question the right of accusers to impose them.[1] Further, of overriding importance, Jesus summarized the Law as loving God and loving one's neighbour—"All the Law and the Prophets hang on these two commandments."[2]

What is particularly severe is Jesus' exhortation to maintain a better standard of righteousness than the scribes and Pharisees. They lived lives that appeared to be above reproach and publicized their piety for all to see. But of all people, they received the greatest condemnation from Jesus. To put it into today's terms, they had a clean face on Sundays in front of others, but in secret, and certainly in their hearts, they were driven by less than honourable motives—in particular, to maintain status.[3] Thus, Jesus characterized them as hypocrites, clean on the outside but dirty within.[4]

Simply put, the Pharisees were playing games with their devotion to God. Unfortunately, we tend to do the same with our wives and husbands, often using poor attitudes or negative actions to manipulate our partners. A husband's anger and violence are not unusual in "Christian" families, yet that husband may project a calm and pious veneer to the world. If we are serious in our faith, we will wish to avoid God's wrath by admitting our games and ending our coercion of those closest to us.

---

[1] John 8:7
[2] Matthew 22:34–36
[3] Matthew 6:2, 5 and 16.
[4] Matthew 23:25–28

Thursday: Matthew 5:21–28

After his instruction to maintain a greater righteousness than the Pharisees, Jesus did not leave us without help. He gave us some examples of the Pharisees' idea of righteousness. They believed that simply complying with lists of laws was sufficient and other actions or attitudes were irrelevant. This led to contradictory results, which Jesus himself pointed out. Pharisees would dedicate money to God that should have been used to assist their parents[1] and ensured accurate tithing without considering the virtues necessary to serve God's people.[2]

Jesus extended the idea of sin to include intents of the heart, explaining that the commandments take account of actions leading to sin or attitudes revealing a desire to sin. While the Law clearly defined murder as killing an innocent party, he considered anger to be equal to murder; similarly, a lustful look at a woman measured the same as adultery. In each case, the sin had been committed already in the heart, whether or not the final action was carried out. If someone had been defrauded, Jesus required repayment to the victim before the victim sued. This involved a change of heart, recognizing the wrong done in order to motivate repayment.

It is easy to consider these requirements unattainable, and if nothing else, they serve to underline the sinfulness of our hearts, making us more reliant on God's grace toward us. As we have received God's grace, we should also give it, for our partners battle the same sinful hearts that we do. But of greater significance is the fact that we need to take responsibility and be prepared to deal with anger, lust and other negative attitudes that precede sinful acts. In so doing, we take a pre-emptive strike against potential sinful situations. Then we are less likely to become entangled in those situations that jeopardize our marriage relationships.

---

[1] Mark 7:10-12
[2] Matthew 23:23–24

Friday: Matthew 5:29–37

In our church there was a lady who was addicted to drugs but had a soft heart towards God. She was aware of the verses we read today and continually threatened to cut off her hands. She was sufficiently unstable at times that we feared she might actually do it. We remonstrated with her on the basis that there are few one-handed Christians around, that most understand the passage as exaggeration to make a point. For instance, we know many people who claimed to "work their fingers to the bone," but few show physical symptoms of it. She would follow our reasoning for a while and then simply go back to square one and state she was going to cut her hands off. Fortunately, to our knowledge she never did.

The great third-century theologian Origen took this passage more literally, castrating himself to eliminate sexual temptation. Certainly, the passage speaks to strictly avoiding situations or practices that may cause us to fall into sexual sin. Wandering eyes are a major cause of divorce, as desire for someone else breeds dissatisfaction with a current wife or husband. Jesus was hard on divorce, recognizing only sexual uncleanness as grounds for it, probably on the basis that the marriage bond has been broken. Apart from this, the marriage is still valid, the divorce void and subsequent marriages adulterous—all a result of lax discipline.

Jesus summarizes these instructions with the advice not to make an oath before God. After all, an oath is only necessary if our normal commitments are not trustworthy, and there is the added danger of invoking God's wrath on us if we break it. His concern is that we keep the promises we make, for in so doing we reflect the image of God, who keeps his promises to us. Following the passages on avoiding sexual temptation and divorce, maintaining our promises to our partners is of primary importance in maintaining those relationships.

Weekend ~ Peace

The name Absalom means "father of peace," and he clearly failed to live up to the hope that David had for him. The earth sorely needs those who can bring peace to a world that has known conflict since the beginning. We know that a final peace will elude the world until the coming of the "Prince of Peace," but how do we find peace amid the current conflicts of life?

Firstly, the world will always have war as long as individuals cannot find peace with their neighbours. While watching the many peace marches worldwide—and even agreeing with their desire—I often wonder if those marching are at peace with their friends and family. It is the height of hypocrisy to berate the leaders of the world for failure to achieve peace when the complainers are at loggerheads with legitimate authorities, adjacent neighbours or family members.

Secondly, those who cannot find harmony with people around them are generally not at peace with themselves. Conflict with others is usually a result of conflict within oneself, internal anger, dissatisfaction, turmoil or resentment that is frequently displaced and directed at others. But how can we find that often elusive peace for ourselves?

Finally, the Bible teaches that the source of peace is outside of ourselves; we can have peace within when we have peace with God. Although the coming of the Prince of Peace will finally bring peace on earth, Jesus has already offered peace with God by his sacrifice on the cross for our sin. We can trust God with the inequities of life that cause conflict—even our own guilt. The knowledge that our status is settled forever gives us an inner peace that we can share with others.

Week Thirty-Nine

Monday: Matthew 5:38–48

How does a Christian live a meaningful life in a fractious marriage? How do you cope with a relationship that has deteriorated into an uneasy co-existence where attempts at communication are more like defending against an enemy rather than communing with a friend? When the Bible says we are to love our enemies—particularly: "If someone strikes you on the right cheek, turn to him the other also"—how does this work out in practice? Does today's reading suggest that we should submit to just any injustice?

Jesus' teaching is best understood by how he responded to his enemies. While on trial, Jesus made sure the record was set straight. He asked for legitimate witnesses and requested just treatment.[1] He made clear statements confirming the truth about himself, based his final exoneration outside of earthly courts[2] and set Pilate straight on the limits of Pilate's authority.[3] Jesus faced his martyrdom with resolution, not resignation. He was silent "as a sheep before her shearers," exhibiting no anger, resentment or revenge, but rather, showing compassion towards his persecutors by praying that they would be forgiven.[4]

---

[1] John 18:20–23
[2] John 18:36–37, see also Matthew 26:64
[3] John 19:11
[4] Luke 23:34

Love for a partner in a broken relationship especially means praying for them as Jesus prayed for his tormentors. It is not possible to pray for someone without loving them, and if we pray in love, we will pray for them as we would pray for ourselves. If prayer is an expression of love, it also increases our love and, consequently, our ability to weather the storm.

But true love is not sentiment but service. Jesus upheld social and moral laws while under oppression. John Stott, in his book on the Sermon on the Mount entitled *Christian Counter-Culture,*[1] gives an example. "If my house is burgled one night and I catch the thief, it may well be my duty to sit him down and give him something to eat and drink, while at the same time telephoning the police." Sitting quietly under abusive and violent behaviour only enables that conduct. If we care for our partner, we will use all the resources at our disposal to bring him or her to acceptable behaviour and reconciliation—and it may mean a partner needs to face concerted intervention or even the requirements of the law for offensive activity.

Tuesday: Matthew 7:13–23

The initial understanding of this passage is the rejection by Jesus Christ of those who have first rejected him by following self-destructive paths or falsely represented him for their own advancement. This may seem reasonable if we view it as a judge convicting the wrong-doer, but suddenly it seems so much more tragic when we conceive of him rejecting his own children by creation. If his love for his creation is as strong as we have previously noted, this cannot be anything but the greatest heartbreak for God. But for parents, it should be encouraging to know that even God, as a perfect parent, did not raise perfect children.

---

[1] John R W. Stott, *Christian Counter Culture: the Message of the Sermon on the Mount* (Downers Grove, IL: Intervarsity Press, 1978), 112.

How often have you beaten yourself up as a parent for the behaviour of your children? We tend to do this whenever we recognize ourselves as imperfect parents, losing patience or making errors of judgment in the raising of our children. Most parents regret something in their handling of the childhood years. While we—as opposed to God—may foster some legitimate guilt, we must realize that our children often make their own decisions, irrespective of our desire for them to make different, better decisions.

But even our mistakes are not completely lost. A child with "perfect" parents would never learn at an early age to face difficulties that later life will present. When our two girls were small, we couldn't afford the heating we would have liked in our home and Ann walked them in the winter air to avoid lighting a fire too early. But the girls were robust and healthy. By comparison, two boys of similar age living in a centrally heated house two doors away were continually weak and sickly, unable to cope with their natural environment. If childhood is in some way preparation for adulthood, then they will learn from our mistakes. Further, if we avoid cosseting and over protecting them, they will be better prepared for hazards in later life.

Wednesday: Matthew 8:5–13

At first glance, it may seem that this passage has little to do with families; however, it reveals an important fact about authority. The centurion clearly perceived that his authority was not inherent in himself. He could only command because he was under the authority of the army he served; he merely wielded that greater authority. Paul elaborates on the same issue, explaining that all earthly authorities are God ordained. To disobey those authorities risks the judgement of God.[1] This does not give them free rein to act as they please, though. They will also be judged according to their record of furthering God's will on earth.

---

[1] Romans 13:1–5

A mother was explaining to her small daughter that God wanted her to act a certain way, and then gave her a specific command. The child, defiant, retorted that her mother was not God. Her mother replied: "I am God to you." The mother had grasped the principle that all authority is derived; we do not wield our own. In that sense she was God to her child as long as she fulfilled God's desire for the child. The centurion realized that Jesus had the Father's full authority behind him just as the centurion represented the authority of the Roman Army. That was the basis of the centurion's faith.

This should give us caution as well as encouragement in the raising of our children—caution that we cannot exploit the authority given to us. To exceed that authority may harm our children and bring us reprisals. But we can be encouraged that we have God's authority to steer our children in the right path as long as we fulfill God's desire for us and our families. As we do, we know that course will be the most likely to invoke God's blessing on them and the future generations to come.

Thursday: Matthew 9:14–17

We have seen how the Old Testament portrayed God's relationship with Israel as a marriage, and Israel's idolatry was reckoned as adultery against God. Jesus uses similar imagery in the New Testament, portraying himself as a bridegroom to his people. But there is a stark contrast between the Husband of the Old Testament and the Bridegroom of the New Testament. Under the Old Covenant, Israel was continually in danger of losing fellowship with God and reaping the consequences of disobedience. But under the New Covenant, the Bridegroom is the one who has already paid the price of infidelity and to be with him is a time for rejoicing, not fasting.

The difference is not just a matter of adding the new ideas to the old. The new is incompatible with the old. To patch the old garment with the new material will tear the old, and similarly, the new wine poured into the old wineskins will burst them. Jesus' coming exploded the old relationship so it could be replaced by the new. This did not mean that the basis of the relationship changed. In both, God loved his people and provided for them according to his character, which *doesn't* change. However, the New Covenant that God has made with his people is one that is free from the fear of failure.

God sets high standards for us and we should expect the same of others. But this does not mean that failure to live up to these standards is cause for rejection. In the same way that Jesus took our failure upon himself and in so doing gave us freedom to fail, so we are able to take our partner's failures without always expecting some form of atonement from them. Of course, in practice this applies generally to minor irritants, not necessarily to major injustices. To simply rearrange the dishwasher our partner loaded haphazardly into a more efficient manner is a form of sacrifice, as opposed to complaining and expecting some form of penance. This can be repeated a dozen times day for a hundred other infractions of our personal codes, letting that spirit of grace and forgiveness give us joy in living with each other.

Friday: Matthew 10:16–25

The persecution of Christians has been an ongoing atrocity since the time of Christ. As he was maligned and crucified, to a large extent, his followers have also been mistreated simply for believing in him. This persecution is not only from outside. The church has also had its own program of martyring "heretics" who held differing views on secondary issues of the faith. The greater tragedy is the splitting of families over the issues of faith as predicted in this passage—in particular, the willingness for parents to put their children to death and vice versa.

A local church in our hometown had a pastor whose daughter befriended a non-Christian man. The pastor decided her "sin" meant that she should be cut off from her family and shunned by all in the congregation. The girl eventually married her choice and the separation from her father was then complete. As far as I know, the father never talked to his daughter again—although by all accounts she had a good marriage—and the church split over the issue and eventually folded. God in Christ had extended his saving grace and forgiveness to the father and practising that same grace toward his daughter might have had far better results.

Conflict between Christian parents and their children is often based on differences of faith. Like the example above, it is not always the children who are entirely to blame. A child's rebellion against the guidelines of faith demands careful insight on part of the parents towards themselves as well as their child. Certainly, it is necessary to extend any discipline required during the early years. But our ongoing attitude to our children as they enter adult life should be a grace of acceptance despite their waywardness, as God granted to us before we returned to him.

Weekend ~ Faith or Works?

Some of this week's devotionals must have raised questions about acceptance by God as a result of obedience—especially the value of that obedience under persecution. The foremost tenet of the Christian faith since its inception has been that faith in God is the means of salvation and reconciliation with him. Yet Israel was continually encouraged to obey the laws given by Moses, particularly the Ten Commandments, which formed the basis of all Old Testament laws. There are a couple things that illustrate faith as the real governing factor, both for Israel and in our relationship with God.

Firstly, if keeping Old Testament laws was necessary for Israel's safety within the covenant, their existence was very precarious, as none of the Israelites could keep them completely. In fact, the sacrificial system was instituted for Israel to provide absolution and forgiveness for sins they committed. Thus, the Israelites' safety was not in keeping the law, which eventually only condemned them,[1] but in believing that God accepted their

---

[1] Romans 7:9

sacrifices as atonement for breaking the law. It was faith in that promise that saved them. You may recall that it was Abraham's faith that God counted as righteousness.[1]

Secondly, actions betray belief. While what we do cannot save us, our actions are evidence of what we really believe—that is, evidence of the faith that saves us. Jesus said, "If you love me, keep my commands."[2] Jesus clearly considered that our actions confirm our love for him. Our children may say they love us, but we judge their claim by their actions toward us. James takes up a parallel idea when he says: "Show me your faith without deeds, and I will show you my faith by what I do."[3] Our claim to believe in God's promise cannot be sustained if we act in a way that is contrary to that belief.

---

[1] Genesis 15:6
[2] John 14:15
[3] James 2:18

Monday: Matthew 11:20–30

Parents have reason to be confused regarding the rearing of children. A billboard recently had a picture of a baby with the caption, "It doesn't come with instructions." Add to that the plethora of advice by "experts" and the bewilderment deepens. The Bible does not place its wisdom on "the wise and learned" but suggests that it has been given to "little children." The message here is that knowledge about the life-giving God is given to "those to whom the Son chooses to reveal Him." It is not some lofty secret to be imparted by a cadre of specialists.

Jesus raises the issue, common in Scripture, of understanding spiritual things. First, understanding of the message that Jesus brought is by revelation, not the result of investigation alone—he has "revealed them to little children." This doesn't mean that only children can understand, but rather that the humility and acceptance practised by young children is the key to understanding. An approach to Jesus based simply on human analytical study will fail to unlock his message, for his message is spiritually discerned.[1] It is acceptance of Jesus Christ at face value that gives spiritual insight and understanding.

It is those who are willing to accept him in this way that Jesus calls to himself, not just to live in fellowship with him but also to find rest in him. It may seem strange that rest is found by being

---

[1] 1 Corinthians 2:9–16

"yoked" to him, indicating that the rest he offers is in work. But being "yoked" means partnership; he takes the heavier part of the work, for "my burden is light." It has been the experience of God's people through the centuries that retreating into him is a place of quietness and rest, a place to unburden and renew strength from him. If you are living in difficult circumstances, this is your inheritance.

Tuesday: Matthew 13:11–17

The heading for today's reading could be: "there's none as blind as those who won't see!" This passage picks up the theme from yesterday's reading that the understanding of spiritual things comes through revelation. Jesus updates the quote from Isaiah's prophecy, where Isaiah is called to speak to a people that will not listen.[1] There are a number of reasons why people won't listen. For many, the gospel message is too simple, even infantile, and they feel it is an insufficient response to a complex world. Its simplicity offends their intellect, which is better served arguing against the gospel in complex terms. For others, the gospel interferes with their desires in life, so they devise arguments against it to bolster their unbelief.

Of course, underlying these evasions—for all of us—is sin. Our sinful nature distorts the real truth about life—even about our own sinfulness. This creates a downward spiral where sinfulness and flawed understanding feed off each other, leading us further from the truth. Those who are seduced from the truth this way are "ever seeing but not perceiving" because their "heart has become calloused." It has even been suggested that some do not want to find the truth because they enjoy the search too much. All of which leaves us with the burning question: How can anyone find God?

As we saw previously, Jesus taught that the understanding of spiritual things was a gift of revelation from God; the Holy Spirit came to convict men and women of their sinfulness and need of

---

[1] Isaiah. 6:8–10

him.[1] Knowing that conversion is the work of God and not our responsibility can bring a great sense of relief. We are in partnership with God to bring the gospel to those God has given to us; we will endeavour to live as Christ, but it is the Holy Spirit that convicts of the truth. If you are in a difficult marital relationship, it is God who can reveal the truth to your partner, and prayer becomes your greatest resource.

Wednesday: Matthew 15:21–28

This may seem like a "run of the mill" story about another healing by Jesus. However, each story has been included for a reason, usually to illustrate something of significance because each healing is different. There are many similar stories not recorded.[2] So what is the significance of this story? There are a number of items that stand out. Jesus initially refused to answer the woman, evidently because she was not Jewish. Was this plain old racial discrimination—especially when he suggested her race was equivalent to dogs?

This woman was persistent and innovative. Perhaps Jesus knew this and responded in a way that drew her out. He may have even enjoyed the brief repartee they engaged in. His initial indifference could not eventually hide his compassion, and in the end the woman's daughter was healed. But the main point of the story is that this woman was an unlikely candidate for Jesus' care. She was outside of the people he was sent to: "the lost sheep of Israel." Even his disciples didn't think she was worthy of attention. So there are two lessons to be drawn from this story.

Firstly, Jesus was illustrating that Gentiles were not outside his care; in fact, as the gospel unfolds in Scripture, it is evident that the blessing of Abraham was to *all* peoples.[3] Those of us outside the Jewish race are recipients of that promise. Secondly,

---

[1] John 16:7–11
[2] John 20:30
[3] Acts 3:25

Jesus' compassion reaches beyond ourselves to those *we* might consider not worthy. Families are his concern, many of whom struggle outside the faith. Are we as willing to engage hurting fathers, mothers and children outside of our faith as Jesus was?

Thursday: Matthew 18:1–7

We have already noted that wisdom is not necessarily to be found in those instilled with human wisdom, but rather, in the heavenly wisdom that is available to all who ask for it. Today's reading views the quality of humility as another asset in the resources of the spiritual person. Jesus compares the humility of children, who naturally defer to their immediate adults, with those who are greatest in the kingdom of heaven. With some exceptions, children are generally content to live an enjoyable life unbothered by ambition for fame or grandeur.

It seems in this context that humility is not to play the "doormat"—as is so often suggested—but to fulfill God's requirements in our life without wanting or receiving accolades that we think should be forthcoming. Jesus is explicit that the desire for public recognition is opposed to spiritual maturity. In fact, those who desire earthly recognition receive their reward in this life; it is those who work for him behind the scenes that will receive God's reward.[1] That is not to say that we should shun public recognition—we all need encouragement at times—but it should not be our motivating force or goal.

We spend a lot of time teaching our children and ensuring what we teach is right, but we spend too little time learning from them. Their qualities of innocence, humility and trust endear them to us, for these are the qualities that we need in relating to our heavenly Father. Those who exhibit these qualities that are the greatest in the kingdom of heaven.

---

[1] Matthew 6:1–6

Friday: Matthew 19:1–12

The first chapters of Genesis describe the creation ideal for the basic human relationship. While a family may be made up of various groupings, the Bible defines marriage between a man and a woman. Marriage is established as a procreative setting,[1] and as such, other unions are to be excluded. But the sexes were also designed for companionship, for it was "not good for man to be alone."[2] After showing Adam all the animals, none was found suitable—that is, similar to Adam—so Eve, made like him, was brought to Adam as his companion.[3] Jesus quotes liberally from the Genesis passages, endorsing the message and therein restating the "one flesh" principle.

The relationship between man and wife is closer than their relationships with their original families. The attraction is so strong it is sufficient to break the bond with parents—to "leave" one and "cleave" to the other as the King James Version of the Bible states. Jesus reminds his listeners that they "become one flesh" to the same degree that Adam and Eve were made from the same piece of clay. This highlights not only the strength of the marriage bond but the pain associated with marriage break-up. In this sense, divorce can be compared to abortion. It is more natural for the unborn child to remain in the womb until birth than to be torn from it. So it is more natural for married partners to remain together than to be torn apart.

In this passage Jesus also recognized singleness as a viable option. There is no reason for singles to be considered as "loose halves." Paul saw a spiritual advantage for those whose energies are not split between family and God's service.[4] In this way he supported singleness without denigrating the family. However, if God has placed us in a family, our service to him is to serve them. Therefore, it is illogical to consider that family is secondary to our

---

[1] Genesis 1:28
[2] Genesis 2:18
[3] Genesis 2:20–24
[4] 1 Corinthians 7:32–35

service to God; this idea has led on occasion to the neglect of family for so-called "ministry." Don't fall into the trap of letting either your family or outside ministry dominate the other.

Weekend ~ He was Ready

A friend of ours, Brad, died recently, leaving a wife and two children. He had lived a precarious life due to sickness, and living until his fifties was a miracle. He had been near death several times earlier in life but had survived long enough to witness the answer to his prayer that he might live long enough to see his children become adults. Brad lived a full and fulfilling life, both in the community and for his family. He worked most of his life in the city building department, and city hall practically emptied out the day of his funeral. His strong faith in God gave him courage to live with his sickness and to face uncertainty with serenity.

Brad, probably spurred by his sickness, continually invested himself in his family, ensuring his home was secure and a place of peace and comfort for its members. He was certainly ready to go when the call came. His wife, a registered nurse, supported him in his infirmity and through numerous medical operations. Together they accomplished what neither could do apart: they established a place of refuge during the distressing times of life, recognising God's grace and affirmation in their lives and marriage.

The story of Brad's last days is an illustration of his entire life. He had come to a place where critical heart surgery was necessary—he couldn't now live meaningfully without it, but he might lose his life through it. He retrieved all his belongings and trophies from his work and finalised all the outstanding matters on his desk at home. He wrote to his church, expressing his gratitude for their support during his sickness, and wrote to his family, thanking them for their love and reaffirming his love for them. He stated his confidence in God for both life and death, for himself and his family. He bought new furniture and appliances for the home so that the succeeding years would be trouble free.

Finally, he emptied his personal bank account, giving his wife the cheque on the day of the operation that took his life. He was ready.

Week Forty-One

Monday: Matthew 19:13–14

What we have read earlier helps us understand Jesus' rebuke of his disciples when they considered him too busy to respond to children. In this story he repeats the basic concept that the nature of children is the quality that gives easier entrance to the kingdom of heaven. But he not only used them as examples, he also cared for them. Before he continued with his work he blessed them. The pictures of children surrounding him, sitting on his knee, seated or standing around him in fascination ring true, as does his enjoyment of children.

His assessment of their qualities also made him angry at their mistreatment. It is not possible to see the suffering of children widely disseminated in the media without a real sense of the judgment awaiting the perpetrators. But it is parents who abuse their children who bear the greatest culpability. Our children are not really "ours"; they are lent to us for a time for our enjoyment. But they are also placed in our care during their vulnerable period, for which we will be held accountable. As we are stewards, not owners, of what we "possess," so we are stewards of the young lives growing in our homes.

While this may seem somewhat daunting, it is comforting to know that the mistakes we make will not be held against us. Children are very adaptable; they rarely hold against us the errors we may occasionally make and can be very forgiving as we admit our mistakes to them. Providing our desire for our children is right, and if we get it right most of the time, they will probably be just fine. And it is comforting to know that when we acknowledge and confess our mistakes, our Saviour covers them with his blood.

Tuesday: Matthew 20:17–28

It is not unreasonable for parents to want the best for their children, but it is often sought at the expense of others. The mother of James and John sought special status for her two sons, obviously at the expense of the other disciples. It is clear that her sons were also complicit in the request and the other disciples were indignantly aware of it. The danger of conflict in this case was only part of the problem. Jesus' first response was that they didn't know what they were asking. So the question arises, what made their request one that had an answer they would not expect?

Jesus had already expressed to his disciples that he would shortly be condemned and crucified, and later in his explanation he indicated that his death was one of service to mankind. This was the "cup" he was to "drink"—one of suffering for the sake of others—one that the disciples themselves would eventually share with him. It was unlikely that James and John understood this. If they wanted to share the places of honour with him it would be because their service with him would accord them the lowest social status.

Perhaps the most well-documented cases of this type of favouritism today are the frequent instances of hockey parents using abusive language and violence at hockey rinks when their children get less than their parents' desire for them. They are following the pattern described by Jesus "that the rulers of the Gentiles lord it over [others]" and unwittingly push their children first in this life. But as Jesus said concerning the next life, "many who are first will be last, and many who are last will be first"[1] This

---

[1] Matthew 19:30

does not legitimise humiliation or deny fairness, but it reminds us and our children that the aim of Christian life is service, not status.

Wednesday: Matthew 21:14–16

Children can often be more perceptive than adults, probably because they are not contaminated with the scepticism that life and living brings to us. This appears to have been the case in this passage: the children saw Jesus healing and simply made four by putting two and two together, as it were. To them, he was obviously the heralded Son of David. The chief priests and teachers, who had far more resources and reason to recognize Jesus' real identity, failed to do so. In fact, they vehemently denied the children's claims for Jesus.

Jesus not only recognized the perceptiveness of the children around him, his response showed that it was God's plan to use children to reveal himself. They would be the ones who would recognize and proclaim the true identity of Jesus to the world. Possibly these children were the ones who had stirred up the populace to welcome Jesus into Jerusalem earlier in the day as he rode into the city on that first Palm Sunday.[1]

It has been said, "Give me a child up to the age of six, and I will have him for life." This acknowledges that what a person learns in childhood is likely to stay with him or her throughout life. Children can understand their relationship to God very early, our youngest daughter making her lifetime commitment to God at the age of three. She needed to rethink her understanding as she approached adulthood, and for some children this is a time to question and possibly even reject their childhood conception of faith. But the reality of the childhood experience remains strong, and many recognize the truth of their faith as they see it anew through adult eyes.

---

[1] Matthew 21:8–11

Thursday: Matthew 21:28–32

In some ways this story has a parallel with the two sons in the parable of the prodigal son. Here are two sons with opposite responses to their father's wishes. The defiant one eventually changed his mind and obeyed his father; the other agreed to his father's wishes but then failed to obey. Jesus explained the basic lesson of this parable by pointing out that the religious leaders of his day failed to fulfill God's desires even while sinners repented and found acceptance into his kingdom.

However, from the different responses of the two sons we can glean insights here into the behaviour of all people, but the second response is certainly the most frustrating. Children frequently give a positive response to a parent's command but through laziness or distractions end up not complying. Dealing with this type of deceptive behaviour is difficult, for the disobedient attitude is harder to establish and resolve. Outright defiance is simple animal behaviour, but deception is a greater fault, for it is a sin of reason—God's gift peculiar to humankind deliberately used to mislead.

A child that lies tacitly admits wrong behaviour and guilt and is using reason to avoid discipline and obstruct the resolution of any injustice. By wilfully failing to carry out an agreed task, a child is mindfully testing a parent's resolve to have the child complete the task. Without compulsion to obey, a pattern of deception—saying one thing and doing another—may be set, one that may earn the Pharisee's reputation abhorred by Jesus. Setting a time limit—even letting the child do so—provides a measurable method of ensuring compliance and will help to discourage similar behaviour in the future.

Friday: Matthew 22:23–33

In today's reading, the Sadducees were wrong on two counts: not believing in life beyond death and in sarcastically postulating marriage beyond death. Jesus responded to their main argument—against resurrection—by showing that the patriarchs, Abraham, Isaac and Jacob must be alive, for God "is not the God of the dead but of the living." The assurance that God's people will survive death has been the solid hope of Christians through the ages, assuring them that those who have gone before will be there to meet us, especially our Saviour, who will be there to greet us in person. But Jesus also corrected their imaginative view of heaven by stating that there would be no marriage in heaven— men and women "would be like the angels in heaven."

It may come as a shock or disappointment that there is no marriage in heaven. For those of us that have had happy marriages on earth, there is a natural hope that the relationship will continue. But even our marriage vows indicate that marriage and the fidelity it demands ends at death. In addition to marriage, there are a host of loved ones that have gone on before us with whom we hope to be reunited. That there will be a reunion is clear in Scripture, which is why we do not "grieve like the rest of men, who have no hope."[1] The reunions will be real, but the relationships will be different because we will be different, and the final union will be with Jesus Christ, whose bride we will be.

We firmly believe that all things of value will survive this life. Does that mean that because the marriage union does not continue into heaven it has less meaning now? There are some who would deny marriage because its earthbound condition appears to lack spiritual roots.[2] But even though the earthly institution of marriage may not survive, there are eternal values and results that will, and these are frequently established through our marriages. These will form the basis of the church's marriage to the Lamb.

---

[1] 1 Thessalonians 4:13–14

[2] 1 Timothy 4:1–5

Weekend ~ Idealism or Realism

Idealism is a feature of youth but realism is a growing understanding gained later in life. Idealism sees "what should be done" while realism perceives "what can be done." These two viewpoints are often the basis for disputes between the generations, the older and "wiser" having the experience to know the setbacks and pitfalls for any project. On this basis, logic says that the older ideas should prevail. But realism often degenerates into "what can't be done." However, all the reasons why something can't be done often require only one reason why it can.

Children and youths see everything through fresh eyes, including methods and ideas not anticipated or available to their elders. They have the advantage of not being restricted by systems and processes gradually adopted by the older and traditional generation, and they are more able to "think outside the box." Prior to the 1851 Festival of Britain in London, a competition was held to determine the design of the main building. Although many architects presented designs, the winning project was a huge steel and glass building (later known as the Crystal Palace) designed by a gardener familiar with greenhouses. He wasn't inhibited by the standard building techniques of his day, and his design was the forerunner of the many later steel and glass buildings.

I am always amazed at the occasional news reports of children who have pioneered a fund collection or humanitarian project, often with remarkable results. It is somewhat humiliating to see children doing what I would probably fail at. It is on these occasions that I note how the child's idealism has been channelled into workable solutions. Rather than recount why a child's idea cannot be done, enable them to think through their own ideas of how problems can be overcome. We may be amazed at what their idealism can accomplish.

Week Forty-Two

Monday: Matthew 22:34–40

You may recall that Jeremiah forecast a time when the Law would be written on hearts, not on stone.[1] Paul understood the meaning of Jeremiah's words when he talked of the New Covenant and reminded us that the letter of the Law kills. The Law only showed us our sin; it could not save us. It is the Spirit of God placing us into the salvation offered in Jesus Christ that transforms the Law into a life-giving reality[2]—love fulfills the Law.[3] Paul did not work this out by himself; today's reading shows that Jesus was the first to place the Law into the context of Love.

Jesus taught that to love God with heart, soul, mind and strength and to love our neighbour as we love ourselves—both quotes from the Old Testament[4]—are the supreme commandments. Today's reading also records Jesus saying that the two commandments to love God and love our neighbour summarize all the Law and the Prophets. Reviewing the Ten Commandments,[5] we note that the first four are about our relationship to God, and the remaining six are about our relationship to our neighbour. These commandments simply tell

---

[1] Jeremiah 31:33
[2] 2 Corinthians 3:6
[3] Romans 13:10
[4] Deuteronomy 6:4–5; Leviticus 19:18
[5] Exodus 20:1–17

us how we will relate to God and our neighbour if we love them. Or put another way, if we love our neighbours, we will not kill them, commit adultery against them or steal from them.

This has far-reaching consequences, for it means we have great flexibility in fulfilling the Law. Jesus completed the Law for us— both by keeping it and dying for our failure to do so. We no longer obey the Law out of fear but in the grace of God's forgiveness, freeing us to love from the heart and not by the letter. Our marriage partners are our neighbours. As we live in the freedom of God's grace and forgiveness, we can love them from the heart, covering them with *our* grace and forgiveness. Their mistakes and faults in trying to love are covered by the blood of Christ just as ours are.

Tuesday: Matthew 23:33–39; 24:1–2

We probably consider that Jesus, being God incarnate, would have had a great many advantages over us. One attribute that we may consider to his advantage was his knowledge of the future. However, a thoughtful reading of today's Scripture should convince us that this may have been a distinct disadvantage. John spelled it out simply in the opening words of his gospel: "though the world was made by him, the world did not recognize Him. He came unto His own, but His own did not receive Him."[1] Jesus knew in advance that the city he loved and cared for would reject him and would shortly be destroyed.

But it was not just the rejection that distressed him, it was also the future that they were bringing upon themselves. He knew the desolation that would come to Jerusalem: it would be sacked by the Roman army and the city's inhabitants scattered to the four winds some forty years later. He describes in chapter 24 the destruction of the temple that would accompany that attack. Today, nearly two thousand years later, only the temple platform

---

[1] John 1:10–11

remains of the original temple—apart from the Muslim Dome of the Rock built later and the Wailing Wall that supports it.

The parent-child relationship that Scripture often uses to illustrate God's relationship to his people is used again here. If Jesus can mourn over the condition of his defiant people, Israel, he can clearly identify with parents of rebellious children. You may have sons or daughters who have cut themselves off from you to seek precarious lives on their own. You not only mourn the rejection and loss of intimacy with your children but you are also painfully aware of the outcome of their poorly chosen lifestyles. Jesus, who has travelled this pathway, feels your pain as you travel this rugged journey with him.

Wednesday: Matthew 24:42–51

There are really two parables in today's reading; one refers to securing the house, the other to maintaining readiness. These two parables are related in their encouragement to ensure that the house is not only secure from outside threat but also protected from failure within. While these stories refer to our readiness for the return of Jesus Christ to earth, there is the timeless truth that we need to be ready for him to take us through death. This not only means that we must be reconciled to him, as critical as that is, but also that all our affairs need to be in order, particularly as the day can come at the most unexpected time. Some may be keenly aware of the possibility of dying because of lingering sickness or other threatening tragedy, but for many of us it is a distant and dormant prospect.

The first parable illustrates the necessity of providing a secure place for our family. Security for a house means locking doors and windows and setting the alarm system. Security for a marriage partner is founded on trust in the faithfulness of the other. It requires that living and working arrangements are set up to reduce the possibility of infidelity and that clear alarms are voiced when risk is apparent.

Even so, securing a home is pointless if there is a threat within it. The second parable describes a large home with servants, probably more than most of us may ever expect. But we do have a great deal of influence over the members of our household, particularly the happiness of our partner. Love makes the lover vulnerable; it places us at the mercy of those we love and gives us power over those who love us. We will be answerable to God—as well as our own conscience—for how we use that power within the household. We can use it to serve and bring happiness to our partner and children and reduce the threat from within, or we can use it for our own self-interest, producing a resentful and rebellious home. If we love our family as we love ourselves, we will endeavour to provide them with all that they need, particularly a sense of security in an insecure world.

Thursday: Matthew 25:14–30

It is important to guard the home and fulfill our responsibility to it, but this parable suggests that this alone is insufficient. The steward with one talent guarded that talent well and produced it intact, but he still fell short of the master's expectations. To care for our families is of vital importance, yet it may still fall short of God's requirements of us. You may ask what more can we be answerable for if we ensure that our partners and children have the protection and provision they need. Surely this is an expression of our love for them? It may *not* be—it is possible to provide these from duty or even compliance to a court order. Love goes beyond what is required; it also seeks to invest in the growth of family, not just in numbers or years but in the growth of each individual's potential through direction, encouragement and purpose for life.

Primarily, this means ensuring they understand that the foundation for life is their personal relationship to God—understanding the need for and accepting the freedom of forgiveness in Christ. But while that is essential, it is following through with that commitment that provides fulfilment in living.

Does your partner have unfulfilled potential that could enhance not only his or her life but also the lives of others—children, family and friends?

We may be left with a sense of inadequacy and failure when we see the tremendous gains for God's kingdom that other individuals are able to achieve. Yet it is the fulfilling of God's will for us as individuals that is the greatest accomplishment, no matter how limited it may seem. None of the stewards in our story were given the same responsibility; only results that were in proportion to their talents were expected. Even the steward with one talent would have been accepted if he had banked the money and provided the interest. If we are married, our primary responsibility before God is not only the wellbeing of our partners and family but also that we invest in the talents God has given them—at least to ensure that their potential is not hindered and God's investment returns interest.

Friday: Matthew 27:19–25

The last verse of our reading today must be one of the most heartrending cries in world history. Despite Pilate's insistence of Jesus' innocence and his request for an indictable charge, the crowd, incited by the Jewish leaders, simply cried for Jesus' blood. On Pilate's warning that the crowd would be responsible for Jesus' death, they willingly took the blame, but in an arrogant and heartless undertaking, they called judgment down on their children too.

A generation in Scripture is forty years, and it seems no accident that the destruction of Jerusalem and the exile of the Jews from Israel for the next 1900 years took place in 70 AD, forty years after Jesus was crucified. The action of the crowd confirms the old adage, "Be careful what you ask for, you might get it." In this case, it could be argued that they spoke in ignorance, not really knowing the One they wanted crucified and being goaded on by their leaders. But ignorance was no excuse; any unfounded accusation and sentence, especially of this cruelty, is subject to justice for the victim.

There is a parallel here: today's generation has largely denied the claims of Christ, and the attendant tragedy is that their scepticism may be passed on to their children with disastrous consequences. Whereas today's parents may not be calling directly for Jesus' death, their rejection of any claim he may have upon their lives is the same as that which instigated his crucifixion. We may have gentler ways of casting him aside, but encouraging our children to reject him is to call judgment down on them.

Weekend ~ Justice

Any good justice system, like any good table, is built on four legs. Firstly, retribution: a debt to be paid, a punishment or penalty. Secondly, restitution: damage to be repaired. Thirdly, rehabilitation: behaviour to be changed or correction to be applied; and finally, deterrence: a warning to others. All these attributes of justice are promoted by Scripture, but our present society only recognises the last two, pays lip service to the second and abhors the first. Punishment is characterised as vindictive and vengeful and generally considered inappropriate. The title of the Canadian prison service, "Corrections Canada," identifies its primary focus.

Yet all sports identify penalty as a necessary part of the game, even though our culture refuses to apply it to life. Offences against the rules of society produce a debt to society that requires repayment. The Bible sees sin—that which produces real guilt—as a debt against God, a wrong for which a penalty must atone. This idea is fundamental to biblical thinking and essential to the Christian faith. Our guilt incurred a debt to God that was dealt with at the cross, the meeting-place of justice and mercy.

The fact that our penalty has been paid at the cross does not absolve us of our debts to society; those that we incur still have to be repaid. Nor does loving our neighbour mean letting a thief who invades our home go free. Our responsibility is to see that he receives the justice he deserves and the help he needs. It is also our responsible care for our neighbour that ensures *their* protection from the thief. Yet we may also forgive the thief and absorb the loss ourselves at times, practising both justice and mercy. Thus, in practical ways we can teach our children how the justice and mercy of God has been extended to us, so they may also understand what God has done for them.

Week Forty-Three

Monday: Mark 5:22–43

As we have noted previously, Jesus not only used children as an example of the simplicity necessary to enter the kingdom of heaven but he also genuinely cared for them. Further, his care extended to families, showing compassion for the parents of children and the pain they endured when their children suffered. This is illustrated in the story of Jairus and his daughter. It should be noted that Jairus was a synagogue leader; he may even have been the type of Jewish leader that Jesus continually reproached. Yet Christ's consideration went beyond concern for their poor theology. Jesus practised what the Pharisees failed to: he had compassion for people.

The unusual part of this story is the distraction Jesus encountered on his way to see Jairus' daughter. Surely he should have made a dying child a first priority and dealt with the sick woman later. In fact, it was while he was engaged in the healing of the woman that the child died. We know that he eventually raised the girl to life, but the fact remains that children still die despite our prayers for their healing. The greatest mistake we can make is to conclude that he does not care.

What is more unexpected is the little time Jesus had for those who came to mourn. It was a practice to employ mourners to wail and cry on behalf of the bereaved, although the mourners probably had little sympathy themselves. It is a reminder that today many who attend funerals have little in common with the one who has passed on and their brief words of sympathy fade during the lonely days that follow. In contrast, Jesus drove out the mourners and spent time with the parents and child in their distress, raising the child to life and ensuring her welfare. He remains with us in our times of grief when the presence of others wanes.

Tuesday: Mark 9:42; 10:13–16

Internet pornography hosts pedophilia sites, including some devoted to incest. The proliferation of these sites across the globe means that they are easily available in countries where the practices are illegal. News reports constantly document cases of men with computers full of pictures of children in sexual poses. These children are obviously trained in adult preferences or may be sexual slaves in some countries. The violation of children in this way offends even the most liberal mind but is still being actively pursued by its practitioners as a legitimate sexual orientation.

The idea of freedom to practice pedophilia may appear preposterous to us, but the practice of pedophilia has a history of legitimacy in various cultures. Liberalization of cultural mores within minorities is a standard way of introduction into society, especially if construed as a religious rite. As arguments in favour of liberalizing homosexuality by activists have carried the day, similar arguments for freedom of sexual expression for pedophiles may be hard for future liberal-minded governments and courts to deny. Even assuming this does not occur, the free dissemination of pedophiliac material can only break down the moral defences in individuals, providing a false sense of legitimacy and widening its practice. This puts all children at increasing risk, beyond those frequently reported in the media.

Pornography is insidious, posing as harmless entertainment when it is actually addictive and destructive. Pedophilia especially rejects the scriptural injunctions in today's reading to protect children from harm. Pedophiles may argue that their practices do not harm children because they are exhibiting a loving relationship. But this is clearly at odds with the results of pedophilia in residential schools in Canada. Your marriage and children are at risk as long as pornography has free reign to infect your intimacy. Pornography may aid sexual arousal and excitement, but it is too easy to become addicted, leading to loss of sexuality without it. Permanent sexual joy is built on personal intimacy in all areas of companionship and not sexual arousal alone.

Wednesday: Mark 12:18–34

I believe in love at first sight. I have to—I fell for my wife, Ann, at our first meeting. From then on I lived in a twilight world without her and a dizzy disorienting daze when with her. The whole universe took its hue from her absence or presence, and concentration on anything else became laborious and half-hearted. It was probably necessary that those times evolved into something more practical or else life would have become virtually impossible.

Strangely, the Bible rarely talks of love like this in passages dealing with marriage—perhaps only "husbands, love your wives."[1] But even here, there is not the sense of physical attraction. Rather, love is revealed as a form of service, feeding and caring for our wives as we do for ourselves.[2] Our reading today also raises the idea of loving oneself as a means of gauging our love for a neighbour. This is frequently cited as a command to love ourselves before we can love others. Loving oneself is then interpreted as having good self-esteem, liking and valuing ourselves, perhaps verging on narcissism but necessary in order to love others the same way.

This interpretation is perhaps understandable in a society that constantly psychoanalyses itself. But loving ourselves more likely

---

[1] Ephesians 5:25
[2] Ephesians 5:28–29

refers to far more practical things. It is simply caring for ourselves, ensuring we have sufficient food, clothing and shelter. This we do almost automatically, before any thoughts of self-esteem or personal dignity. The latter are important, but Jesus' priority was for the physical well-being of our neighbour—don't talk to him of self-esteem if he is hungry or cold. Jesus drew a parallel point regarding tithes. They are important, but they are hypocritical without the priorities of justice, mercy and faithfulness.[1] When the Bible tells us to love our wives, that is what it means.

Thursday: Luke 2:8–20

As we have alluded to previously, the trauma of an unwanted or inconvenient pregnancy eventually gives way to rejoicing over the birth of the child and then years of pleasure watching the child develop. Today's reading is the ultimate example of this; the heavenly angels themselves rejoiced over the birth of the Saviour. Perhaps the birth of your child does not herald the same fortune for humankind, but the birth of every child is a potential joy to the parents and a benefit to the world.

God brings no one into this world by chance. Each of us is a unique creation of God. He loves us, cares about us, and wants us to know him as he knows us. God is able to use every life to benefit the world and to make his great plan known to each generation. But how that child responds to God's call to follow him instead of wasting the life he has given is their choice to make, not ours to assume or terminate for personal reasons.

However, in some cases individuals believe it would have been better not to have been born. Both Job[2] and Jeremiah[3] felt that way that during times of personal distress, yet their lives had a resounding value in promoting the knowledge of God in perilous times. During the ordeal of navigating through the problems that

---

[1] Matthew 23:23
[2] Job 3:1–26
[3] Jeremiah 20:14–18

an unwanted pregnancy entails, never lose sight of the joy that awaits the arrival of the baby and the potential that child may have for the gospel and the world.

Friday: Luke 2:21–24, 39–40

Following the birth of Jesus, Joseph and Mary fulfilled the requirements of the Old Testament law by having Jesus circumcised and redeeming him with the sacrifice required for the firstborn. The consecration of the firstborn was a sign to remember that the firstborn of Israel were spared when the destroying angel killed the firstborn of the Egyptians.[1] These acts showed not only Mary's and Joseph's devotion to God but also ensured that Jesus was included within the covenant God had made with the Israelites.[2] It was an act of faith in the promises of God.

Most Christians either have their children baptised, common in liturgical churches, or dedicated to God, mostly in the non-conformist traditions. Either way, there is a desire on the part of parents to bring their children into the family of God for his oversight or direction of the children's lives, similar to that of Joseph and Mary and others of their time. Child baptism or "sprinkling" parallels the Jewish rite of circumcision to bring the child into the New Covenant, which he or she confirms later at a ceremony of "confirmation." Children who are "dedicated" at birth confirm their parents' desire for them later in baptism by immersion.

If we believe that God answers prayer, then we will follow through on these procedures as a way of seeking God's intervention in the lives of our children. The last two verses of our reading indicate not only Joseph and Mary's fulfilment of the Law's requirements but also the growth of Jesus in wisdom and the grace of God. We can be reasonably certain that Jesus, knowing his destiny, would grow in this way. However, his parents' role at birth

---

[1] Exodus 13:1
[2] Genesis 17:9–14

for *him* underlines the importance of placing *our* children in God's care, especially as their destiny is far less certain.

Weekend ~ Some Limits in Raising Children

These limits are not a string of don'ts to be avoided, but rather, certainties not available to us. Unless we have a clear understanding that there are some expectations that are outside our control, we set ourselves up for disillusionment and frustration.

Firstly, there are no formulas for raising children. Certainly there are guidelines, but no two children are the same, so they require different handling. What our oldest child took as a warning, our second accepted as a challenge. This meant that even experience was a limited asset. Our third—the ultimate strong-willed child—was different again. That strong will would be invaluable when well directed in later life and needed to be moulded, not broken.

Secondly, we have no final control over our children. Of course, in the earliest years we have some control, but in the end we can only influence our children. We are not creators, making others into our own image; each child has their own God-given personality and decision-making ability. This is true from early childhood on, and increasing independence only lessens our power over them. In fact, good parenting will prepare them to channel their independence into constructive and creative endeavours.

Finally, there is no guarantee that our children will turn out the way we desire. We are all aware of children from good families that turn out badly and vice versa. Perhaps our biggest mistake is in planning to bring up good children. As we have seen, this is outside of our capability. What we can do is plan to be good parents, praying for God's wisdom and direction for us in these uncharted waters, for his call upon their lives at an early age and for his guidance in their major choices in life.

Week Forty-Four

Monday: Luke 2:41–52

There is nothing recorded in Scripture about Jesus' growing up years except this one passage. We have to assume that Jesus did not go through the rebellious "teens," but today's reading does suggest that his parents had their times of frustration, caused mainly by their limited understanding of his role on earth. It is easy to consider Jesus thoughtless for his lack of sensitivity to his parents' worry for him, and Mary minced no words in expressing this—after all, he was missing for three days! One wonders how he ate and slept during that time, although his debating the teachers of his day probably comes as no surprise.

What is surprising is the fact that his parents left Jerusalem without him, assuming he was in the company of their friends. This may be partly explained by the culture of the day and the intermingling of travelling companions. I always found it hard to accept their leaving without him until the day Ann and I left church without our four-year-old daughter. We had driven halfway home before we realized she was missing. On returning to the church, we found her happily in the company of friends, probably unaware that we had left. Being a gregarious type, she felt as comfortable in their company as in ours.

Our experience reminded us that we all make mistakes with our children, often inadvertently or under stress. The experience of Mary and Joseph underlines the fact that our mistakes may also be a lack of understanding of our children's grasp of events and feelings during their childhood and teen years. Although discipline is a necessary ingredient in forming a child's character, it is not a substitute for empathy with their evolving situation and needs.

Tuesday: Luke 6:46–49

This parable is often misused, suggesting that faith in Christ is the foundation for building a secure life. But hearing, even believing, the message that Christ came to bring does not constitute a sufficient foundation for life. It is the person who "puts them into practice" who mimics the man that built on the rock. It is action, not just knowledge or belief, which is the basis of security in life. Certainly, practice is an outcome of faith, but practical experience also reinforces faith. It is easy to accept Jesus Christ but not really change our lives until some adversity hits us. However, strength for the troubled times is gained from practical experience in the easier times. It is important that we set a firm foundation for life at its beginning, not at some later time when difficulty arises.

This is especially true of marriage. It is doubtful that the needs of an enduring marriage and family are in the forefront of a couple's thoughts when engaged to be married. It is the "heady time" it should be, but it should also be a time of commitment for both to place faith in Christ. Additionally, a pledge to put his Word into practice in their life together will lay a foundation upon which they can build their marriage, family and even old age together. Further, putting the words of Christ into practice also means letting the whole Bible be the guide for life, just as Jesus himself regularly quoted the Old Testament to support his teaching.

But Jesus not only gave sound advice, he also gave warning of the consequences of not acting upon his instruction. A house built on sand may last for a long while because it is the absence of the storm, not the foundation, that maintains the house. Many marriages based on the wrong values may seem secure and may endure for a time, but they may not stand the attack of adversity. Certainly, adversity will bring reflection and even a possible recognition of God's claims upon us, but it may mean starting from scratch, learning anew how to sustain a marriage—even building a new foundation.

Wednesday: Luke 7:11–17

The raising of Jairus' daughter is not the only record of Jesus raising the dead. It could be contended that Jairus' daughter was not actually dead—Jesus himself suggested she was only sleeping. But today's story proves his power over death, Scripture clearly stating that the son was dead. In this case, Jesus' concern for the mother is also clearly recorded: "His heart went out to her and He said, 'Don't cry.'" He again raises a child—in this case somewhat older than Jairus' daughter—in order to end the grief of the mother.

In a church that we pastored, a young couple had several children and expected another. Early in the pregnancy, the child was diagnosed with no brain, only a brain stem, and the couple were advised to have an abortion. Their faith made this option unacceptable for them, although it would have reduced the heartache they knew would come. The child, a daughter, was born to them and I had the privilege of being in the hospital room as they nursed her for the few hours that she lived. At the funeral, the young father carried the tiny coffin down the church aisle, weeping as he came.

God loved this helpless child and took her to be with him, letting her stay with her parents for that brief time, although she would remain in their hearts for life. Our reading today emphasises the compassion that Jesus had for this lad's mother, illustrating for us the compassion God has for all bereaved parents. How could it be otherwise? God knows firsthand what it is to see his own Son die—worse still, to die a cruel and ignominious death at the hands of evil men.

Thursday: Luke 14:25–33

The standards in this reading that Jesus requires from those who would follow him appear to challenge the need for cohesive and loving families. It has been the contention of our writing that God is intimately concerned with families and to require hatred of them as a stipulation for discipleship, as stated in today's passage, is against his nature. Attempts to reconcile the conflict from today's reading generally elicit two responses. Either the conditions are unattainable for the average person and refer to exceptional calls of God, or they are an exaggeration to make the point that we all need to have clear priorities.

There is probably truth to both viewpoints. In places where it is dangerous to propagate the Christian faith, a parent may court death or imprisonment and possibly leave the family neglected as a result of God's call. Children may follow God's call to foreign, even hazardous lands, and lose regular contact with their family. The cause may not be *hatred* of family but a priority to follow Christ in these ways, which risks great heartache for them.

Life does not require extreme sacrifices for the majority of Christians in the Western world. Nonetheless, while love for our families is evidence of our love for God, it cannot supplant it. In setting family priorities, we need to ensure that God's desire for our lives is placed before our own, particularly when differences in belief within a family may promote different goals for life. Not only is this fulfilling the command to "hate" our families, but Jesus promised that God will provide alternate "families" to replace the ones we may lose for the kingdom, both in this life and for eternity.[1]

Friday: Luke 15:11–24

This parable of the prodigal son is probably one of the best known stories of Jesus. The stupidity and rebellion of the son

---

[1] Luke 18:29–30

are contrasted with the love and acceptance of his father. This story illustrates the love of God for his stray children. But the comparison to an earthly father also illustrates the strength of love a natural father has for his child and shows the sense of belonging that the son retained despite his foolish and divisive behaviour. For all fathers of stray children, the connection is rarely totally lost; a desire for reconciliation lurks in the subconscious of every child.

What is probably most instructive in this story is the father's willingness to let the son go. He freely gave the son his share of the inheritance, possibly knowing the dissolute use to which it would be put. There is a time in every child's early life when we have the ability to control and influence. But the hard time comes when the child reaches the age of independence as a fully fledged human being capable of making his or her own choices. How do we react then? Can we respect their choices even when we disagree? Even more, are we prepared to receive and support them upon their desire to leave a destructive lifestyle?

Perhaps there is wisdom in giving freedom to a child who opposes parental advice, remaining open to receive that child again later when, of his or her own volition, they return. After all, that is the way God has dealt with us, maintaining both his requirements of us and his love for us. He will leave us to our own devices as long as we want to live our own way, but he is amazingly willing to receive us upon our repentance.

Weekend ~ Growing a Teenager

The growth of children into adolescents is a voyage into uncharted waters for both child and parent. But the best protection for the teen years is training from the earliest years. If a child has not learned respect for a parent, it is less likely he or she will heed instructions as a teen. Respect has to be earned, and it is established in two ways. First, a child must develop a confidence in consistent and equitable treatment of both failures and successes—sanctions   when   guidelines   are   flouted   and encouragement when they are met or exceeded—and secondly, this treatment must always come with genuine respect towards the child.

But respect is also taught by instilling obedience to authority during childhood. A child who can disobey or manipulate his or her parents with little impunity will carry that attitude into the teen years and adulthood with potentially disastrous consequences. This does not mean that as an adult he or she should obey all authority regardless, but rather, that authority will be obeyed even if it becomes necessary to dispute the directive with thoughtful respect.

Obedience is not generated because you love the child, even if the child knows it. It is because the child loves you that he or she will obey.[1] It is a false notion that discipline will undermine a child's love for his or her parent. Certainly, abuse of any sort will distance a child from a parent, but a child feels safe and is happier within secure boundaries. It is more likely that love for parents by children who continually get their own way will be undermined by contempt for parents, and they will develop the practice of setting their own boundaries. Weak and vacillating parents will leave a teen uncertain of their counsel and result in his or her experimenting with alternatives.

If this sounds like you need to be a perfect parent, take heart. Children have an amazing capacity for adaptability and forgiveness, especially if we are honest with them. It should encourage us to know that we need to get it right most, not all, of the time to maintain a bond that lasts.

---

[1] John 14:15

Week Forty-Five

Monday: Luke 15:25–32

Of course, the story of the prodigal son is really the story of two sons and a prodigal father. Prodigality is the opposite of frugality, simply meaning extravagance, which may be wasteful or generous. In the generous sense, the father was prodigal with his love for the wayward son. In contrast, the older son had very little of the extravagant love his father had for his brother and himself. His attitude toward his younger brother is probably the more natural human response—why should a waster be given so much welcome and the devoted son apparently ignored?

This problem of sibling rivalry fed on false perceptions. The older son sensed unfairness in the celebration of his brother's return home and it fostered his jealousy. Really, he had little to be jealous about. His inheritance was now everything his father owned, the younger having had his share. His father recognized the older son's loyalty; he had his father's favour. The younger son was entitled to nothing save what the father graciously provided him. They both shared equally in their father's love. What more could the older brother desire?

Sibling rivalry is a constant in all families; from the youngest age particularly, children squabble constantly. Because children are different, they often need to be treated differently, but this can be misconstrued by a child as *better* treatment even though they are dealt with fairly. To help a child understand that they are being treated fairly, although perhaps differently, may help to head off some jealousy. In the story before us, the father took similar pains to mollify his elder son's anger, noting that in this case, because of the younger son's actions in frittering away his inheritance, the older brother was actually far better off.

Tuesday: Luke 20:20–26

The image of Caesar stamped on Roman coins reminds me of the image of God created in humankind. This has far-reaching relevance to life, particularly family life, yet Scripture gives little indication how that image of God shows itself in us. We can take some educated guesses. We are certainly creative like he is; the character of God shows dimly through our fallen condition. Perhaps self-knowledge and understanding reflect him as well.

As we found in earlier readings, Adam and Eve's joint responsibility over the earth was also a reflection of the image of God. This shows in us by how we care for those things given to us. We do not own those things; they are lent to us for the duration of our lives and we cannot take them with us. Thus, we are only stewards of all that we possess, responsible to God for our use and treatment of them. This applies supremely to the people for whom we have responsibility, especially our families, and we will be held accountable for the way we have served or used them.

Jesus, upon hearing his opponents affirm that it was Caesar's image stamped on the coins of the day, identified the coins as belonging to Caesar. In the same way, the image of God within men and women signifies his ownership of each human being. "My" wife, husband and children are not "mine," they are his, bearing his stamp upon them. As Adam and Eve were responsible for tending the Garden of Eden, so we are responsible for caring for those God has placed in our care. If we fail to care for our families, we risk an impaired relationship with God by rejecting his image in them. This may reduce our ability to care for them, leading to a downward spiral. This worrisome scenario should encourage us to be vigilant of our treatment of those closest to us.

Wednesday: John 1:9–13

We have referred to this reading previously, noting that Jesus was rejected by his own people, which parallels how many youths reject their parents in today's Western culture. There comes a time when children evaluate their parents in the light of their maturing understanding. It comes as a shock to the children to find that parents are flawed individuals and not the final authority on everything they had assumed as a youngster. For the most part, children retain their attachment to their parents, perhaps with a few bumps along the way as they pass through puberty.

But there is a significant minority that reject their parents, despite the parents' best efforts. Many of you reading this will have been through such an experience, and it is indeed a heart-wrenching rollercoaster ride of hope and despair for which entreaties and prayers appear to be unanswered. You hesitate to open the door on arriving home from work, fearful of what new trouble may have transpired that day; every ring of the phone brings a new jolt of apprehension or you are exhausted by living in a state of daily tension.

Recall that Jesus still walks the same road himself; his deity does not soften the despair he feels over those who reject his call. The greatest comfort for parents is found in seeking him to walk with us on the road he knows so well, developing the sense of the presence of God on an ongoing basis. Prayer is the key, for it is natural to pray under stress and to silently call on him in moments of crisis. But also pray for reconciliation with your child. Our reading reminds us that many accepted Christ and became his children, and his joy at their response can also be yours when a child returns.

Thursday: John 4:9–30

The woman in this story had several things against her. First, she was a woman. At that time women did not have the status that Jesus gave to them and the disciples were surprised that he was even talking with her. She was also a Samaritan, a member of the impure race that the Jews despised, so she was surprised that he made a request of her. But worst of all, she had a disreputable background, having been through five marriages and now living common-law with a man—and Jesus knew about it. Yet all these factors did not prevent Jesus from seeking to draw her into his kingdom.

She could not help being a Samaritan or a woman, but her lifestyle was largely a result of her choices, and thus, her responsibility. Jesus did not gloss over these facts; he clearly expressed them to her. His attitude toward her was one of care and respect, and her response was joy that overflowed to others. In fact, in her excitement she brought others to meet him who in turn invited him to stay with them. The record states that many believed on Jesus because of the woman's testimony; still other Samaritans believed on Jesus as they listened to his words.

Race, sex and colour are no bar to receiving Christ. His approach to the despised Samaritans made this clear. In the same way our lifestyle, which may be largely of our choosing, is also no barrier. You may have been involved in life experiences that you now regret and feel that this prejudices your chances of a stable future. But becoming acceptable in Christ is not just receiving his forgiveness. Jesus Christ gives us a new life, for "if anyone is in Christ, he is a new creation; the old has gone, the new has come"[1] Your desire for a stable relationship, possibly marriage and family, can come alive as you commit yourself to him and his care for you.

Friday: John 4:43–54

John is very sparse with his report of miracles, recording only six or seven in his gospel. He called them "signs," recording those that had special significance in revealing the true identity of Jesus Christ. This miracle, like many others, has characteristics that make it unique. He often dealt with people of status as this man

---

[1] 2 Corinthians 5:17

was, a royal official, although in this case Jesus began by rebuking the man, finally healing the man's son from a distance.

Jesus' attitude to the miracles he performed was ambiguous. He refused to perform miracles just to prove his identity. He was no travelling showman.[1] Yet he suggested on one occasion, when accused by the Jews of blasphemy for claiming to be God, that if they could not accept his words they should at least believe on him because of his miracles.[2] The Samaritans in our last meditation showed that belief was prompted by both Jesus' words and his prior knowledge of the Samaritan woman's status.[3] Thus, John saw Jesus' miracles as confirmation of his deity, although it was his words that were the primary source for belief.

But despite John's claim that miracles were signs of Jesus' deity, we have also seen that they were performed out of compassion for the bereaved. He clearly wanted this official to understand that the basis of belief was not the miracle he was about to do for the official's son: "Unless you people see signs and wonders . . . you will never believe." Despite this rebuke, the man continued his entreaty and Jesus caringly responded to his request. As a result of the healing of the official's son, "he and his household believed." Because we generally consider we have life under control when all is going well, it is usually adversity that wakes us up to our need for God. It is far better to seek God's direction for our lives at all times than to wait for family dilemmas to drive us to seek him and believe on him.

Weekend ~ Provoked Parents

At times it seems that the blessing children are claimed to be is replaced by the trials they incite to cultivate our patience. No circumstances in life can bring more turmoil to our emotions than our children. But the range of emotions we feel changes as our

---

[1] Matthew 16:1–4
[2] John 10:31–38
[3] John 4:39–42

children move into the teen years. Our earlier frustrations with them turn to fear for them, and earlier anger toward them turns to mistrust and suspicion. Our ability to assert ourselves gives way to inadequacy as the control we once had lessens. While we were able to be emotionally detached in directing our small children, teens evoke a greater emotional response.

We have high expectations for our children. But in the early teen years those expectations can appear to be disappointed. At that age many youths consider themselves to be adults and able to make adult decisions, exhibiting a confident folly stereotypical of the years between childhood and adult maturity.

At the same time, our limitations begin to show as we discover we don't have all the answers and find ourselves with an empty authority. We may discover our lack of communication skills—particularly active listening—and find that we have previously not really heard *and* understood.

The teen years will find the weak spots in our marriages. Marriage conflict is a prime source of insecurity in teens, and they are old enough to try to find that security elsewhere. Parents should have their acts together after at least a dozen years of child raising, and during this time of greatest stress they must also learn to operate together, giving no opportunity for a child to divide and conquer. Scripture's picture of the Trinity is our guide—to offend one is to offend all.

Monday: John 9:1–23

This passage raises the question of the lengths that parents are willing to go to support their children. These parents had grave difficulties with a son blind from birth. Apart from the obvious problem of providing for a son who would normally have helped to support them, they probably had to bear the taunts of those who assumed that the blind son was punishment for some sin of theirs. And the healing of their son by Jesus only added to their woes.

The son was feisty enough to stand up for himself; he didn't really need his parents, but the Pharisees' need to establish the son's identity drew them in. The son had a personal experience with Jesus and so decided that he no longer needed the approval of the Pharisees. But his parents were still dependent on the synagogue for acceptance, so their answers were non-committal so as to avoid disgrace in the community. Thus, the son was left to defend himself and was eventually thrown out of the synagogue.

There is often a fine line between recognizing a child's unacceptable public behaviour and maintaining support for him or her as a person. Some scold their children in public, leaving the child isolated. Others will deny the child's responsibility, tacitly condoning the behaviour. Still others may virtually disown the child as these parents did, leaving the child to defend himself or herself. But something like: "Son, let's go home and work this out together," may provide support and dignity for the child while still leaving the appropriateness of the behaviour to be dealt with. How would you normally respond?

Tuesday: John 11:17–37

The home of Mary, Martha and Lazarus was a place of rest and recuperation for Jesus, and they were certainly a family that had his compassion. Even so, he was pointedly questioned about failing to heal Lazarus before he died. Both Martha and Mary accused Jesus of the same thing: "Lord, if you had been here, my brother would not have died." Some voiced the thoughts of many: "could not He who opened the eyes of the blind man kept this man from dying?" Certainly, if Jesus had healed Lazarus before he died rather than bringing him back to life after, he would have saved the sisters much misery.

This raises the age old question of why God does things the way he does when we can see no reason for it. At least in this case we have some explanation. Jesus indicated that this event was to glorify him.[1] Jesus' response to Martha clarified it further: he proclaimed himself as "the resurrection and the life" and raised Lazarus as proof he could back up his claim. It reminds us that God's primary purpose is that his "will be done on earth as it is in heaven."[2] As we are part of this process, we may experience situations that we cannot understand, like Martha and Mary, but unlike them, receive no explanation.

The answer that God has his reasons for our distress may add to our stoicism, but it is rather cold comfort. Of greater reassurance is the fact that Jesus is the resurrection and the life and he can breathe new life into seemingly dead situations. Hope for the future is what the Christian faith is all about; it is as we trust him that we begin to understand God's plan and see him working in our lives and that of our families. But it is at the resurrection to our final destiny that all things will become clear

---

[1] John 11:4
[2] Matthew 6:10

and be restored. For what we see and understand now is temporary; it is the unseen that is eternal.[1]

Wednesday: John 14:15–24

We have noted previously that the Bible refers to physical love very infrequently when talking about marriage. This may seem like a strange omission, especially when the Bible is a book about love—God's love for us. Perhaps one reason we consider this strange is our misconception of love, relegating it primarily to a "feeling" word. We are all aware that the feeling is not permanent, so what happens when the feeling is gone?

There are several Greek words used to describe love: *Eros* refers to sexual attraction or desire, often pictured as the small angelic being with a bow and arrow. *Philos* deals with the love between friends and family, hence Philadelphia is called the city of brotherly love. Both of these concepts deal with natural affinity derived from feelings. However, *agape*, frequently used in the Bible, expresses love as an act of the will, replacing desire with decision. Thus, our reading today reveals a responsive relationship; God will commune with those whose love is manifested by their obedience. In this way, our relationship to God is not conditioned by our feelings but by our commitment. Our feelings may vary, but our commitment can remain strong irrespective of how we feel.

Feelings can change both ways, from love to indifference and vice versa. A change of feelings can be generated by the will, not in determination to *feel* different but by a decision to *act* in a way that displays love. Feelings or attitudes are helpful but not necessary to generate actions. In contrast, actions can generate feelings; hence the importance of understanding verse 15, where obedience and love act as a double spiral, each reinforcing the other. God's love for us is not just the communication of his feelings but also his action in sending Jesus to die for us. Actions

[1] 2 Corinthians 4:16–18

that demonstrate love—emotions aside—will help to keep the feelings alive in our relationships.

Thursday: John 16:16–22

Carrying and having a child is—at least at the time—a long period of relative discomfort followed by several hours of painful labour. There appears to be little of redeeming value in the whole process except the hope of birth. This is specifically true for women who bear the burden of the trauma. Men can only relate vicariously, unaware of the real difficulties women have to tolerate, and bringing their husbands into the delivery room enables them to share some of it. One woman put it this way: "My husband was happy enough to be present at the conception; he can be there at the delivery as well."

Many might debate whether a woman completely forgets the trauma of childbirth once the little one is in her arms, as today's reading suggests. To be fair, the Bible doesn't mitigate labour pains, in fact, they are mentioned as an illustration of severe suffering.[1] But the general idea is that the joy a child brings eventually outweighs past pain. Thus, for the Christian, the Bible refers to the pain of childbirth as a symbol of the difficulties that will eventually give way to the joy of final union with Christ.[2]

All who have lived for a time on earth know that we will always be subject to adversity. But all Christians live in hope—not the earthly wish that things *may* improve but the *certainty* of the promises of God. Whether it is the loss of a loved one to death or to the failing attractions of the world, we do not "grieve like the rest who have no hope."[3] We know that our suffering is of temporal duration and joy will last forever.[4]

---

[1] Isaiah 13:8; 21:3; Micah 4:9–10
[2] See Matthew 24:8, where the misery of earth is a prelude to the return of Christ.
[3] 1 Thessalonians 4:13–14
[4] Romans 8:18; 2 Corinthians 4:17

Friday: Acts 2:14–21

In addition to what we noted about the next life yesterday, today's reading describes God's intervention in this life: there is hope for coming generations who accept and honour Christ. The context of this passage is the "coming of the great and glorious day of the Lord." The first coming of Jesus to earth and his return to heaven led to the day of Pentecost and the indwelling Spirit promised to all believers. In the intervening time until his return to earth, coming generations are promised the inspiration of God's Spirit in visions and dreams.

Although this passage has been mainly co-opted by Pentecostals, who regard the promises as miraculous phenomena, it is a promise given to all Christians that God will work in their lives to accomplish his will on earth. It is given to all, irrespective of age or sex, referring to "all people . . . sons . . . daughters . . . young men . . . old men . . . men and women." Dreams and visions may be not just visible spiritual manifestations but also clarity of what the future could be and understanding of the outcomes of various plans or actions.

For those of us who recognize that our own sin involves us in Jesus' crucifixion, the forgiveness he promises can bring a rich heritage to our children. Unlike those who sought his crucifixion, it is not condemnation for shedding Christ's blood that we bring upon our children but the promise of the Spirit coming upon them and his involvement in their lives. Their dreams and visions will contribute to God's plan to bring hope to a fallen world and even change the course of world history as "everyone who calls on the name of the Lord will be saved." Isn't this what we desire for our children?

Weekend ~ Pornography

Of the many forms of aberrant sexual behaviour, we need to look at pornography, which is a major driving force in the decay of Western society. At one time it was generally found only in magazines hidden from public view and generally considered unacceptable by the mainstream, with schoolboys sneaking a mischievous peek. Today it is totally different. The internet inserts pornography into the mainstream of communication; it is instantly accessible with the click of a mouse to be indulged in complete privacy. It is no longer limited by the printed page from the corner store; the full range of global deviancy is instantly available.

As pornography becomes easily available to youth, impressionable young males begin to view females as objects for sexual pleasure. The impact of this is sexual exploitation of juveniles, spoiling them for sustainable marriage. Over time this has dire consequences for families at large and, consequently, eventually society as a whole. But pornography also has its effect on marriages. It can redefine the wife as a sexual object rather than developing sexual union through personal intimacy. Constant use of pornography to initiate sex can be addictive, becoming increasingly necessary—and possibly increasingly deviant—to promote sexual activity.

In addition, use of pornography may also reinforce sexual deviancy that a married partner may already have—male or female. The variety of sexual practices on the internet becomes a smorgasbord of ideas to highlight and legitimize aberrant sexual preferences and so undermine the marriage relationship. The internet not only provides definition for these fantasies, it also provides opportunity for practice by connecting to likeminded individuals. For a constant user, the ever present temptation to practice deviancy increases the chance for sexual misbehaviour that threatens marriage.

Week Forty-Seven

Monday: Romans 1:18–32

This passage is perhaps the most quoted for demonstrating the steps of descent into sexual adventurism. We have previously raised the issue of the normalisation of current sexual practices and the compassionate response we are constrained to make as sinners ourselves. However, this passage claims that homosexuality is a direct result of refusing to acknowledge God and a lack of thankfulness to him for life and its provisions. The latter part of our reading also traces the confusion between good and evil and the increasing approval of evil that follows an increase in unnatural sexuality.

Eliminating God from our thinking leads to fuzziness between right and wrong and the eventual approval of evil. The current idea in Western culture is that an action is good or evil depending on the circumstances—little is evil in itself. This idea is basically from Eastern mysticism, the notion that "all is one," that there is no distinction between good and evil. It is certainly not biblical, as today's passage shows, and as Isaiah records, it is not confined to our age.[1] Our reading labels this confusion about good and evil "depravity."

It should go without saying that not having a clear understanding of good and evil is not going to help any relationship, particularly the intimate one of marriage. A positive

---

[1] Isaiah 5:20

approach to today's reading indicates that acknowledgment of God and thankfulness to him will clarify our thinking on sex and other issues. That clarification is to be found in the Bible: there are 22 verses in the New Testament citing good and evil, sometimes more than once in some verses, ten of which were spoken by Jesus. This emphasizes that continual reference to the Bible by study and daily reading is invaluable in maintaining a healthy marriage.

Tuesday: Romans 2:17–24

The first human disobedience to God recorded in Genesis has affected the lives of us all. That event is known as the "fall" — not the autumn of existence but certainly the heralding of a long winter of earthly toil and distress. We no longer exhibit the true image of God but a distorted version of it, perhaps more discernable in some than others. Unfortunately, the distortion of God's image is more clearly seen in close relationships, tempting us to judge and act accordingly. Yet it should evoke pity, even empathy, and a corresponding humility, for we are in the same condition. It was because God loved us and looked on us in pity instead of judgment that he made the ultimate sacrifice to reconcile us back to himself. If we are to display the image of God to others, it must be a reflection of God's concern for them illustrated by his sacrifice.

This may be old news to you, but do you practice this with your partner? Today's reading was written to the Jews who considered themselves superior to the Gentiles because of their relationship to God. It can just as easily apply to us when we place ourselves in judgment over our partners. God does not recognize or accept this kind of superiority, for he sees each of us in need of his continuing forgiveness and grace, finding us all on level ground at the foot of the cross.

None of this detracts from the responsibility of a man or woman for their sin, having to cope with the fallout from it and to rectify it where possible. However, if we are to be a supporting member of our marriage team, we can only approach the other person's failure with the recognition of our own. Motivation based on superiority or judgment will maintain inequality in our marriage and ensure a dysfunctional relationship. It will also foster similar behaviour in our children and in their marriages as they learn from us and mimic our attitudes.

Wednesday: Romans 5:1–11

God's love is not blind. Yet his love for us acts as though it was. As we grow more accustomed to our partners and the glow comes off the relationship, we are each seen as we really are, warts and all. This is not a matter of coming from a poor environment or having handicaps that are unavoidable, but rather, clear faults in the character of the beloved. Celebrating differences is critical to keeping a relationship alive, but it does not mean tolerating bad behaviour or slovenly habits. Yet love blooms in spite of them, and love will continue despite them. Every couple may deal differently with the shortcomings of each other, but failure to hold our partners accountable may harbour resentment in us, fail our partners and leave the marriage vulnerable.

It is often the little things, not dealt with, that can destroy a marriage. Even in the midst of her love song, the beloved in the Song of Solomon recognized that it was "the little foxes that ruin the vineyards."[1] One lady, when asked what irritated her about her husband, replied that it was his habit of peeling grapefruit like an orange. In dealing with irritants in a marriage, it is critical to decide what is really important and what is not. Consider together the things that may bring conflict to your relationship. In the small annoyances there are two options—for the complainer to accept them or the perpetrator to stop them. What is not an option is to break up a marriage over them.

---

[1] Song of Solomon 2:15

God loved us, demonstrating "His own love for us in this: while we were still sinners, Christ died for us." Without having the human advantage of an infatuating courtship, even while we were still rebellious to God he loved us enough to go to extraordinary lengths to reconcile with us. This is a pretty tough act to follow. Most of us have a limit to patience and tolerance, and some marriages cannot be saved when debilitating dynamics such as illegal drug use, alcohol abuse or infidelity continue. Relationships should be built on grace as much as love, fostering the ability to forgive and accept non-critical conduct in a marriage.

Thursday: Romans 8:12–17

The Bible frequently talks about our relationship to God as that of child to parent. The New Testament defines this in two ways: being born into God's kingdom or becoming children by adoption. While adoption may seem like a secondary attachment, there is no difference between natural born or adopted children under the law. Further, the parental attachment is no different. In fact, many adopted children consider themselves more fortunate than natural children in that they were *chosen by* as opposed to *given to* their parents. The Bible makes no distinction between the two—both have the same privileges and inheritance.

Today's reading highlights the idea of adoption—being drawn into God's family by his choice and calling him "Father" with the full benefits of a child. One of the benefits is knowing that he has the same interest and heartache over us as we do over our children. Our pain, waywardness or foolishness affects him just as we are affected by similar behaviour in our children. If the way he guides us is similar to how we need to raise our children, then there is much he can teach us about bringing up our family.

How does God work with us to encourage, mature and discipline us? The answers are in Scripture, which "is God-breathed and is useful for teaching, rebuking, correcting and training in righteousness, so that all God's people may be thoroughly equipped for every good work."[1] An increasing knowledge of God's Word and regularly seeking him and his ways will give us resources for ensuring our children's happiness and fulfilling our God-given role.

Friday: Romans 14:1–12

In a church we pastored there was young couple that had a remarkable ability with children. They had three of their own and adopted two more, one with foetal alcohol syndrome. Rick was a gung-ho Christian, clearly demonstrating his commitment to God in outspoken ways. Mary was more subdued, fulfilling her responsibilities in practical ways. Much of the commendation for the children's growth was hers. However, Rick complained of her lack of spirituality, meaning of course, that it did not measure up to his. Eventually he left her, taking the children with him and joining up with an unmarried mother with four children of her own. Mary, feeling betrayed, promptly divorced him.

When I asked Rick for his reasons for this move, he indicated that he and his new partner "were one," meaning one in spirituality, enabling them both to serve the Lord. This rationale apparently trumped the obvious injustice against his former wife Mary. I heard from Mary many years later, by then living a single but fulfilling life while remaining in touch with her children. One daughter was living with her but had tried to commit suicide several times. No one can tell what the outcome would have been had Rick remained faithful to Mary—it most likely would have been better—but the outcome was not the problem. While the act of desertion was wrong, it was built on a mistaken judgment Rick was not qualified to make.

It is all too easy for us to judge another's spirituality, which means we assume ours to be superior. To do so fails to take into account differences in temperament and the fact that we cannot see the other person's heart, which God alone judges. But above

---

[1] 2 Timothy 3:16–17

all we have no right to judge those whom God has accepted—they stand or fall before him, their only Master. We become hypocrites, well-deserving of being called Pharisees. How do we feel about our partners? If they have made a commitment to God but fail to attain our expected standard of spirituality, this reading reminds us that God is able to make them stand. Why not celebrate and extol their manner of devotion? It stems from the difference that drew us together in the first place.

Weekend ~ Celebrate the Difference

Common remarks heard about a marriage often refer to the difference between the partners—"How could two people be so different and still get along?" or "What does she see in him?" As a rule of thumb, it is preferable for marriage partners to have common interests as a bond between them. Common beliefs would probably top this list, but other shared dynamics—culture, education or hobbies, for instance—are helpful. When it comes to temperament and abilities, the picture is quite different. We tend to admire—or resent—in others those things that are absent in ourselves, and we tend to fall in love with individuals who are opposite to us, coveting their differences. This is probably the reason that a reclusive, self-contained young man attracted to a vivacious young socialite is astonished that she should fall for him. She is drawn to his steadiness and self assurance.

Sexual attraction is essential for a good marriage, but sex alone cannot hold the relationship together without the attraction of personality—which raises a critical point. The differences in temperament that initially attract can become the source of irritation as the relationship matures because each does things differently. It is at this point that the husband may try to make his wife over into his own image, perhaps even with her compliance in her anxiety to please. In doing so, the difference that attracted him fades, the source of excitement is lost and boredom sets in. Thus, he sets up for himself the perfect scenario for venturing outside of marriage for that lost attraction. In another couple, the wife might try to do the same.

The disordered way in which the dishwasher is loaded (compared to my efficient arrangement, of course) is not an appropriate issue for expressing irritation or rebuke. Rather, it is a time to rejoice that the vitality I most admired is still in the house, both physically and temperamentally. The French would say, "Vive la difference," referring to the sexes. We should incorporate that idea as we consider the differences in personality that first drew us together.

Week Forty-Eight

Monday: 1 Corinthians 1:18–31

Why is the wisdom of the Bible superior? Are there not other resources that can bring the same benefits? While many would claim there are, none has provided a better or lasting alternative. Certainly, our permissive culture has been destructive rather than beneficial to human relationships. Today's passage warns us of the arrogance of claiming our own wisdom above that which comes from God. Actually, developing our own ideas of what constitutes wisdom can lead us away from God.

Our ideas of wisdom start with our sense of independence from God. We cannot in the long run develop sound wisdom for living if it is not founded on truth. The Bible maintains that God exists and he responds to those who seek him.[1] If this is true, to consider God non-existent or irrelevant to life is to build on an insecure foundation, because all that is built on a false belief must inevitably be flawed and eventually unsustainable. That is why our reading maintains that "God chose the foolish things of the world to shame the wise" and "the weak things of the world to shame the strong." Realizing their lack of wisdom drives the foolish and weak to One outside themselves.

Perhaps you have sensed this feeling of inadequacy. Despite the variety of voices offering guidance, you don't know where to turn for lasting direction. If you feel this places you among the

---

[1] Hebrews 11:6

weak and foolish, then be encouraged, because this opens the door for our Creator's wisdom to enter your reasoning and bring joy and meaning to your life and relationships. It has been our belief and practice to pattern our marriage and family after the guidance given in the Bible. As our Creator is the wisdom within the Bible, so he can also guide and sustain all the relationships of our lives.

Tuesday: 1 Corinthians 6:8–13

This passage includes homosexuality in a list of unacceptable practices. But the burden of this passage is not so much a rebuke as a reminder that these practices can be changed. The propensity to sin is in all of us, and it is not hard to find tendencies within ourselves that are unacceptable and need to be curbed, such as adultery, pornography or other unacceptable sexual practices. Unfortunately, some consider them harmless personal preferences to freely to engage in rather than avoid. Despite claims that homosexuality is genetic, it is still debated, and Paul lists homosexuality under the category of sexual preferences that can be resisted or reversed.

Jennifer married a fine man; both were Christians at the time and they had several children together. One day, her husband notified her that he was gay and was leaving the marriage, and divorce followed. The question remains: was he really gay or did he give in to temptations outside of his marriage covenant with Jennifer? He was clearly straight, as many years of marriage to a woman and several children attested. Assuming that the claim of homosexuality was his real reason for leaving the marriage, it was basically simple adultery and equal to leaving for another woman. Both homosexual and heterosexual dalliance outside of marriage breaks the marriage vow through adulterous sexual choices.

However, it is critical for us to realize that the tendency to homosexuality is not a sin. Temptation is not a sin—Jesus was tempted as we are, yet without sin.[1] We all have temptations to deal with, and in this way we are all in the same category as homosexuals. Unacceptable sexual orientation of any sort only reminds us that we are all "oriented" towards sin, whether sexual or not. It is the indulgence of our tempting desires that converts them into sin.

Wednesday: I Corinthians 7:1-9

This passage deals primarily with sex—the need for it, the provision for it and consent to it. Paul claimed that remaining unmarried like him was a gift, but for others marriage was also a gift. While he clearly saw advantages to personal faith and action in being single as he was,[2] he also recognized the need for some to marry rather "than to burn with passion." In this he identifies sex as good, and an outlet is provided for it in marriage. This means that sexual co-operation is a condition of marriage, and his instructions are that each should fulfill their marital duty; to deprive the other of sexual intimacy is fraud, a refusal to abide by the marriage vows.

However, this does not mean that a couple cannot limit sexual contact for an agreed period for prayer—a type of fasting to concentrate on spiritual matters. But the period cannot be indeterminate or too long or it may result in "lack of control" and cut short the agreed devotional time. But even this suggestion of mutual abstinence is given "as a concession, not as a command." Clearly, Paul believes that mutual satisfaction in the marriage relationship is critical to maintaining the fidelity and permanence of the union.

I'm sure that this is a message that the guys want to hear. If there are any complaints about the lack of sex, they usually come from men who are frustrated with their wives. Yet, as someone said, there are no frigid women, only inattentive men. Men may

---

[1] Hebrews 4:15
[2] 1 Corinthians 7:32–35

be turned on by sight, but women respond to more intimate companionship. Warmth towards a husband is fostered by a wife's sense of being looked after, protected and cosseted, knowing she and her ideas are valued and that her needs and desires—besides sex—are important to her husband.

Thursday: I Corinthians 7:10-14

Today's reading discusses mixed marriage—not between people of different colour but between a believer and an unbeliever. Two kinds of mixed marriages are possible: one where a Christian man or woman marries an unbeliever and the other where one partner becomes a believer after marriage. The former is inadvisable, because mixed marriages entered into knowingly statistically favour the unbeliever as the believer usually loses faith. This may be a result of persuasion from the unbeliever or attempts to mollify him or her. Worse, marriage entered into on the promise or hope of the other's conversion is a form of spiritual blackmail.

But given the condition of a mixed marriage, particularly if one partner becomes a believer while married, what are the responsibilities of the believer? Paul is trying to combat the idea that a new Christian should opt out of such a marriage because it seems more appropriate to his or her new spiritual position. Rather, in verses 12-15 Paul lets the unbelieving spouse set the agenda to continue in the marriage or leave. There are many mixed marriages where there is genuine love between the partners, even if the intimacy of faith is missing. To destroy these relationships on the basis of faith is irresponsible, especially where there are children from the marriage. In fact, Paul shows his concern for children, indicating that they are under the umbrella of the believer's faith by the extension of his or her sanctification to the partner— presumably for the period of the children's dependence.

Paul's exhortation for the new believer to "retain the place in life that the Lord assigned to him"[1] is good advice for the married

---

[1] 1 Corinthians 7:17

or single. It is too common for a new believer to equate new life in Christ with a need to change his or her living situation. This may be necessary if a Christian is living an unacceptable lifestyle, but it is preferable to retain legitimate relationships or vocations.

Friday: 1 Corinthians 7:15–16

As we noted previously, the decision regarding the future of a mixed marriage is left to the unbeliever. The Christian is under no compulsion to persuade the partner to stay or leave. But if the unbeliever decides to leave, the believer "is not bound" to try to save the marriage. The desertion of an unbelieving husband is grounds for the dissolution of the marriage. Thus, Paul adds desertion to infidelity as the basis for divorce. Although not covered by Paul's discussion, this would probably apply equally where a believer leaves a marriage. Unless he or she leaves for legitimate reasons, by taking that initiative the action becomes that of an unbeliever.

The rationale for this approach is that marriage is not meant to be an evangelical institution. By saying, "How do you know . . . whether you will save your [partner]?" Paul is indicating there is no guarantee that the unbelieving partner who wishes to leave will be saved if constrained against his or her will to stay in the marriage. Even though the Bible gives guidelines for ending a marriage, the possibility of reconciliation is the first option. For this reason, Paul indicates that where a believer takes the initiative to leave a marriage that may be intolerable, he or she should remain unmarried, for it provides the option for reconciliation.[1]

Two phrases in the Corinthian passage that often cause confusion are the statements "not I, but the Lord" and "I, not the Lord,"[2] which qualify Paul's writing. Some assume this to mean that what the Lord has said takes precedence over what Paul has written, disqualifying the options that Paul gives. In fact, Paul in

---

[1] 1 Corinthians 7:10–11
[2] 1 Corinthians 7: 10, 12

the first instance is simply quoting Jesus,[1] and in the second, he is writing as the Holy Spirit leads him. Both are the Word of God to us and are there for our guidance and benefit.

Weekend ~ Remarriage

There has always been some debate in Christian circles about divorce and remarriage. Some will deny the possibility of divorce for the believer because God hates divorce.[2] Others will agree that God has made allowance for divorce because of the hardness our hearts[3] but deny the possibility of remarriage. Still others maintain that the reason for divorce is to allow remarriage; divorce is unnecessary if remarriage is disallowed. This debate stigmatizes those who have sought divorce for legitimate reasons and casts an additional pall of suspicion on those who remarry.

It is one thing to be passionate about marriage and its permanence, as we all should be, but it is cruel to translate that into lack of compassion for those caught in intolerable marriages. It was our practice during our time of ministry to remarry those who had been divorced, and a close friend castigated me roundly for doing so. How could I marry those who had been divorced when it was clear that God hated it?

I could not argue that divorce was what God wanted, but it was clear to me that God's provision for it was an act of grace towards us all, for none of us would make the perfect marriage and some of us could not sustain one. But God's grace provided more than that; it was the source of forgiveness for all sin, and I had accepted that grace for me personally. How could I not pass the same grace of God to those coming to me? If I was to err at all, it had to be on the side of grace and not the law.

---

[1] Matthew 19:9
[2] Malachi 2:16
[3] Matthew 19:8

Week Forty-Nine

Monday: I Corinthians 13:1–7

No review of love would be complete without a reference to this passage. In a book that deals primarily with the love of God, this passage is unique in that it deals in depth with our love for each other. While it does not deal with marriage in particular, it does hold key advice for the marriage relationship. However, in contrast to the previous passages we have looked at, it reverses some of those ideas. While we have recognized that love without actions is dead, this passage reminds us that not all actions are motivated by love. In fact, lesser, even offensive, motives can provoke seemingly good actions. What motives might these be?

It doesn't take long to look around us, or even inside us, to find some answers. Desire for personal recognition, fanatical dedication to an ideology, creating a sense of indebtedness to oneself or even plain old manipulation can provoke seemingly loving actions. But these actions can be done without care or concern for the person to whom they are directed. The problem with these motives is that they are not long term. Once the desired end is gained or found unattainable or irritation or impatience sets in, the actions cease. On the other hand, "love never fails."

In support of the permanence of love, Paul lists qualities of love in verses 4–6 that reveal attitudes that cannot exist with the lesser motives listed previously. Love "always protects, always trusts, always hopes, always perseveres," for love does not require other motives to support it; it is sufficient in itself. This does not mean that, in practice, our earthly relationships are totally altruistic. Most of us need a "pay-off" somewhere along the way to keep us encouraged, and fortunately, most of the time real love gains a response. But if genuine love for the object of our actions is the primary motivation, it will stand the test of time, displaying— for the most part—the characteristics that Paul lists.

Tuesday: 1 Corinthians 13:8–13

Paul not only sees love as a primary motivator in relationships and actions, he also sees it as a priority for life. Christians invest heavily in the knowledge from the Bible about God and how to live, but Paul sees this as temporary and limited. What we know now is but a "poor reflection as in a mirror," inadequate for the life beyond this one. In fact, knowledge can become a problem. While knowledge is necessary and commended by the Bible, it can give rise to the pride of being right and acting as a gauge of another person's spirituality. The man who claims to know it all is simply unaware of what he does *not* know.[1] Similarly, the gifts of the Spirit—prophecy, tongues and so on—are temporary and not indicative of special approval from God.

Am I proud of my greater spiritual progress than my partner, using it to control or browbeat her, pointing out her deficiencies or lack of devotion? Paul points out in this passage that the difference between my partner and me is insignificant compared with my near complete ignorance of spiritual things. But what I know is not insignificant when used in love to encourage and commend my wife. Then it can be of great benefit to our relationship. If my gift of knowledge or other spiritual gifts are used without love, they are empty and eventually ineffective.

Of real significance in this passage is the listing of the primary virtues of Christianity: Faith, Hope and Love. They are worth comparing with the Greek cardinal virtues: Wisdom, Moderation, Courage and Justice. All the latter do not require an object—they can

---

[1] 1 Corinthians 8:1–2

be practised personally without a necessary connection to someone else. The Christian virtues, however, need an object. We need to have love and faith in someone outside ourselves and we need to have hope in something beyond us. God did not plan for us to be independent beings; rather, we were designed to be interdependent with each other and each of us dependent upon Him.

Wednesday: 2 Corinthians 5:1—10

We touched previously on how provision, protection and purpose are required in all families. Today's reading focuses on the need and formation of purpose, probably the most important of the three. In this passage, Paul sets out God's purpose for us—that we might be with him in heaven. This is parallel to the purpose given to Israel: they would be God's people[1]—and as we are also God's people, heaven is our final destiny. While it is our desire to be with him, at present we are confined in this earthly body, looking forward to our final rest with him, for which the Holy Spirit, given to us, is our guarantee.

Thus, whether at our final destination or during this interim sojourn on earth, Paul reminds us that it is "our goal to please him." Hopefully we do this out of love and not coercion; Paul reminds us that we will have to give an account of our time and actions while on earth. For some of us, the value of our work may be counted in straw, not valuable stones.[2] This may be a fearsome notion: have we fulfilled the task given to us? What if we have missed God's calling for us? If we are not sure of God's requirements of us, we could be in trouble.

Part of the reason for these meditations is to show that the initial purpose for our existence to please him can be found at home. In the relationships closest to us, where we live moment by moment, we find our first opportunity to please God. This makes it attainable for everyone. Whatever else we may feel called to do,

---

[1] Exodus 6:7
[2] 1 Corinthians 3:10–13

fulfilling God's requirements to our partners is the start of a life pleasing to God. In fact, to fail in this area may nullify all the other efforts we make to please him.

Thursday: Galatians 3:23–29

A lthough we have seen that creation defines the nature and roles of men and women as equal, it is clear from experience that this is not true in practice. Even so, our reading today shows how God's intervention in human history has begun to restore it. The equality of all human beings is in view here, not just the sexes. The short list given—Jew and Greek (Gentile), slave and free, male and female—represents all classes of people as a wider reading of the New Testament shows.[1] Whatever was lost at the fall has now been recovered in Jesus Christ, for we "are all sons (or children) of God through faith in Christ Jesus."

It is lamentable that some groups who base their conduct on the Bible deny full fellowship to others on the basis of race. White supremacists come to mind, as do the South African churches that supported apartheid. It is also true that within North American Christian churches there are many that are all-white or all-black— less by design than by attitude, for while many of us pay lip service to the idea of equality in Christ, we are hesitant to associate with those different from us.

It is to the credit of some streams of secular thinking, including moderate feminism, that they have led the way toward redressing the inequality between men and women, recognizing the unnaturalness of this imbalance. While the role of women in the church is beyond the scope of these notes, the equality of women is often seriously undermined in otherwise faithful churches by restrictions placed upon the service of women. Even this pales into insignificance alongside the attitude of some Christian husbands that their wives—and their children—are simply adjuncts to themselves. Apart from the inequality this fosters, the greater

---

[1] For instance: Luke 14:7–14; James 2:1–4

tragedy is the loss of companionship and efficiency in the family unit when a form of dictatorship is the basis of family life.

Friday: Ephesians 5:15–21

The verses that follow today's reading (verses 22–33) are probably the most referred to in establishing a marriage relationship, yet they are also frequently misapplied. Firstly, in these verses it is significant that men have far more instructions than women, possibly because they are harder of hearing. Secondly, the standard set for men is supremely higher than that for women; men have no cause for superiority. But of greatest concern, today's passage sets the context for the marriage relationship but is rarely connected to it. Of particular interest, the passage is centred on wisdom: how to act "not as unwise but as wise." We are urged "not [to] be foolish, but understand what the Lord's will is" as we understand and apply the counsel that follows.

Thus, these verses set a standard for relating to others in the body of Christ. It is instructive to read these verses as though they refer specifically to husband and wife—avoid drunkenness, be filled with the Spirit, rejoice and be thankful to God for his goodness together. The passage concludes with a simple charge to "submit to one another out of reverence to Christ," which then becomes the context for instructions on married life. In marriage both wives *and* husbands, as part of the body of Christ, are to submit to each other.

So the following verses seen in this context are a description of how each—both man and woman—submit to the other. Contrary to some views, it particularly means that the husband will submit to his wife as a sister in Christ. This submission is obviously out of consideration for one another, but particularly "out of reverence for Christ." To submit to one another is a Christian's duty, for it follows the example given by Christ[1] and is part of the growing image of God in us.

---

[1] Philippians 2:5–8

Weekend ~ Anger

Anger is like fire and is as common and deadly. It harms those who harbour it as well as those at whom it is directed. As a motive for violence, it is the most destructive force on earth, although it is rarely dealt with as such. In the moment anger seems reasonable, for anger always has a reason—but seldom a good one. The issue is not whether our anger is justified but what we are going to do with it. Anger is not a sin in itself—God has anger—but it is a temptation to sin with violent words or actions, often irrespective of justification.

Anger is like pain, an indicator that something is wrong. If we are to do what is right we should initially avoid the cause of anger if possible, but if this is not possible, we need to deal correctly with the anger when it arises. Anger is often triggered by failure to deal with a situation or our sense of the helplessness or meaninglessness of a situation. But even anger at ourselves or circumstances beyond our control can be transferred to others. We must not only evaluate our anger but *own* it and deal with it ourselves. We are responsible for our *re*-actions as well as our actions. Provocation is a cause, not a justification.

Anger is like alcohol—a way of escape, of avoiding reality. Anger becomes comfortable, like a warm coat on a cold day, and when continuously indulged, anger reinforces itself. How can we deal with it? We have three choices: express, repress or confess. We may express it and risk injuring others; expression may release tension, but it reinforces the anger and its justification. To repress anger risks injuring ourselves; it may avoid injury to others in the short term but threatens depression or a later explosion. As Christians, we have an alternate recourse: we may confess our anger to God and leave the issue that provoked it in his hands. This will help diffuse our anger and direct it into constructive channels.

Monday: Ephesians 5:22–24

These verses, given as instructions for the wife, have been widely used to establish a sort of lordship of the husband over the wife so that she becomes a resource for the husband's own advancement. The repetition of "submit" and the phrase "for the husband is the head of the wife" enhance this idea. As the church is obedient to Christ, so the wife needs to be obedient to her husband. Even assuming the husband has the best interests of his family at heart, it is interpreted that his wife's resources must necessarily be devoted to *his* pursuit of advancing the cause of the family. This is how these three verses have frequently been explained.

But this interpretation raises some problems. If Scripture interprets Scripture—the traditional way of understanding the Bible—then how does this line up with the equality of the sexes we have already seen? In addition, equating the husband with Christ does not take into account man's imperfection and difference from Christ. Ann puts it concisely: "I will submit to my husband when he loves me as Christ loves the church." Fair comment. But probably the most revealing difficulty is the relation of this passage to the ideas discussed from yesterday's reading. The idea of the wife's subservience is totally out of keeping with the instructions to the husband. How do we reconcile these two ideas?

Paul was writing from Rome, where there was an almost total breakdown of the concept of family. Both men and women often named past years by the names of their wives and husbands rather than by date. William Barclay cites several Roman writers as evidence that having a score of marriages and divorces was not uncommon.[1] Paul's concern was the sanctity and durability of Christian marriage as opposed to the surrounding culture. His instructions to both husband and wife were designed for this achievement—by the wife remaining faithful and respecting her husband and the husband assuming responsibility for his wife's welfare. It was not to be achieved by control of one over the other, but rather, through showing mutual love and respect.[2]

Tuesday: Ephesians 5:25–33

As we noted previously, the context for today's reading in husband and wife relationships is the charge to "submit to one another." This necessarily includes the husband, but how does a husband submit to his wife? Does this mean obedience to her claims or some secondary place in the marriage? Clearly, equality of the sexes precludes these ideas. Marriage is a partnership of equals. Submission by the husband is painstakingly described in our reading and it adds up to recognizing his wife as his first priority.

Thus, my wife's well-being and fulfilment comes before anything else, on the basis of an ultimate standard—for me to love her "just as Christ loved the church." If I fail to accomplish this, I can hardly expect my wife to fulfill her role. Here are three suggestions on how to fulfill our obligation as men to our wives, based on this passage. Firstly, we are responsible to protect and provide for our wives in the same way that we look after ourselves, for everyone "feeds and cares" for his own body. That's simple enough. Secondly, we need to give our lives for our wives as Christ gave himself for the church, for this is how Christ loved

---

[1] William Barclay, *Letters to the Galatians and Ephesians*, Reprinted Edition (Edinburgh: Saint Andrew Press, 1972) 202.
[2] Ephesians 5:33

the church. Not so simple. As we have previously suggested, it may not mean dying for our wives, but it certainly means living for them. Despite other legitimate calls on our time, their need of us outweighs them all—their welfare is our first priority.

Lastly, we have the opportunity to present our wives to Christ as he will present the Church to himself. It should be my supreme service and joy to present my wife to Christ complete in him. I will certainly rejoice at the work of God's grace displayed in her, but will I regret her unachieved potential because I failed to sufficiently invest my life in her?

Wednesday: Ephesians 6:1–9

This is one of the few Scriptures that give specific instruction regarding the relationship between parents and children. Perhaps this scarcity points to the fact that guidance for life is to be found in God's dealings with us, his children by creation, rather than by his specific instruction. Even in the detailed instructions regarding relationships between masters and slaves, the relationship between each is based on their relationship with Christ.

However, there is an interesting twist in this instruction to children. We know that for children the promise of reward can be a greater incentive to obedience than punishment for non-compliance, and it is noted that honouring parents is the one commandment that has a promise attached. There is, of course, a practical application of this promise: a child who rejects a parent's advice is more likely to develop a lifestyle that may risk health and even life. On a more positive note, a child that learns respect for parents is more likely to carry that respect into life and create a stable and safe society.

But there is a reciprocal requirement that parents also respect their children. Parents that treat their children as commodities or personal belongings are also more likely to generate rebellion from them later. A child will learn respect for parents by the respect he or she receives from them. While this may seem obvious, the way many parents humiliate their children would suggest they believe that respect is gained from intimidation, like bullies the world over. To bring children up "in the training and instruction of the Lord" is to treat them with the fairness and justice that God grants us.

Thursday: Philippians 1:12–26

If we are true Christians, we will have committed our marriages and families to God and endeavoured to serve him by serving them. But when we are finally reunited with our loved ones in the next life, we will then see clearly that Christ was the one who gave us each other and our children, and we will also see him as the source of our joy in those relationships. Thus, being "married" to him will fulfill all the desires of our hearts that we felt so inadequately on earth. The longing to be reunited with an absent loved one is symptomatic of our desire for God, for him to fill the "God-shaped" void within us.

Paul was not married (as far as we know) but sensed the conflict between his desire to be reunited with God and the benefit of staying so that he could continue his ministry. While it is true that our relationship with our partner is a partial fulfilment of our relationship with God, it is our bond with God that gives depth and stability to our marriage. Thus, our relationship with our partner is dependent on our relationship with God. Our desire to remain on earth is because we wish to fulfill our responsibility to God by serving our partners, but it does not and should not preclude our desire to be with God.

Paul felt the tension between the two but recognized both to be legitimate. There are times when we may feel that we enjoy our families or sense their need so much that we are loath to leave them for the final joy of direct fellowship with God. On the other hand, to desire to leave for our final rest may seem like a betrayal of those we love and who love us. Paul resolved it in his own mind by accepting that his staying would increase the joy in Christ of those who depended on him. In the final analysis, the choice is not ours anyway. God will decide when our work is done and take us to be with him at the appropriate time. So we have the peace of resting by faith and without guilt in the decision that he deems right for us.

Friday: Philippians 2:1–8

Given the equality of the sexes in creation and the image of God in both, how does this work out in practice? What attitudes and conduct express these characteristics? Many years ago, I heard an eminent Christian psychologist explain that he sought early in his counselling practice for a common thread in all relational breakdowns. At first he thought there was none, but he later found an attribute that was common: a lack of respect—treating others as inferior, unworthy or inadequate and using words that degrade, insult or injure. In fact, lack of respect to some degree is usual in all marriages. Familiarity can breed contempt, and too often we treat our partners in a casual and cavalier manner.

Today's reading gives some ways in which we can emulate the image of God seen in Jesus Christ. Verse 5 points out that the same servanthood shown by Jesus to the human race can be seen in us by the actions listed in the first four verses. As Jesus is the express image of the Father,[1] our imitation of him reflects the image of God in ourselves. In this way, showing respect means treating each other with deference, esteem and honour and considering the other's views, concerns and ideas all worthy of a conscious and deliberate hearing. How often have you been accused of answering without hearing?

Shared decision-making is an essential skill to nurture as we endeavour to respect each other and share responsibility for our assigned tasks. This means that no decision will be made unless both partners are agreed. Where there is disagreement on a course of action, compromise is usually required. In mutual respect, both will embrace the outcome fully, even if either or both are somewhat dissatisfied. Where disagreement is fundamental, it may mean making no decision or deferring it. When a decision is

---

[1] Hebrews 1:3

unavoidable, one may defer to the other in mutual respect but consider the decision a joint one to deny future recriminations.

Showing respect and sharing decisions reflects the equality God has built into the sexes, the image of God placed in both and the charge we have to care and value each other in our lives together.

Weekend ~ Agreeing Together

Equality in marriage means unanimous agreement on decisions that affect the marriage. The importance of agreeing together cannot be overemphasized. It means that each has a veto over the other, which you may consider unworkable. But it has the clear advantage that neither partner can carry resentment over a decision that the other has made. Let's look at a couple of examples to illustrate how constant agreement may work.

Ann and I attended an investment seminar together but I was very sceptical of the excessive claims made for property investment. However, it seemed good to Ann and important to her, and in the end I thought there was a possibility it might work so we went ahead. As it turned out, the decision was a poor one due to a downturn in the markets and it caused us financial headaches for years. But despite my original misgivings, we made the decision together so we weathered the difficulties together.

During a period of time spent on the west coast of British Columbia, we searched for a house to buy. Our agreement to only buy a house that we both liked meant that it took over a year to find the right one. Each of us found places that we liked but didn't suit the taste of the other. The home we finally settled on was perhaps one of the best we have owned. When we decided to move back to the prairies, the situation was different. Due to various restraints, we needed to move quickly and Ann went ahead to find a place to live. I gave my agreement to her choice before she made it, on the assumption that her choice would be a good one. She bought a house that was an ideal unit for us, and it turned out to be good investment. I had finally learned to trust Ann as she had trusted me.

Week Fifty-One

Monday: Philippians 3:1–11

The ability to respect others frequently hinges on the status that we accord ourselves. Being popular, attaining social or career position or influence over others, having recognized gifts or achieving other personal success can lead us to disparage others less privileged. Paul was a Jew of great intellect and status in the Jewish hierarchy of his time. He had all the qualifications required by Jewish law to place him in this privileged position: physical circumcision, a Hebrew of the tribe of Benjamin, a Pharisee, zealous and faultless before God.

Yet in this passage Paul recognized that all his personal, particularly religious, assets meant nothing apart from his relationship to Jesus Christ. For him, none of these things had any value before God; only the righteousness of Christ could replace his sin. This drove Paul to participate in the risen life of Christ—to experience the power of his resurrection but also to share in his sufferings. This all meant that Paul had nothing of his own to bring to his relationships, only the fellowship that he had with Christ. He had confidence that the power of God was able to change the circumstances in which he found himself. Yet there were times that he experienced some degree of the sacrifice that Jesus made in order to bring about the change that God's power could bring.

The relationship between achievement and suffering is not uncommon in the New Testament.[1] The history of the early church as well as modern China, for example, is that the church flourishes under persecution. All this reminds us that personal achievement, ability or knowledge cannot necessarily promote success in our relationships, particularly with our partners. To depend on these alone is to assume personal superiority over circumstances and perhaps our partner as well, methods that Paul found did not accomplish lasting results. It is only as we recognize our need to seek God's direction of our knowledge and talents— perhaps calling for sacrifice on our part—that we will see the power of the risen Christ evident in our lives and marriages.

Tuesday: I Timothy 3:1–5

Here's a passage that we may assume does not apply to us; however, the requirements listed are not exclusive to leadership, although necessary for it, but are clearly required of all who profess to follow Christ. Most of us can probably comply with the faithfulness to one partner requirement, but perhaps we may have more difficulty obtaining children's obedience. From our experience, many are tempted to exempt themselves from leadership because of this requirement.

Does this really mean that disobedient children indicate unacceptable Christian character in the parents? If this is so, then perhaps to a greater or lesser degree none of us fulfill this requirement in our parenthood and none of us are eligible for leadership. What is more likely in view here is that when children are disobedient, parents should deal with it in a way that garners respect from their peers and is also respectful to the children: "In a manner worthy of full respect." The emphasis is on management of the household, not on attaining the perfect family.

For those currently in or considering leadership, recall that God, as the perfect parent, still encountered disobedience from his

---

[1] Romans 8:17-18; 2 Corinthians 4:17

first created "children." That episode and the way God has interacted with mankind since should be the pattern for our parenting. Remember also that leadership is not just a calling for directing the affairs of his church on earth but is a calling for all that have others, especially children, dependent on them.

Wednesday: I Timothy 5:4–8, 16

The relationship between parents and children is given clear direction in today's reading. There is an echo here of the fifth commandment, to honour one's parents, extended in this case to the needs of other family members. Clearly, the divide between members of the same family was as prevalent in Paul's time as it is now, making this passage just as relevant today. The necessity of caring for others, especially our parents, is part of our Christian duty.

The irony of this, both then and now, is that it is natural to love our children and parents, which should make the requirement unnecessary. But prevailing conditions in our society betray the basic selfish instinct that many of us cannot or will not suppress. We are only too aware of the number of elderly folk who are generally ignored by their children until the pension checks arrive or they die. This is not to be unaware of the fact that an increasing life expectancy makes some children seniors themselves, often less able to cope with sick and aging parents. Increasing life expectancy has created the difficult "sandwich" generation: those endeavouring to look after feeble parents while still raising their own family.

Scripture neither recognizes nor downplays the difficulties in looking after parents and grandparents, particularly those who are widowed, but it does require children to take responsibility for their aged forbears at a level they can manage. This may mean taking steps unpopular with both the parent and others—putting him or her into a senior's home is a particularly divisive decision—to ensure the elder is properly looked after. One who ignores the plight of an elderly family member "has denied the faith and is worse than an unbeliever."

Thursday: I Timothy 5:11–15

It is pretty certain that Paul would be in hot water today for setting the stereotyping apparent in this passage: "counsel younger widows to marry, to have children, to manage their homes . . ." It could certainly be argued that he had a poor opinion of women who succumb to "their sensual desires," or who are "idle" and "busybodies." All these are listed in opposition to "their dedication to Christ." However, it is fair to recognize that this was at least partly Paul's experience, as some had "already turned away to follow Satan."

We should also distinguish between the culture of Paul's day and ours. In his time, widows may have had few options, whereas the opportunities generally open to women in Western society are many. Paul's main concern was that younger widows who had youth and health on their side should not think that their widowhood entitled them to become wards of the church. While Paul does not specifically mention divorcees, divorce was not uncommon—particularly men divorcing their wives for frivolous reasons—so divorced women could also have been in view.

Today, with the high rate of divorce and increasing number of single mothers in society and in our churches, similar guidelines may well apply. I have great admiration for single mothers who, under great handicap, work and often pursue professional goals while raising their families alone. I also applaud those parents of single women who, in an apt reversal of Paul's advice and despite their age, pitch in to assist in stabilising their daughter's family and create an environment that will foster responsible citizens. I'm sure Paul would feel the same way.

Friday: 2 Timothy 1:1–5

You may recall that Timothy was a "son in the faith" to Paul. The amount of ministry that Paul left in Timothy's care reflected not only a close relationship, but more importantly, Timothy's clear understanding of the faith and its practical application. From reading Paul's other letters, it is clear that he had many whom he commended in the faith, but Timothy stands out because of his great administrative qualities, which Paul used extensively.

What is noticeable in this passage is Timothy's genealogy as listed by Paul. It must be remembered that this letter was written only about 36 years after Christ's crucifixion. While we know that Timothy was young,[1] his mother Eunice and grandmother Lois must have been converted to Christianity during those years, both women obviously coming to a clear understanding of their newfound faith. So Timothy was probably brought up from early childhood in a Christian household, where the faith of his mother and grandmother was clearly expressed.

Here is a plain record of transmitting the need to seek God through the generations. One assumes that Timothy was generally a compliant child and that he easily adopted his mother's faith, eventually firmly making the faith his own. The ability to carry out the tasks allotted to him, especially during a time of persecution of the church, could not have been accomplished through a second-hand faith. Lois's and Eunice's faithfulness to God had great outcomes in Timothy; his work for the early church is a continuing legacy for us today. What sort of legacy will we leave to our children? This example from Timothy should be an encouragement to us that our faithfulness to God may produce children of similar influence.

---

[1] 1 Timothy 4:12

Weekend ~ Raising Children: Then and Now

Most parents need all the help they can get. Raising children today is a particularly hazardous venture, for there are so many dangers to which they can fall prey. I remember an incident in my teen years in England in the 1950s. Watching a television program one day, there was a story about a person admitted to hospital with injuries but feeling no pain. It turned out that he was addicted to heroin, a so-called "dangerous drug." That was my first introduction to recreational drugs—they were unheard of in my childhood. Life is different in the new millennium.

That is one example of the difference between now and then. Although Ann and I spent our young childhood in England during World War II, we always knew who and where the enemy was. Today's terrorist warfare is an unpredictable dread. The England of our childhood was a Christian country—not that all were Christians; they were a similar minority as today but Christian values were universally held. This meant that sex was meant for marriage, children obeyed their parents (not the other way around) and divorce and children out of wedlock were almost unheard of. It wasn't that rebellion did not exist or the moral code was never broken, merely that infractions were stigmatised and restrained.

I have great concern and admiration for those who are raising children at the beginning of this century and facing challenges we escaped in our era. In fact, there are some who refrain from having children at all because they consider the world too awful a place for them. Understandable. But for those of you with children, you have already found out that some of the greatest joys as well as heartaches accrue to you from your family. You have learned that your closeness to God and prayers for your children are not optional but a necessity. Raising children *is* a risky journey, but it may be *your* child that leads the way to a better world.

Week Fifty-Two

Monday: Titus 2:1–8

Titus, like Timothy, was a "son in the faith" to Paul and was committed to similar work,[1] and much of the letter to Titus contains similarities to Paul's first letter to Timothy. It is likely that the criticism against a passage that we reviewed previously[2] could be levelled at this passage also. There is clear stereotyping, particularly of female roles, that is offensive to some in today's Western culture. A similar defence could also be made that the culture of Paul's time had few options for women and most would have fallen into the "wife and mother" category.

However, we must look beyond the culture of the day to Paul's purpose in this passage. He is not necessarily defining roles but rather the behaviour expressed within them. For today's men and women, the message is the same irrespective of their function in society: behave in a way that does not malign the gospel. None of Paul's exhortations are arguable. We can probably identify best with the encouragement for young men to be self-controlled, for the older women to be mentors of the younger and the older men to be sound in faith. Moderation and faithfulness to each other and to God are the keys that Paul uses to reflect the truth of what they believe.

[1] Titus 1:5
[2] 1 Timothy 5:11-15

Two words stand out in this text. Firstly "self-controlled," which is used three times in the admonition to teach the older men and both younger men and women. The Greek word suggests sober clear-headedness that reflects a trust in God's control of life's situations. The other word is "integrity," which simply requires both belief and practical life to be integrated. These two passions are symbiotic, and as we practise them in our family and extend them into other situations, they will reinforce each other and strengthen our faith and witness to those whose lives we touch.

Tuesday: Hebrews 5:5–10

Here is one of the most difficult passages to understand, particularly that Christ *learned* obedience though suffering. As the perfect Son of God, why would he have to learn obedience? Surely his obedience was inherent in his perfection. The answer lies mainly in the fact that he was a Son with a responsibility to his Father. He could not adequately fulfill his mission on earth without complete earthly obedience to his heavenly Father. Whatever plans the Trinity had made together depended on Jesus becoming a man and then listening to and obeying his Father to ensure those plans succeeded.

This meant that he had to be successful where Adam had failed. He was to be put to a test that Adam failed but that he would not. Only in this way could he become the perfect substitute for humankind. His earthly ministry began with his being "led by the Spirit" into a place of temptation.[1] Where Adam succumbed to the desire to "be like God,"[2] Jesus, despite great need, refused to use his divine powers for his own benefit. Adam found that he could not be like God, whereas Jesus became the perfect man.

---

[1] Matthew 4:1
[2] Genesis 3:5

Obedience to parents is not easy, particularly during puberty, when questions about life and peer pressure create an environment of challenge. Of course, parents are not perfect, being susceptible to errors and subjective decisions. Perhaps this is the basis of *our* suffering in learning obedience. Our obedience to instructions that may be incorrect, mistaken or unjust reflects the obedience of Jesus to his Father's instructions. Those instructions seemed manifestly unnecessary and unjust for Jesus, but he obeyed purely so that he could be our perfect sacrifice.

Wednesday: Hebrews 12:4–13

The writer to the Hebrews brings home the necessity of discipline. For the Hebrews in their time, the writer is thinking of persecution as he tells them, "you have not yet resisted to the point of shedding your blood." Thus, in verse 7 he equates hardship with discipline from God, a concept our soft Western culture would find hard to accept. Surely, we reason, if all good things come from God, how can we expect pain and suffering from him too?

The New Testament recognizes that adversity will often accompany our faith, whether by persecution, sacrifice or simply the effects of living in a broken world. This passage adds the notion that adversity is also a form of discipline. Discipline falls into two categories. Either the discipline is punishment from others for a wrong committed or it is a self-imposed routine of training for some endeavour. Here Paul suggests both are included in the adversity that we experience, a discipline that later on "produces a harvest of righteousness and peace."

But what is emphasised is not so much the outcome of discipline but the fact that it is a product of love. Furthermore, Paul maintains that without discipline there is no love. Apart from some misguided individuals that may still think that "free expression" is the ideal for raising children, the vast majority see the need for shaping a child's behaviour. While parents may occasionally react in exasperation, most discipline is born of a desire to prepare a child for life in the real world. Children who learn that there is conduct that is unacceptable in both the family and society—that not everything they want is immediately available and personal desires have to be balanced with service to others—will be provided with a foundation for a well adjusted and happier life for themselves and those around them.

Thursday: Revelation 12:1–17

The lines of symbolism in this reading are generally clear. The woman about to give birth is the nation of Israel, the sun, moon and stars referring back to Jacob—renamed Israel—his wife and twelve sons.[1] The dragon is clarified as "that ancient serpent called the devil, or Satan, who leads the whole world astray." The son that was born is Jesus, whom Herod sought to kill at birth. Herod—knowingly or not—acted for Satan, who knew the coming King would be the one to destroy him. Throughout Jesus' ministry, evil men sought to kill him and thought they had triumphed at the crucifixion. But the resurrection changed it all, and eventually Jesus "was snatched up to God and his throne."[2]

This passage also sets the basis for the persecution of the Christian church. It is not one ideology pitted against another, although that is the way it is often portrayed. It is a spiritual battle, won by the King himself but now waged against those who follow him—the woman's offspring: "those who keep God's commands and hold fast their testimony about Jesus."

But why wait to persecute until men and women grow and make a commitment of faith in Jesus Christ? Satan is totally non-discriminatory. His campaign against the unborn, newly born and young children is an attempt to kill off any who might make an allegiance to Christ. Herod set the pattern, killing off a generation of infants in trying to ensure the death of one. Likewise, by infanticide widely practiced in China and India; by abortion, the

[1] Genesis 37:9
[2] See Acts 1:9–11

scourge of the West; and by indiscriminate suicide bombing of women and children, the enemy of God tries to ensure that children cannot turn to Christ and the potential births of others who may do so are eliminated.

Friday: Revelation 21:1–10

No discussion of marriage would be complete without meditating for a while on the real marriage that earthly marriages illustrate, however poorly. The holy city of Jerusalem, here called and adorned as the "bride of Christ," represents all those who have entered that symbolic city by their acceptance of and allegiance to Jesus Christ.[1] It is a time when Christ himself will present his bride to the Father as those he has drawn to himself by his work on Calvary.[2] At the consummation of all things, the final marriage, which contains within itself all marriages, will be completed. The bliss of the marriage we have with him will surpass any union we may have known on earth, maintaining forever all that a marriage provides for its partners.

Entry into that marriage will be like true marriage on earth; it will be a desire of both partners for union. It will not be based on the purity of the bride but the beauty that the groom sees in her and his willingness to provide her with fresh clothing.[3] The parable of the king's banquet, while not a full analogy, provides a picture of those unworthy of the wedding banquet receiving invitations and appropriate clothing to wear.[4] But the work of the bride does not go unrewarded; her clothing also represents the fulfilment of her commitment to the Groom during her engagement.[5]

Perhaps our marriages on earth would improve if we would see them through the image of that final wedding. That final

---

[1] Revelation 19:7–8
[2] Ephesians 5:27
[3] Revelation 7:13–14
[4] Matthew 22:1–14
[5] Revelation 19:8

union is based on the Groom's love for the bride and his acknowledgment of her failures. While that is the position of Christ for us, it should be the attitude of both partners in an earthly wedding. Men have no advantage over women when it comes to sin—perhaps less—and also need acceptance of their male frailty from their wives. But as men, will we have the same pride in the presenting our wives complete in Christ as he will have in presenting his bride to his Father?[1]

Weekend ~ That Final Reunion

When our youngest daughter and her husband put their house up for sale, they had a number of people view it. There was one couple from an Eastern background who were familiar with artefacts having meaning rather than just being ornamental. As they passed the dining room table, the wife noticed a centrepiece with three candles and asked if there was some meaning for that display. For most of us in the decorating mode of Western culture the answer would probably have been: "It's just an ornament."

In this case, that answer would have been wrong. Alexandra and her husband had been trying to have children for some time, and the last three pregnancies had resulted in miscarriages. Most would have put these behind them as part of life's misfortune; after all, our culture considers the unborn child as a non-person, with no human rights or significance. However, Alex kept these three candles as a reminder of the three children that she had lost, despite the fact that they had not been born. Apart from giving honour and respect to the unborn, they kept alive another Christian belief—that of final reunion.

Those three children that God took home to be with himself for reasons best known to him had not been lost—they will be there to greet their parents in the place where all tears will be wiped away. None of us who have lost children or other loved

---

[1] Ephesians 5:27

ones in the Lord will be deprived of a final, complete and eternal fellowship with them. That is why we "do not grieve like the rest who have no hope."[1] The reunion with Christ and loved ones who have gone before is one of the most precious expectations of all Christians. We may look back at events in life with sorrow, but we look forward to that final reunion with joy.

---

[1] 1 Thessalonians 4:13–14

Old Testament References
Includes References in Footnotes

New Testament References
Includes References in Footnotes

Index of Weekend Comments